THE POLITICS OF DISCOURSE:
THE STANDARD LANGUAGE QUESTION IN BRITISH CULTURAL DEBATES

Tony Crowley

MACMILLAN

First published 1989

Published by
MACMILLAN EDUCATION LTD
Houndmills, Basingstoke, Hampshire RG21 2XS
and London
Companies and representatives
throughout the world

Typeset by Wessex Typesetters
(Division of The Eastern Press Ltd)
Frome, Somerset

Printed in China

British Library Cataloguing in Publication Data
Crowley, Tony
The politics of discourse: the
standard language question
in British cultural debates
1. English language. Historical linguistics
I. Title
420
ISBN 0–333–45470–7
ISBN 0–333–45471–5 Pbk

Contents

For My Father
Cornelius Crowley
Sí teanga na muintire a shlánós an mhuintir

Preface

If I were to thank all those who have helped me to write this book it is possible that this preface would be longer than the main body of the text. So I shall have to apologise in advance to anyone I leave out. My first thanks are to Professor Roy Harris of the University of Oxford who supervised my doctorate on a related topic; and to Alan Ward and Raymond Williams who examined it. Thanks of this order are also due to Dennis Horgan who helped me start this project, and to Kate Belsey, Terry Eagleton, Cathy Fuller and Andrew Thacker who read and gave me help with later work. My colleagues and students at the universities of Oxford and Southampton have my gratitude for putting up with me and for giving me the intellectual space and time in which to work. Special thanks in this respect to my special option group of 1986–7. And my very, very special thanks to the secretaries at the Department of English in Southampton: Sheila James, Jill Bennett, and in particular Norma Martin who provided such cheerful and indispensable help.

My thanks are also due to all those who friendship and good advice made it worth undertaking this project: Sue Forber, who gave me great friendship, support and encouragement in times of doubt; Isobel Armstrong, Debbie Cameron and Edmund Papst who often, in different ways, made me think things through again when I wrongly thought that I had proved my point; Courtney Greenaway and Kadiatu Kanneh who have made me think in new and better ways; Tom Mulhearn who has long given me the benefit of his friendship and logical skills. Also Angela Poingdestre, Steve Sheedy, and all the Prangleys: Clare, Paul (the boss), Ged, Ant, John, and most of all Kate, who have long supported me.

Perhaps my deepest debt can be acknowledged last. To my brother and sisters, Nicky, Collette, Terry and Jacky, and my father, Cornelius Crowley, I offer my thanks and love.

T.C.

Acknowledgement

I would like to thank Oxford University Press for their permission to include the diagram from the 'General Explanations' in volume 1 of *The Oxford English Dictionary*, ed. J.A.H. Murray.

T.C.

Introduction

Language, knowledge, power

> In appearance, speech may well be of little account, but
> the prohïbitions surrounding it soon reveal its links with
> desire and power.
>
> (M. Foucault, 'The Discourse on Language')

The aim of this introduction is to give a brief sketch of the
sort of theoretical work that has helped me with this project.
The work was drawn principally from the work of three
writers: Foucault, Vološinov and Bakhtin. Their investigations
were of interest not in the fact that they mapped out a certain
field that could then be taken over and the details filled in,
but in that they offered a direction in which to proceed. In
fact their texts are very dissimilar and often contradictory in
terms of the aims and methods of their studies. However, I
found that there were sufficient similarities to suggest that a
number of fairly basic points could be drawn together in order
to provide a theoretical starting point. Those similarities and
that starting point are my concern in this introduction.

In his inaugural lecture delivered at the Collège de France
in 1970, Foucault took as his topic the order of discourse. The
lecture ranged across a number of disciplines but returned
constantly to the principal theme of the 'subjection of discourse'. The lecture investigated this process of subjection by
outlining some of the ways in which discourse was controlled
and delimited: principally the systems of exclusion, the principles of classification, ordering and distribution, and the rules
determining the conditions under which, and by whom,
discourse could be deployed. In a sense then we could use
another of Foucault's own terms and sum up his project in

this lecture as a preliminary investigation of the disciplining of language.

That language is disciplined in Foucault's view is evident in his tracing of the web of prohibitions that surrounds discourse, 'prohibitions [that] interrelate, reinforce and complement each other, forming a complex web, continually subject to modification'. It is a complex and unceasing process of permission and denial, an ordering of what can be said and what not, of who can speak and who is to remain in silence. It is also a project that appears to have a distinct purpose in Foucault's view since he argues that,

> in every society the production of discourse is at once controlled, selected, organised and redistributed according to a certain number of procedures, whose role is to avert its powers and dangers.   (Foucault, 1972, p.216)

But then the question might be asked – what are these powers of discourse that have to be averted, and what are the dangers which it has in store if it is not disciplined? Who is it exactly that has to be wary of the powers and dangers of undisciplined discourse? It would be naïve to expect simple answers to such questions from Foucault's text since he was careful, in this text and elsewhere, to avoid the assignation of power in any restricted sense to a particular group. His aim instead was to trace the set of processes, practices and institutions by which power was disseminated. And in so far as his object of study in this lecture was the subjection of discourse, he had to concentrate on such dissemination in the system of education.

It may be taken as axiomatic that the system of education is concerned with the dissemination of discourse, and it is hard in fact to imagine what other aim the education system as constituted at present could have. It has to concern itself with how different branches and levels of knowledge are organised, presented and assimilated. Yet the aims of education and their enactment in reality are clearly distinct. For example, liberal theories of education are grounded upon the concept of open access to discourse and free choice in what, and how, learning takes place. Radical theories on the other hand indicate the essential naïvety of such a view by pointing up the limitations that operate upon discourse and the ways in which discourse is not open but delimited and constrained. They argue that it is often not only not free choice that operates, but sometimes no choice at all. Foucault makes precisely this point about education and discourse when he concludes that:

> Education may well be, as of right, the instrument whereby every individual, in a society like our own, can gain access to any kind of discourse. But we all know that in its distribution, in what it permits and prevents, it follows the well-trodden battle lines of social conflict. Every educational system is a political means of maintaining or modifying the appropriation of discourse, with the knowledge and powers it carries with it. (*Ibid.*, p.227)

Education for Foucault is not a free area in which all can participate but yet another site upon which wider social conflicts are fought out. In the precise distribution of discourse that takes place within education is reflected the distribution of knowledge and power which is characteristic of modern societies more generally. Which means of course that it is distributed according to principles of exclusion and inequality.

Foucault's arguments in this text are not in one sense new, although they clearly have a novel methodology and distinct implications. They can be linked to that tradition of thought which has long questioned the nature of institutions (particularly those belonging to the state) and their role in the distribution of knowledge and power. They could for example be compared to the scepticism demonstrated by the English radicals towards the introduction of state education in the early nineteenth century.[1] Yet Foucault's arguments can also be related usefully to another strain of radical thought and one that has only recently appeared in western Europe. It is a field which concentrates on language and the social foundations of discourse and is best formulated in Vološinov's *Marxism and the Philosophy of Language* and Bakhtin's *The Dialogic Imagination*.

As readers in this field will already know, the question of the authorship of these texts is a subject of contention but it is a problem that can be left to one side here. What is interesting about both these texts is their common starting point which holds that 'verbal discourse is a social phenomenon – social throughout its entire range and in each and every one of its factors, from the sound image to the furthest reaches of abstract meaning' (Bakhtin, 1981, p.259). As with Foucault, both of these writers see discourse as subjected to the forces and conflicts of the social history which produces it, though both are much more forthright than he in specifying the nature of those forces and conflicts. From this starting point it follows that Vološinov will argue that the social context of an utterance – 'the immediate social situation of the broader social milieu' – determines *from within* the forms of discourse. Moreover, given the unequal distribution of power that characterises our present social context in its largest sense, it is no surprise to find that he agrees with Foucault's contention that the present distribution of discourse is unequal and hierarchical. He argues that any detailed analysis would demonstrate 'what enormous significance belongs to the *hierarchical factor* in the processes of verbal interchange and what a powerful influence is exerted on forms of utterance by the hierarchical organisation of communication' (Vološinov, 1973, p.21).

The texts of Vološinov and Bakhtin are useful since they have a novel and specific approach to the study of discourse. They are concerned both with the social nature of discourse and with identifying and investigating the historical processes by which particular forms of discourse are brought into existence and others rejected. In a sense then they are both theoreticians and historians of discourse and its conflictual and power-laden nature. An example of such thinking is Vološinov's argument that within any particular sign-community there will be different classes who use more or less one and the same language. Yet given the conflictual nature of social relations those classes will accentuate the signs of the language in different ways and thus the signs become multiaccentual and sites of conflicts in themselves. In fact such multiaccentuality for Vološinov is what maintains the vitality and dynamism of the sign and gives it the capacity for further development. However, in order to naturalise social processes, which is the principal function of ideology, a disciplining of language has to take place. For the necessary task of stabilising 'the dialectical flux of of the social general process', the multiaccentuality of signs has to be banished since multiaccentuality is a reminder that there are conflicting groups and interests and that yesterday's history was different from today's and tomorrow's could be altered again. It is an ordering of discourse that Vološinov sees in terms of the interests of a specific class:

> The ruling class strives to impart a supraclass, eternal character to the ideological sign, to extinguish or drive inward the struggle between social value judgments which occurs in it, to make the sign uniaccentual   (*Ibid.*, p.23)

It is the attempt to take the social and historical processes out of discourse in order to make a certain order of things appear natural and given.

One of the most interesting aspects of their work is the way in which these theorists give an historical account of their own discipline as they specify the forms of study that have created the particular ways of thinking about language which they have inherited. In particular Vološinov singles out the nineteenth and twentieth centuries as being concerned with abstractive and decontextualising methodologies in the study of language. Saussure is subjected to a rigorous critique by Vološinov as a pre-eminent figure who is hailed as having thrown off certain of the methods of nineteenth-century philology but who in fact simply rejects certain of the concerns of such work while retaining its essential methodology. Vološinov's claim is that theoretical abstraction is justifiable only in the light of a specific theoretical and practical goal. He then criticises Saussure's abstraction of the synchronic *état de langue* as a system of 'normatively identical forms' on the grounds that it does not offer a way of analysing social verbal discourse but is derived precisely from the methodology of the study which had been so decidedly renounced by Saussure – 'the study of defunct, alien languages preserved in written monuments'. For Vološinov philologism is the dominating trend that gave birth to the modern science of linguistics and both fields are characterised by a rejection of social discourse in favour of the study of the 'dead, written, alien language', and in particular the 'isolated, finished, monologic utterance, divorced from its verbal and actual context and standing open not to any possible sort of active response but to passive understanding on the part of the philologist' (*ibid.*, p.73). Now such a charge against a certain school of philologists is permissible from Vološinov's point of view since it is undoubtedly the case that the philologists were often interested in dead languages and the history of particular forms rather than how a specific form was produced in a particular context. To accuse the so-called father of modern linguistics of this, however, is perhaps to overstate the case. It was after all Saussure who had claimed that:

> for obvious reasons linguistic questions are of interest to all those, including historians, philologists and others, who need to deal with texts. Even more obvious is the importance of linguistics for culture in general. In the lives of individuals and societies, language is a factor of greater importance than any other. For the study of language to remain solely the business of a handful of specialists would be a quite unacceptable state of affairs. In practice the study of language is in some degree or other the concern of everyone. (Saussure, 1916, p.7)

Nonetheless Vološinov makes his charge against Saussure precisely by arguing that in making linguistics the study of the synchronic *état de langue* he had managed to reject precisely what motivates verbal discourse in the first place: social and historical forces. The attempt to ground the study of language by clarifying what it was that linguists were supposed to take as their object of study turns out in the end to undermine the whole project since:

> With each attempt to delimit the object of investigation, to reduce it to a compact subject-matter complex of definitive and inspectable dimensions, we forfeit the very essence of the thing we are studying – its semiotic and ideological nature.   (Vološinov, 1973, p.46)

The Saussurean disciplining of language is held to be unproductive in that it ends up returning to an account of language that sees it in terms of autonomous, rational, fixed forms. Thus Vološinov's critique consists of four points. First, that Saussure's model sees language as a stable system of normatively identical forms which is presented as a 'social fact' to the individual consciousness and which is thus unalterable by the individual. Second, that the laws of language are viewed as akin to the laws that govern the symbols in the system of mathematics and are thus self-enclosed laws. Third, and following from the second point, that linguistic laws and relations are wholly independent of other social or historical forces. And finally, that individual utterances (parole) are often distortions of the normatively identical forms and thus unstable tokens of the fixed types. These four fundamental points of the Saussurean model led Vološinov to characterise it as an 'abstract objectivist' paradigm and to classify it as closely related to the work of the earlier philologists. Following Saussure, Vološinov alleges, 'linguistics studies a living language as if it were a dead language, and native language as if it were an alien language'.

According to his own account of the way in which discourse is controlled and delimited it is clear that Foucault can be described as dealing primarily with systems of discursive exclusion in 'The Discourse on Language'. Vološinov on the other hand could be characterised as being concerned principally with the principles of the classification, ordering and distribution of discourse. Finally in this brief sketch of these analysts of discourse we turn to a writer whose work covers both of the areas already specified and goes further in concentrating on the conditions under which, and by whom, discourse is deployed: Bakhtin.

One of Bakhtin's central arguments is that language is stratified in a number of ways and in fact he goes so far as to say that what has so far counted as *a language* is a fiction which can only appear as a result of an active process of repression. As with Vološinov's monologic utterance which is formed by repressing the dialogic context in which it was created, the notion of a single and unified language can only result from a similar repression of the heteroglossic reality of its historical setting. Bakhtin argues that:

at any given moment of its historical existence, language is heteroglot from top to bottom: it represents the co-existence of socio-ideological contradictions between the present and the past, between differing epochs of the past, between different socio-ideological groups in the present, between tendencies, schools, circles and so forth, all given a bodily form. These 'languages' of heteroglossia intersect each other in a variety of ways, forming new socially typifying 'languages'.   (Bakhtin, 1981, p.291)

The nature of language is that it is constituted by centrifugal forces which operate in a ceaseless flow of becoming and which are in constant dialectical tension with each other to produce new languages and forms of heteroglossia. However, against these centrifugal forces are ranged the centripetal forces of language which attempt to unify and centralise over and above the heteroglossia of the historical becoming of language. These are the forces which attempt to discipline the forms of discourse in various ways and they are to be met with most clearly in the philological study of language. Just as Vološinov had noted the abstract objectivising tendency of philologism, Bakhtin argued that the concept of a 'unitary language' was the result of similar processes of repression:

Unitary language constitutes the theoretical expression of the historical processes of linguistic unification and centralisation, an expression of the centripetal forces of language. A unitary language is not something given (dan) but is always in essence posited (zadan) and at every moment of its linguistic life it is opposed to the realities of heteroglossia. But at the same time it makes its real presence felt as a force for overcoming this heteroglossia, imposing specific limits to it, guaranteeing a certain maximum of mutual understanding and crystallising into a real, although still relative, unity – the unity of the reigning conversational (everyday) and literary language, 'correct language'. (*Ibid.*, p.270)

The unitary language is a result of the regulation of discourse in which the centralising forces of language impose a thin though durable web over the surface of heteroglossia. Yet as with Foucault's description of the distribution of discourse by means of the institutions of education, Bakhtin does not see this struggle between opposing forces as involving purely linguistic forces. Both writers clearly argue that such a conflict follows, and is determined by, forces that have other than linguistic existence. Foucault argued that the distribution of discourse within education takes place in the 'well-trodden battle lines of social conflict'. And Bakhtin also argues that the disciplining of language is determined by larger historical forces. He specifies, as forces that have served the project of centralising and unifying the European languages, 'Aristotelian poetics, the poetics of Augustine, the poetics of the medieval church, of "the one language of truth", the Cartesian poetics of neoclassicism, the abstract grammatical universalism of Leibniz (the idea of a "universal grammar")' and so on. The list seems a little obscure in so far as it seems to consist largely of various intellectual and discursive movements. However, Bakhtin insists that these movements and their effect on the distribution of discourse are also engaged in the warfare of social conflict. The centripetal forces embodied in this list are also described as bringing about:

> The victory of one reigning language (dialect) over the others, the supplanting of languages, their enslavement, the process of illuminating them with the True Word, the incorporation of barbarian and lower social strata into a unitary language of culture and truth, the canonisation of ideological systems. (*Ibid.*, p.271)

The search for linguistic unity and identity is one that is founded upon acts of violence and repression: a denial of heteroglossia – discursive and historical – in favour of centralising, static forms. And the victory of one dialect or language over others produces an hierarchy, an ordering of discourse which excludes, distributes and defines what is to count as discourse and what is to be relegated to oblivion. It brings into being the 'authoritative word':

> The authoritative word demands that we acknowledge it,

that we make it our own; it binds us, quite independent of
any power it might have to persuade us internally; we
encounter it with its authority already fused to it. The
authoritative word is located in a distanced zone, organically
connected with a past that is felt to be organically higher.
It is, so to speak, the word of the fathers.   (*Ibid.*, p.342)

There is then no possibility of challenging this discourse, of
questioning it or of being persuaded by it. Its authority is
already borne along with it and it is the authority of the ruling
patriarchal tradition.

The theories of discourse embodied in the texts of the three
writers considered in this introduction are important for two
principal reasons. First, they each give valuable insights into
the social nature of discourse, in particular how it is constituted
in its various forms and the importance which those forms
have. Second, although there are problems with each
approach, they all insist upon a dialectical relationship
between language and history. It is not a question of holding
that history determines the forms of discourse, or that the
forms of discourse determine history. The relationship is
complex, often difficult to trace, never unidirectional, and
always at work. These seem to be the necessary starting points
for any investigator of the politics of discourse.

This introduction has attempted to set out what is useful
and enabling in these theories in order to prevent the argument
that follows in the subsequent chapters becoming merely a
'practical' illustration of the theories. The aim is not to give –
a major problem with so many 'theoretical' texts – a slavish
account that vindicates the theory which it sets out to illustrate.
Rather it is to point out to the reader the sort of analytical
tools with which this book was begun and then to present as
far as possible the results which those tools helped to discover.
The results may well not be compatible with some of the
theoretical positions with which it began but that is not a
problem in my opinion since it may lead to modifications in
such positions.

The theoretical positions which are set out in this introduction (and they are by no means a full account of the texts
from which they are taken) are starting points, categories

which enable us to sift through the multifarious and fascinating phenomena which are the reward of anyone investigating the historical formations of language. They are tools that enable us to construct a narrative, to discern a pattern, and to make connections amongst apparently unconnected words and things. That is, they have allowed the writing of a cultural history of a set of processes which centre around the distribution of discourse and the disciplining of language. And like any cultural history there is much that has been left out and many conflations in this account. There were points, for example, at which it was felt that the direction of a particular writer's work in relation to the main concern with the politics of discourse, worked against the massive and often brilliant contribution to scholarship that it makes. In such cases attention has been paid to the direction of the work rather than to the contribution to scholarship and on occasion that has meant that there is a failure to highlight the difference between those who made genuine contributions to their field and others who diligently popularised received positions. However, no apology is made for that since it was often, by definition, the popularisers who were most influential in determining public opinion on such questions, and the question of intellectual acknowledgement is far less important than the other issues at stake in this text.

A second and more glaring omission in a text that uses Bakhtin's insight into the authoritative word of the fathers is the lack of more than an unextended account of the exclusion of women from discourse, or at least from certain forms of discourse, which is an important distinction. There are various reasons for this. First, there are a number of texts which have begun to explore this area from a theoretical perspective, and an introduction to such attempts is given in Debbie Cameron's *Feminism and Linguistic Theory*. Second, such a project demands not only a theoretical clarification but a large-scale empirical investigation of the gendered ordering of discourse in the sorts of debates which are presented below. And finally, in this work the run of the argument in the texts investigated has been followed. That argument did not usually ground itself upon a gender-based distribution of discourse but on a class-based ordering. That is not at this stage to give class a theoretical precedence in our investigations but it is to be quite specific about, and insist upon, the historical moment, and the forces operating within it, of the texts and debates under view.

Finally it is argued that although the cultural history presented below is rather bleak, it is also accurate. That has certain advantages: first it sets out the historical ordering of discourse which has taken place within specific institutions and forms of practice. That in itself should be enough to banish certain forms of nostalgia. And second, it attempts to demonstrate precisely the processes by which such ordering has taken place. It is even possible that this might suggest possibilities of resistance.

Foucault contends that 'historians have constantly impressed upon us that speech is no mere verbalisation of conflicts of domination, but that it is the very object of man's conflicts' (Foucault, 1971, p.216). The aim in this text has been to chart the recent history of such conflicts.

1

A History of 'The History of the Language'

When you speak of a 'wide eyed presentation of mere facts', you characterize the true philological attitude. . . . The appearance of closed facticity which attaches to a philological investigation and places the investigator under its spell, fades to the extent that this object is construed in an historical perspective.

(Walter Benjamin, letter to Adorno, 9 December 1938)

Introduction

For historians of the study of language in Britain it has become a commonplace that the eighteenth century, in which the discourses of prescriptivism predominated, was superseded by a nineteenth-century reaction against such discourses. One such historian has declared that, 'perhaps the greatest legacy of the nineteenth-century philologist was the study of language from an objective point of view, a view that has been adopted by twentieth-century linguists'. The cause of this shift, he argues, is that, 'for the philologists, the study of language became removed from the social and rhetorical concerns of the eighteenth century, and thus became an abstract and objective study' (Stalker, 1985, p.45). However, it will be the major contention of this text that no such shift from prescriptivism to descriptivism took place. Rather the study of language in Britain was to be still, in significant respects, as concerned with 'social and rhetorical concerns' in the nineteenth and early twentieth centuries as it had been in the eighteenth. The objectification of language, it will be argued, is a construction of the history of the study of language in Britain that cannot be supported by the evidence. Moreover, it is a discursive construction that serves particular social and rhetorical purposes.

The appearance of historicity

According to such historians, the nineteenth century saw language demoted to the status of object and thus subjected to the positivistic gaze of 'scientists' and historians. Language became the object of a new field of study within which 'scientists' and historians (both to be subsumed under the later title of 'linguist') were to work. Such a shift is attested not merely by the historians of the new field but by its very practitioners. Thus Max Müller, first Professor of Comparative Philology at Oxford, asserted in one of his Royal Institution Lectures of 1861 (a version of which was presented to Queen Victoria in 1864) that:

> Language, the living and speaking witness of the whole history of our race, was never cross-examined by the student of history, was never made to disclose its secrets until questioned and, so to say, brought back to itself within the last fifty years by the genius of a Humboldt, Bopp, Grimm, Bunsen and others. (Müller, 1862, p.27)

He continued to argue that, 'in the science of language, languages are not treated as a means; language itself becomes the sole object of enquiry . . . . We do not want to know languages, we want to know language' (*ibid.*, p.23).

The nineteenth century believed (and many in the twentieth century continue to believe) that a significant shift in language studies had taken place; the eyes of the observer of language now remained fixed on language itself rather than straying beyond it. Developments in the nineteenth century brought language 'back to itself' through the desire 'to know language' rather than to know *a* language, or languages. In this process of questioning language rather than *a* language, it is held, the nineteenth century witnessed the birth of a new discourse: a language dedicated solely to language. Or to put the point in a different way, the nineteenth century saw the appearance of a language about language, described wholly unselfconsciously by Müller as the 'science of language'.

Of this account one might ask: if language had to be brought back to itself, where had it been? From which disciplines did language have to be wrested in order that the discipline of the 'science of language' could appear? The answers to such questions are complex as Aarsleff points out in his pioneering work *The Study of Language in England 1780–1860*. When mentioning but a few of the eighteenth- and nineteenth-century writers on language he asserts that, 'it is characteristic that Dr Johnson, Sir William Jones, Friedrich Schlegel, Jacob Grimm, and N.F.S. Grundtvig all considered language study a means to an end rather than the end itself, though they differed somewhat in their conceptions of that end' (Aarsleff, 1967, p.5). Before it was wrested 'back to itself' then, language had been instrumental, a means by which distinct types of knowledge could be derived.

Of the different areas of knowledge that the study of language benefited two were predominant in the eighteenth century. The first was General or Universal Grammar, and the second was the field that concerned itself with the origin of language (involving problems of reference, logic, meaning, as well as origins). Both are subsumed under what Foucault has described as the episteme of *Representation*. However, rather than dealing with problems that would now be described as lying within the 'philosophy of language' and related largely to the question of how language referred to an external world, the nineteenth century was to witness language being 'brought back to itself', since as Foucault pointed out language folded in upon itself and thus inflection rather than reflection was to be the order of the day.[1]

On this point there seems little disagreement among two of the major historians of language study in the nineteenth century. Aarsleff held that:

It is universally agreed that the decisive turn in language study occurred when the philosophical, a priori method of the eighteenth century was abandoned in favour of the historical, a posteriori method of the nineteenth century.   (Aarsleff, 1967, p.127)

And Foucault argued in his archaeology of the human sciences that:

From the nineteenth century language began to fold in upon itself, to acquire its own particular density, to deploy a history, an objectivity, and laws of its own. It became one object of study among others.   (Foucault, 1974, p.296)

Although the emphases of their accounts (and what Foucault calls the 'fundamental codes' that inform their work) differ, there is a clear consensus that language became 'objectified', an object of the science that wanted to 'know language'.

For Foucault the development of the 'science of language' was linked to the shift from what he calls the classical period to the modern period. The new order of things, the new structure of knowledge as Foucault argues, was arranged not in relation to the classical problem of Representation but to the modern problem of *History*. History, in this sense, is to be understood as neither teleological progression nor as 'the compilation of factual successions or sequences as they may have occurred', but as 'the fundamental mode of being of empiricities, upon the basis of which they are affirmed, posited, arranged and distributed in the space of knowledge for the use of such disciplines or sciences as may arrive' (*ibid.*, p.219). For Foucault, history has been the 'fundamental code' that has structured the cultural knowledge of western Europe from the early nineteenth century. Thus, across a number of apparently distinct fields of knowledge can be traced a unifying theme: the appearance of 'historicity'. He argued that around the end of the eighteenth century, 'a profound historicity penetrates into the heart of things, isolates and defines them in their coherence, imposes upon them the forms of order implied by the continuity of time' (*ibid.*, p.xxiii). With this there follows the appearance of new disciplines as 'words, beings, and objects of need' begin to take their place within new discursive fields, within 'those now familiar forms of knowledge that we have called since the nineteenth century, *philology*, *biology* and *economics*'.

A similar view was also held by cultural historians of that time; for example, E.A. Freeman argued that there was a contemporary recognition of a shift in the field of knowledge. The Regius Professor of Modern History at Oxford declared that:

> On us a new light has come. I do not hesitate to say that the discovery of the comparative method in philology, in mythology, let me add in politics and history and the whole range of human thought – marks a state in the progress of the human mind at least as great and memorable as the revival of Greek and Latin learning. The great contribution of the nineteenth century to the advance of human knowledge may boldly take its stand alongside of the great contribution of the fifteenth.

The shift that occurred across the field of cultural knowledge was, at least for this practitioner, as great as that brought about by the Renaissance. Moreover, as with the Renaissance, the shift brought into focus new objects, new relations between objects, a new historical order and therefore a new order of values:

> Like the revival of learning, it has opened to its votaries a new world, and that not an isolated world, a world shut up within itself, but a world in which times and tongues and nations which before seemed parted poles asunder, now find each one in its place, its own relation to every other, as members of one common primaeval brotherhood. And not the least of its services is that it has put the languages and history of the so-called 'classical' world into their true position in the general history of the world. (Freeman, 1873, p.302)

Direct engagement with Foucault here will be limited though it should be clear by the end that the main thrust of the argument is both for (in general terms) and against (on specific questions) Foucault's reading. However, at this point Foucault's insight into the early development of language studies is used since it is clear that within western Europe generally the study of language did indeed become historical in the nineteenth century. The new 'science of language' that was to be known as Comparative Philology compared nothing but the historically variant forms of different languages in order to derive general and later (for the neo-grammarians) universal linguistic laws. History, we may agree with Foucault, was the 'fundamental mode of being of [the] empiricities' of language that delivered to the science of philology its material. And once again we may cite contemporary evidence since in his *Principles of The History of Language*, Hermann Paul asserts that:

> Language like every other production of human culture falls under the general cognizance of history; but the history of language like every other branch of the science of history has running parallel with it, a science which occupies itself with the general conditions of the existence of the object historically developing.   (Paul, 1890, p.xxi)

This is an interesting statement since evidently history is taken to be dominant in the study of language on the grounds that all human cultural production is historical. But along with the 'history of language' he also argues for a field of study that is occupied with 'the general conditions of the existence of the object' of linguistic history. That is, as well as 'the history of language' there also exists the possibility (or the necessity) of a 'science of language' that specifies the 'general conditions' of its object. The 'history of language' would determine the specific conditions of existence and the 'science of language' would determine the general conditions. This distinction is also of interest in that it demonstrates that the epistemological distinction between diachrony and synchrony was not conjured out of the air by Ferdinand de Saussure, the father of modern linguistics, as is so often claimed. And in fact the type of distinction made here by Paul was quite common to the nineteenth century though it appeared in differing forms. One example is the distinction between 'historical grammar' and 'grammar'. Another instance is given in the 'anthropological linguistics' of many late-nineteenth-century British linguists, which evinces a clear interest in synchronic study. In any case this was not a complete breakthrough by Saussure since, as with most 'revolutionary' changes of this type, there was much preparation in advance. His use of the distinction did, however, produce novel possibilities and problems for the study of language.

One of Paul's opponents objected to his emphasis by declaring that the historical perspective is not the fundamental basis of the study of language. To this Paul replied by reasserting the general cognisance of history and therefore the necessary ubiquity of historicity:

> I must contradict this. What is explained as an unhistorical and still scientific observation is at bottom nothing but one incompletely historical. . . . As soon as ever we pass beyond the mere statements of single facts and attempt to grasp the connexion as a whole and to comprehend the phenomena, we come upon historical ground at once, though we may not be aware of the fact.   (Paul, 1880, pp.xlvi–xlvii)

In a totalising Hegelian movement the historical science of language passes beyond 'statement of single facts' in order to organise such facts and to point out the relations between formal elements in historical (diachronic) terms. By comparing distinct elements and forms the new 'science of language' imposed historical order and constructed a history: which is to say that comparative philology started with analysis of the disunited elements solely in order to restore them to an ordered totality. As one of the first comparativists F. von Schlegel put it analogically, 'the structure or comparative grammar of languages furnishes as certain a key of their genealogy as the study of comparative anatomy has done to the loftiest branch of natural science' (Schlegel, 1808, cited in Foucault, 1974, p.280). Schlegel's comparison was frequently used in the nineteenth century. For example, James Ingram had deployed it a year before Schlegel in his lecture on *The Utility of Anglo-Saxon Literature* (1807). In this text Ingram recommends the study of, 'if I may use the expression the comparative anatomy of human language; we must dissect, we must analyse, we must disunite and compare' (Ingram, 1807, p.30). Yet this methodology was undertaken only with the aim of a final restoration, a last return to a unified totality that could then be described as a language, a history, or a system. Later Kemble also refers to the 'comparative anatomy of Anglo-Saxon' (Kemble, 1845, p.131) and Latham points out similarities between studying 'the structure of the human body' and 'the structure of human language' (Latham, 1855, p.98). In various ways each of these references lends support to Foucault's argument that historicity became the 'fundamental mode of being of empiricities to be traced across various fields'. Thus at least part of the concern of this text will be to demonstrate how and to what effect this appearance of historicity underpinned the study of language in Britain.

The term 'comparative grammar', first coined by Schlegel in 1808 (Pedersen, 1931, p.18), is held to mark the appearance of the study that was to objectify language. That study, comparative philology, gained the status of being the principal mode of linguistic study in western Europe for the next century. Until, that is, diachrony was replaced by synchrony and the history of forms by the structural relations between them. However, there is an important point to be made here since although comparative philology dominated the nineteenth-century study of language in western Europe, and although the study of language in Britain was diachronic at this period, it does not necessarily follow that comparative philology was the predominant mode of linguistic study in Britain. And in fact we shall argue that it was not. The remainder of this first chapter will be given over to that peculiarity through an examination of the appearance of a distinctive discourse on language in Britain. And the rest of this text will be concerned with examining the importance of the distinctive British discourse in terms of its academic, social and political effects.

History and language in Britain

The term 'linguistics', used to refer to a 'science of language', was Germanic in origin though it was first widely disseminated in other continental languages. In French for example, A. Balbi in his *Introduction à l'atlas ethnographique du globe* wrote of 'cette science nouvelle que les Allemands, par une dénomination plus juste et beaucoup plus convenable, apellent linguistique' (Balbi, 1826, p.ix). The term itself was worthy of an entry in the sixth edition of the *Dictionnaire de l'Académie* giving its date as 1835: '*linguistique*: Etude des principes et des rapports des langues, science de la grammaire générale appliquée aux diverses langues'. And P. Leroux in his *De l'Humanité* of 1840 refers unself-consciously to a field within which there are established positions and controversial counter-positions:

> Tout ceux qui s'occupent de linguistique aujourd'hui, savent que les prétendues differences infranchissables qu'on avait voulu établir entre les langues qu'on appelle semitiques et celles qu'on derive du sanscrit n'existent pas à une certaine profondeur.   (Leroux, 1840, vol. II, p.637) [All those concerned with linguistics today know that the alleged insuperable differences which scholars had sought to establish between those languages called the semitic languages and those traced from the sanskrit, do not exist if one delves deeper.]

By the mid-nineteenth century, M. Cournot in his *Essai sur les fondements de nos connaissances et sur les caractères de la critique philosophie*, was able to write of the worth of linguistics as a field of research:

> La linguistique, . . . cette science toute récente et si digne d'interêt, dont l'objet est de mettre en relief les affinités naturelles et les liens de parenté des idiomes.   (Cournot, 1851, p.252) [Linguistics . . . that science of such recent date and so worthy of interest, whose aim is to highlight the natural relationships and family resemblances between languages.]

However, although the terms 'linguistik' or 'linguistique' were in increasing use on the Continent in referring to the new 'science of language', the situation within Britain was different. In Britain no such term was in use although there was one contender: 'philology'. 'Philology' in the first half of the nineteenth century in Britain still had the sense of 'the general study of classical literature – scholarship *tout court'* (Burrow, 1967, p.180). That is, the study of literature with a stress on polite learning as it was defined by George Campbell in 1776: 'all the branches of philology, such as history, civil, ecclesiastic and literary: grammar, languages, jurisprudence and criticism' (Campbell, 1776, p.56). Yet by the mid-nineteenth century the term had become more specific in its range of reference in Britain, since according to J.S. Blackie writing in 1852, 'philology unfolds the genesis of those laws of speech, which Grammar contemplates as a finished result' (Blackie, 1852, p.7). However, even this specialisation was not enough to enable 'philology' to become the dominant name for the new field. The new 'science of language' in Britain went under various names and in 1821 Sir James Mackintosh described it as 'a science so new as to be yet without a name' (Aarsleff, 1967, p.142). As late as 1862 Müller wrote that:

The Science of Language is a science of very modern date. We cannot trace its lineage much beyond the beginning of our century, and it is scarcely received as yet on a footing of equality by the elder branches of learning. Its very name is still unsettled, and the various titles that have been given to it in England, France, and Germany are so vague and varying that they have led to the most confused ideas among the public at large as to the real objects of this new science. We hear it spoken of as Comparative Philology, Scientific Etymology, Phonology, and Glossology. In France it has received the convenient, but somewhat barbarous, name of *Linguistique*. If we must have a Greek title for our science, we might derive it either from *mythos*, word, or from *logos*, speech. But the title of *Mythology* is already occupied, and *Logology* would jar too much on classical ears. We need not waste our time in criticising these names, as none of them has as yet received that universal sanction which belongs to the titles of other modern sciences, such as Geology or Comparative Anatomy; nor will there be much difficulty in christening our young science after we have once ascertained its birth, its parentage, and its character.   (Müller, 1862, pp.3–4)

The name with which the new science was eventually christened was of course linguistics, a version of which had been used by Whewell in 1837 when he asserted that 'we may call the science of languages linguistic, as it is called by the best German writers' (Whewell, 1837, vol. i, p.cxiv). However, this direct importation of the German *linguistik* demonstrates the novelty of the term and it was not until the last quarter of the century that the now familiar form appears in common use.

Müller's comment on the difficulty of setting a name for the 'young science' points out one of the differences between Britain and the rest of western Europe. In Britain not only had a name not been settled upon, there was as yet no overwhelming acceptance of the 'young science' as a 'modern science'. Unlike geology or comparative anatomy, the science of language had not yet been subject to the ascertainment of 'its birth, its parentage, and its character' and thus did not have the status of scientificity thrust upon its methods. The 'science of language' had certainly begun to dominate intellectual thought in western Europe but not, it is argued, in Britain. By 1820 the first major works in the field had been completed: F. von Schlegel's *Über die Sprache und Weisheit der Indier* (1808), Rasmus Rasks' *Undersøgelse om det gamle Nordiske eller Islandske Sprogs Oprindelse* (1814, pub. 1818), Franz Bopp's *Über das Conjugationssystem* (1816) and Jacob Grimm's *Deutsche Grammatik* (1819). In Britain, however, the new science was only to be taken up seriously, and then not comprehensively, in the late 1830s and 1840s; moreover, the greatest part of this British work in Comparative Philology was derivative of the earlier continental work.

There were a number of reasons for this tardiness, which have been treated at some length by Aarsleff (1967, ch. 5). One of the principal reasons was that the scope and ambition of the continental work daunted many British scholars. This is a point well illustrated (albeit retrospectively) in Thomas Hardy's poem 'Liddell and Scott, on the Completion of their Lexicon'. The subjects of the poem are the lexicographers who produced the *Greek–English Lexicon Based on the German Work of Francis Passow* (1843), constructed on the continental philological principles. In the poem Liddell bemoans having left the safe ground of theology for the uncertainties of the 'young science':

> And how I often, often wondered
> What could have led me to have blundered
> So far away from sound theology
> To dialects and etymology;
> Words, accents not to be breathed by men
> Of any country ever again.

To which Scott consents with the further complaint:

> That German has read
> More than we! . . .
> Yea, several times did I feel so.
>
> (Hardy, 1979, 828)

Liddell's complaint also points to a further obstacle to the reception of comparative philology, which was the threat that it presented to the established opinions of 'sound theology'. The anti-intellectualism of one section of Victorian Britain was to provide little space for an analytical and rationalist 'science of language' that for some was later to outrank even geology and the theory of evolution as the chief focus of religious doubt. Though of course the picture was not as clear as this might suggest since language was also used by some to defend theological claims, as will be shown in Chapter 2. The point in regard to that argument, however, will be that although the study of language was used in defence of theology, it was not the analytical and rationalist form of that study that was used but a specific British form. The sort of distinction referred to here is made by a later commentator when reviewing the period; he asserted that 'to poetry and humour the English will respond, ideas they find inhuman' (Granville-Barker, 1929, p.164). It was, to adapt Müller's phrase slightly, more the mythological than the scientific aspects of the new study that interested such theologians.

The distrust of the more rationalist continental approaches is also captured in the lines of Browning's poem 'Development':

> What's this the Germans say is fact
> That Wolf found out first? It's unpleasant work
> Their chop and change, unsettling one's belief
> . . .
> Why must he needs come doubting, spoil a dream?
>   (Browning, 1981, p.918)

However, although the new science did not gain much of a foothold in Britain it is important not to overstate the case since it did win significant victories and many of its results were absorbed into British scholarship. For example the Anglo-Saxon Controversy of the 1830s, in which the new and old methods of linguistic study were opposed to each other with the new methods emerging victoriously, ensured that the backward state in which most students of language found themselves in Britain would at least partly be modified by an awareness of the merits of continental work, even if such work was not taken up extensively.[2] However, such victories were minimal since at the established universities the distrust of German scholarship was deep-seated. One instance of this fear was the rejection of Max Müller's candidature for the Boden chair of Sanskrit at Oxford on the grounds of fears about rationalism and atheism sparked off by his surnominal umlaut (Dowling, 1982, pp.160–78). More concrete evidence is demonstrated in the fact that the Philological Society, formed in 1842 'for the investigation of the structure, the Affinities and the History of Languages; and the Philological Illustration of the Classical Writers of Greece and Rome', hardly concentrated at all on the theoretical objects or methods of comparative philology and worked instead in a much more empirical fashion than the comparativists. The concerns of the society were much wider than those of the European linguists, as is shown by the contents of volume I of their *Proceedings*. The *Proceedings* included articles on English orthography, Welsh onomastics, English etymologies, European grammars, lexicons of Sanskrit, the language of the Papuan or Negrito race in the Australian and Asiatic islands, the origin of the phrase 'wager of law', the classification of Chinese roots, Welsh derivatives, the inflection of Old English adjectives, the languages and dialects of the British Isles, the probable relations of the Picts and Gauls with the other tribes of Great Britain, Plato's Number, remarks on the statute of Endymion, the Berber language, Herodotus and the Athenians, the reformation of the English alphabet, the origin and import of the Augment in Sanskrit and Greek, and English Pronouns Personal (*Proc. Phil. Soc.*, 1, 1842–4). This staggering range of empirically investigated cultural and anthropological topics was not peculiar to the first volume and work of this type was to be published in the *Proceedings* (and later, *Transactions*) of the Philological Society throughout the century. What should be clear from this is that the study of 'the history of language' (as Paul was to describe the new theoretical science), was not taken up in Britain in the manner in which it had so successfully been taken up throughout Europe. The new science may have gained respect but not discursive hegemony, and this fact is puzzling. Given its advantageous position in its relation to the 'old philology' (as exemplified in the results of the Anglo-Saxon Controversy), there remains the need for an adequate account of the relative neglect of the new science of language in Britain. This account can only be provided by a close analysis of the relations between history and language as perceived by British linguists of the mid century.

Although British linguists of the period did not, on the whole, take up the theoretical and historical perspective of the comparativists they did not reject history either. Indeed the failure of the science of language, more than by reference to its novelty and fears of its rationalism, can best be explained by reference to its displacement by another linguistic and historical discourse. Instead of the study of 'the history of language', British linguists worked within the study of 'the history of the language'. The evidence will not support Müller's claim for the desire for knowledge of language rather than knowledge of a language: in mid-nineteenth-century Britain the converse was true.

Appeals for 'the history of the language'

In Britain a distinct type of interest in history was to dominate linguistic studies in the nineteenth century. A relationship between language and history was to be developed that was linked to, but significantly at variance with, the relations between language and history that lay at the foundations of the work of the comparativists.

The names of at least the early comparativists are familiar from the often repeated brief histories of the subject that appear in introductory textbooks: Jones, Bopp, Grimm, the Schlegels, Rask, Verner, and so on. All have their allotted space and role. There is another set of names or designations, however, familiar to readers in the field of British cultural history over the past 150 years. Bradley, Craigie, Ellis, Furnivall, Morris, Murray, Onions, Skeat, Sweet, Trench, Wedgwood, the Wrights, and Wyld: these are the names of the British linguistic historians whose texts are read or cited in even the most recent of historical accounts of this field. It is the appearance of these writers and their particular concern with the relations between history and language that will be explored in the remainder of this chapter.

Within the texts of this group of writers there is another pattern of familiarity since the subject matter (and its arrangement as will be argued later), is again recognisable. Frequent references are made to specific texts of particular authors in an ordered chronology: Higden's *Polychronicon*, Chaucer's comments on linguistic diversity in *Troilus and Criseyde*, Caxton's Preface to *Eneydos*, Waller's complaint about English orthographical mutability, the Royal Society's desire for simple prose, Swift's *Proposal*, Johnson's *Dictionary* and so on familiarly. The pattern of repetition set out in this taxonomic classification (itself familiar to the nineteenth century), clearly delineates a designated field of knowledge as it traces the outlines of a structure that holds these texts together. This is a set of texts whose importance is created precisely by their arrangement within this field of knowledge since their relation to each other, and their relation to other texts, gives them particular values and enables them to carry out specific tasks within this field. This is not just a random selection of texts but a structured arrangement, and these texts are given order in the structure of the discourse that we now know as 'the history of the language'. In fact what is remarkable about these texts is not the repetitious use made of them to 'illustrate' 'the history of the language' used in England, but the fact that they can be made use of to perform such work at all. Describing this as remarkable is seeking to call attention only to the novelty of such a possibility since these texts have been able to be deployed within 'the history of the language' only relatively recently since the field itself as an academic and cultural discourse is a comparative newcomer. 'The history of the language' is perhaps 150 years old but certainly no more; once this is appreciated, it follows that such texts as those cited above could not have been used to 'illustrate' 'the history of the language' before that date, or at least could not have been used in any systematic way.

Evidently more will have to be said before such a claim can be allowed to stand. Therefore I propose to look at linguistic texts from the 1830s and 1840s in order to demonstrate that 'the history of the language' as a specific field of knowledge (distinct of course from work upon the history of the language), is of recent date. Edwin Guest, for example, whose work was later described by the dialectologist and etymologist Walter Skeat as 'pioneering', had argued for the need for greater research in his *History of English Rhythms* (1838). Guest had written:

> The history of our language has suffered, equally with that of our poetry, from overlooking the peculiarities of our poetic dialect. . . . A complete history of our rhythms would probably lead to a very satisfactory arrangement for our poetry; and enable us to trace, with more truth and precision than has hitherto been done, at once the progress of our language, and the gradual development of our inventive genius.   (Guest, 1838, p.301)

Evidently, neither the labour nor the materials for such work had yet been furnished since Guest bemoaned the fact that:

> Unfortunately, the published specimens of our early litera-

ture are so scant as rarely to furnish us with an unbroken series of early rhythms. Large gaps occur, which can only be filled by a laborious search into MSS scattered through the country and not always very easy of access.   (*Ibid.*)

The appeal for work in this general area was also made by Hensleigh Wedgwood (Darwin's brother-in-law), who argued for research into English etymology as the means of preserving 'much valuable knowledge' and of accumulating 'materials for an etymology of the English language, for which at the present day, we have little to show beyond the uncertain guesses of Junius and Skinner' (Wedgwood, 1844, p.2). In the same volume of the *Proc. Phil. Soc.*, J.M. Kemble argued for work on the 'comparative anatomy of the Anglo-Saxon' since:

In spite of a certain outward activity which has always existed and does yet exist in England with regard to that language, there is reason to suspect that very few persons indeed have penetrated its secret, or possess any beyond the merest superficial acquaintance with its philological character.   (Kemble, 1845, p.131)

Two years later, James Halliwell commented in his *Dictionary of Archaisms and Provincial Words* on 'the general history of the English language'. He described it as 'a subject of great difficulty, and one which requires far more reading than has yet been attempted to develop satisfactorily, especially in its early period' (Halliwell, 1847, vol. 1, p.x).

It is possible to read in these texts of the 1840s a clear anxiety: an anxious recognition of gaps, neglect and superficial acquaintance in works on the history of the language. Yet these texts and others are set within the early formations of the discourse that was to fill gaps, rectify neglect and render more than superficial knowledge. In the 1840s and 1850s a number of texts were published that signalled the appearance and rise to rapid hegemony of the new discourse: 'the history of the language'. From that point on all work on the history of the language was conducted from within 'the history of the language' and texts, institutions and various forms of discursive practice bore witness to the importance of the new field of knowledge.

R.G. Latham's *The English Language* (1841) was perhaps the most popular of the early texts, its first Part being an 'Historical and Analytical View of the English Language'. Moreover, the dominance of the new discourse and the importance attached to it are signalled by Latham's publication of what is essentially the same material in texts of varying form for different levels of readership. For example, within a period of eight years he had published much the same materials in texts such as his *Elementary English Grammar* (1843), the *Elements of English Grammar for the Use of Ladies' Schools* (1849), *The History and Etymology of the English Language for the Use of Classical Schools* (1849), *A Grammar of the English Language for the Use of Commercial Schools* (1850), and *A Handbook of the English Language* (1851).[3] Latham's texts were clearly designed to be used at specific levels in the educational system and the intended audience dictated the textual presentation of the material. Thus the history of the language, in the form of short histories and overviews, was to be taught and learnt by rote: elementary schools, 'ladies schools', 'classical schools', 'commercial schools', and the universities, were to be the sites of its dissemination.

It has been argued so far that one accepted account of the history of the study of language in the nineteenth century is inaccurate if we consider Britain, in that it reductively neglects the specificity of British historical work on language. Comparative philology was not the dominant mode of linguistic study in Britain, since on the contrary, the concern for the relations between history and language in Britain produced a novel and powerful discourse, that of 'the history of the language'. It is intended next to indicate why 'the history of the language' became such a powerful cultural discourse in nineteenth-century Britain, relegating on the way not only comparative philology but many other cultural discourses to an inferior status. 'The history of the language' and the texts it produced held sway in a specific sphere of cultural activity until one of its own progeny rose in turn to displace it. This was, of course, English studies.

The birth of 'the history of the language'

In his Romanes Lecture of 1900, *The Evolution of English Lexicography*, Sir James Murray (the first major editor of the *New/Oxford English Dictionary*) asserted that, 'the evolution of English lexicography has followed with no faltering footsteps the evolution of English History and the Development of English literature' (Murray, 1900, p.51). For our purposes, Murray's claim for lexicography will be broadened to a claim for the study of language generally. If Murray was correct, then we could usefully investigate relations between language study, literature and history and this section will concentrate upon the conditions that made the birth of the new discipline possible in the mid-nineteenth century.

Thomas De Quincey's essay 'The English Language' (1839) is a text that characterises much of the contemporary thinking about language in Britain and indicates the future direction of such work. In the essay, De Quincey notes (and is pre-emptively at one with Foucault in this) how a particular discipline comes to take its place within the field of knowledge, and how, once established, it becomes difficult not to think of it as always having been in place. Moreover the example that De Quincey cites is one that also concerns Foucault in his archaeology of knowledge: economics. De Quincey argues:

> For example, odd as it may seem to us, it is certain that in the Elizabethan age, Political Economy was not yet viewed by any mind, no, not by Lord Bacon's, as even a possible mode of speculation. The whole accidents of value and its functions were not as yet separated into a distinct conscious object, nor, if they had been, would it have been supposed possible to trace laws and fixed relations among forms apparently so inpalpable and combinations so fleeting.   (De Quincey, 1890, vol. xiv, p.148)

The tracing of hitherto unnoticed 'laws and fixed relations' was not to be restricted to political economy at this time since students of language were also concerned for the first time with tracing precisely such organising principles in their object. As one of De Quincey's contemporaries wrote in 1839, students of language were concerned with:

The dignity of human speech, [and] of perceiving how little of the casual and capricious there is in language, and of convincing themselves that in this, as in other things, there are laws to combine, regulate and vivify the seemingly disjointed, scattered and lifeless phenomena. (Donaldson, 1839, p.vii)

For Foucault it was the appearance of historicity that made the new sciences such as economics and philology viable; and De Quincey was also concerned with history but in a different sense. For De Quincey the new order of things, the emergence of new methodologies and therefore new sciences, caused problems. He saw the new methodologies as disturbing historiography itself in that they revealed the deficiencies in contemporary thinking about the past and the past writing of history. Therefore he expressed concern with regard to current historiography, particularly with reference to the nations of England and France, as he argued that 'the history of neither kingdom has yet been written in such a way to last, or in a way worthy of the subject' (De Quincey, *op. cit.*, p.148). Specifically, he criticised those histories 'written without knowledge as regards the political forces which moved underground at the great eras of our national development'. Therefore he appealed for a new type of concern with history, and a new historiography that would concern itself with those forces moving underground to produce particular effects. However, this is not to claim that De Quincey sought a crudely economic form of history since, it will be argued, his appeal for a new form of history was cultural rather than economic in its focus. He cannot be accused anachronistically of accepting the cruder version of the unfortunate base-superstructure model of the social formation familiar to critics of 'vulgar Marxism' since he specifies that his historical attention is to be focused upon 'political forces' rather than economic forces. However, it is important to bear in mind that he does maintain the radical distinction between the material world and social consciousness that was to be central to the text of one of De Quincey's later admirers, Marx. In fact he even expresses tentatively the crucial view that it is social being that determines consciousness, rather than vice versa, as he argues that:

> Possibly the aspects of society must shift materially before even the human consciousness, far less a human interest of curiosity, settles upon them with steadiness enough to light up and vivify their relations.   (*Ibid.*, p.147)

For De Quincey a new sense of historicity had to be introduced into language studies, but not in the sense of encouraging the historical perspective of comparative philology in Britain. His purpose was quite different, and novel, in that he proposed the political and cultural project of the writing and rewriting of the history of the English language and therefore the formation of 'the history of the language'. What he exemplified (rather than initiated) in this gesture, was the concern with the appearance of a new academic discipline, a new field of knowledge to be worked upon by the enormously energetic cultural producers of Victorian Britain. He announced (though its appearance was not dependent upon him) the arrival of 'the history of the language' and therefore, for the first time proper, historians of the language.

It is important to make clear the point being made here. The claim is not that there had been nothing written about 'the language' before 1840, or even that there had been nothing written about the history of the language before that date. The claim is that before this period there had been no historians of the language simply because there had been as yet no 'history of the language' as a field of knowledge, no discourse that could operate under such a title. In the same way, there were no natural scientists before the appearance of 'the natural sciences' as a distinct field of knowledge, a field related to other fields in particular ways and one whose relative position could change. To claim that there were 'natural scientists' in the sixteenth century, for example, is to neglect the differences of history since it is to subsume wholly differing practices and activities under a sort of Platonic 'form' in order to unify them. It is to say, in effect, that there have *always* been 'natural scientists' and that in turn relegates history to a subsidiary place. In this view, the category 'natural scientist' is fixed and it is the simple role of history to inform us of what the 'natural scientists' did at any specific period. For this reading differences are unimportant and are mere variations within an eternal verity. However, the argument here is against this reading: the claim is that 'the history of the language' is a specific textual, institutional and discursive practice that appears at a particular period, one that has specific types of relation to other discourses, and one that is deployed in certain ways. Before that period it is certainly true that there were writers upon the history of 'the language' (as will be illustrated) but there were no historians of the language any more than there were 'natural scientists' in the sixteenth century simply by dint of the fact that there were people interested in the natural world and its composition. To argue for this reading of the appearance of 'the history of the language' is not, however, to hail De Quincey as the initiator of the discipline since such attributions are at best highly reductive. It is to claim, rather, that a new field appeared which in turn enabled new categories and new types of cultural production. De Quincey lay within that field rather than outside it, a participant rather than an originator.

In fact De Quincey met the objection that has already been specified, that there had been many previous writers on the history of 'the language'. He acknowledges the work of Jonson, Wallis, Nares, Webster, Murray, Priestley, and, of course, Johnson. After reviewing their work he commented, 'there we have the total amount of what has hitherto been contributed towards the investigation of the English language'. He then went on to draw a distinction between that work and the new type of work he envisaged:

> As to the investigation of its history, of its gradual rise and progress, and its relations to neighbouring languages, *that* is a total blank; a title pointing to a duty absolutely in arrears rather than to any performance ever undertaken as yet, even by way of tentative essay.   (*Ibid.*)

The point was reinforced by Guest in his *History of English Rhythms*, also published in 1839, in which he asserted that, 'the little attention that is paid to the critical study of our language, and the slight regard which attempts to investigate its history have met with reflect no less a discredit on our patriotism than on our scholarship'. He continues by comparing this with the situation in France and Germany:

> While Frenchmen are sending agents over Europe to scrutinise every MS which may shed light on their early literature, Englishmen are satisfied with knowing that Anglo-Saxon MSS may be found in France, in Holland and in Sweden. The German publishes the most insignificant fragment connected with the antiquities of his language, while *our* MSS lie mouldering in our libraries, and our critics – some of them of no mean reputation – content themselves with the vague and scanty notices of a Hickes and a Wanley. (Guest, *op. cit.*, pp.702–3)

Work on the history of 'the language', or at least on what was considered to be the earliest stages of 'the language', had been sporadically undertaken, as Guest's last line indicates. The earliest work in this area had been undertaken during the Reformation for explicitly radical political purposes in order to prove the continuity and stability of the English church and nation. And nineteenth-century linguistic historians were fully aware of this earlier work and its political import, as evinced when G.L. Craik, writing of that 'form of the national speech' known as Anglo-Saxon, argued that the English Reformers had studied it 'for evidence of the comparatively unromanized condition of the Early English Church' (Craik, 1861, vol. 1, p.33). In fact the Reformation period saw a number of works on earlier writers. John Leland collected materials for a history of English writers which was later incorporated into Bale's *Illustrium Maioris Britanniae Scriptorum Summarium* (1548). And in 1566 the first work printed in Anglo-Saxon letters (a reproduction of Aelfric's 'Easty Homily'), appeared in *A Testimonial of Antiquity*. However, most of this work began to appear only in the seventeenth century and began to gain wide recognition only in the eighteenth. In 1638 Sir Henry Spelman founded a lectureship at Cambridge to be concerned with 'domestick antiquities touching our church, and revising the Anglo-Saxon tongue', although the lectureship dropped into obscurity. Other isolated seventeenth-century figures were Wallis, Skinner, Junius and Hickes; the chief of these was Hickes, whose major works included the *Anglo-Saxon Grammar* of 1689 (used as a basis for their work by Rask, Grimm and Bopp), and his *Thesaurus* of 1703. Swift's *Proposal* (1712) included elements of historical sketching, and Johnson's *Dictionary* (1755) was prefaced by a 'History of the English Language' including specimens of earlier texts. Two interesting texts that appear to have escaped the notice of most historians of the language actually bore titles that might lead the careless reader to date the appearance of the new discourse in the mid-eighteenth century. These are John Free's *An Essay Towards an History of the English Tongue* (1749) and V.J. Peyton's *The History of the English Language* (1771). However, the most interesting thing about these texts is that Free's is not concerned with English but with the ancient languages of Britain – the Roman (Latin), British (Welsh), the Pyntas (Pictish), Scots (Erse); and Peyton's only offers a short sketch followed by a long plea for the superiority of English and for its study. In the literary field also, Thomas Percy's *Reliques of Ancient Poetry* (1765) and *Northern Antiquities* (1770), along with Warton's *History of English Poetry* (1774–81) bear testimony to an interest in giving a history to earlier writing. And by the end of the eighteenth century, such work was becoming more familiar and frequent. The most significant of this work was that of Sharon Turner (*History of the Anglo Saxons*, 1799–1805), and James Ingram (*The Utility of Anglo-Saxon Literature*, 1807), along with John Josias Conybeare (Ingram's successor in the Oxford Rawlinsonian Chair), Joseph Bosworth (one of the last of the old school philologists), and John Kemble and Benjamin Thorpe (bearers of the New Philology from the continent). In his inaugural lecture Ingram gave his own short history of Anglo-Saxon studies in Britain and summarised the increasing importance they were gaining. Interestingly too, he defended the utility of studying Anglo-Saxon precisely on the grounds of its political importance. Anglo-Saxon, he commented:

> is of the greatest importance to Englishmen, in that it is intimately connected with the original introduction and

establishment of their present language and laws, their
liberty and their religion.   (Ingram, 1807, p.2)

The sheer increase in the volume of such work, the constant
stress on its significance, and the frequent references to the
small amount of earlier work indicate the growing importance
attached to this field of knowledge. Anxieties about the status
of British scholarship in its study of the native language,
combined with an increased sense of the 'patriotic' importance
of such work, led to repeated appeals for new work, new
studies, and a new field of history.

However, despite the increasing volume of such work, there
was as yet no field to which it could properly be said to belong
since the aims and methods of those who wrote upon such
topics were so diverse in this early period. Was their work
literary, philological (in the old sense), comparatively philological, philosophical, political, literary, historical, or . . . ? Well,
or what? The work seemed as yet not to fall into any specific
field since its aims and methods spanned so many. No category
could as yet be assigned since the work lacked, so to speak, a
unifying subject. However, the appearance of that unifying
force was signalled by the novel project that was to make the
English language an object to be constructed and ordered
according to the continuity of what may be called 'national
time'. To accomplish that task the project would have to be
ambitious and it was in fact astounding. The project was to
make the English language its own meta-language; or to put
it another way, to construct a history of the English language
simply by using ordered examples from the language itself. It
is significant that allegorically linked to this new historical
and 'scientific' investigation that was to be embodied in the
discourse of the 'history of the language', was the similarly
newly developing field of symbolic logic. Symbolic logic,
apparently the most a-historical of signifying systems, was to
be described repeatedly as *the* meta-language, the transparent
system by which the historically untainted but obscure workings of the rational mind could be made clear. Within the
'history of the language', however, it was not the symbols of
logic but the familiar terms of the language itself that were to
be both subject and object of the study. That is, linguistic

terms (from within the language) were to be used to construct a history (that is to stand outside the language), in order to permit the new discourse. So ambitious was the project that it can be said to have eclipsed all other linguistic projects within Britain for the next century. From that point on, any piece of writing – past, present, or future – had at least a dual function since whatever other status it had, it was henceforth assured of its importance to the historians of the language. As T.L. Kington-Oliphant argued, the new discourse created new interest in a diverse field of objects as now, 'poems, scriptural and profane, epics, war-songs, riddles, translations of the bible, homilies, prayers, treatises on science and grammar, codes of law, wills, charters, chronicles set down year by year, and dialogues, all these . . .' had become of interest. The list is, of course, potentially infinite: treatises on rainfall in tropical rainforests, medieval tracts, philosophical speculations, gravestones, advertisements for children's shoes, the Daily Mirror, lists of the fishes of the sea and birds of the air, even a literary text: all had lost their innocence. The humble art of writing was humble no more since each and every occurrence was now, at least in one respect, equally important since nothing was to escape the scrupulous net of the historian of the language. From now on all writing in English became at least potentially the object of the 'history of the language', and the new discourse was to unite various types of cultural products that could not previously have been brought together.

Herman Paul was later to set out 'the true object of philological study' as:

the entire sum of the products of linguistic activity of the entire sum of individuals in their reciprocal relations. All the groups of sounds ever spoken, heard, or represented, with the associated ideas whose symbols they were; all these belong to the history of language, and must, properly speaking, all be thoroughly apprehended to render a full apprehension of its development and possibility. (Paul, *op. cit.*, pp.2–3)

Clearly the ambition of 'the history of language' as a

discipline was all-encompassing, but the ambition of 'the history of the language', though grand in itself, was not quite so great. Instead of the 'linguistic activity of the entire sum of individuals in their reciprocal relations', the object of 'the history of the language' was simply to be the linguistic activity of the entire sum of English-speaking individuals in their reciprocal relations. Thus 'the history of the language' was to create a necessary methodological unity: if it was to have as its subject of study 'all the groups of sound ever spoken, heard or represented, with the associated ideas whose symbols they were' of English-speaking individuals, then it had first to organise these individuals into a unity. That unity was the nation, and thus it was that the language was to serve as a crucial focal point of national unity as it bound all English-speaking individuals together at the present and gave them a sense of a common past history. Each English-speaking individual was a member of a synchronic, collective 'social fact', and a diachronic, continuous evolution. Thus 'the history of the language' was to become a unifying tendency not just in the area of knowledge but in important cultural and political areas too.

The study of language and British history

The new cultural project had been specified clearly by De Quincey in his call for a 'monument of learning and patriotism' to be erected to the vernacular language. He asserted that:

> The most learned work which the circumstances of any known or obvious case will allow, the work which pre-supposes the amplest accomplishments of judgement and enormous erudition would be a history of the English language from its earliest rudiments, through all the periods of its growth, to its stationary condition.   (De Quincey, *op. cit.*, p.149)

He saw it as a serious fault that we 'possess at this day no history, no circumstantial annals, of its growth and condition at different eras'. That fault, that absent history so often remarked upon, was to be rectified by the construction of an area of knowledge whose development was to be dependent on recognition of the importance of the project in cultural and political terms. As with the 'discovery' of the Anglo-Saxon texts in the reformation period, their nineteenth-century rediscovery was laden with political significance. Therefore, as De Quincey appealed for the project to be undertaken, he simultaneously signalled the value of its object:

> Let us recognise with thankfulness that fortunate inheritance of collateral wealth, which, by inoculating our Anglo-Saxon stem with the mixed dialect of Neustria, laid open an avenue mediately through which the whole opulence of Roman, and ultimately, of Greek thought, play freely through the pulses of our native English.   (*Ibid.*, p.151)

This coupling of the classical world and contemporary Britain in linguistic and literary terms was to prove an effective rhetorical strategy in various forms of political discourse over the next century. Matthew Arnold was the major proponent of such linkage, particularly in *Culture and Anarchy*, and one of his editors was to make use of the same strategy for cultural and political purposes during the First World War. Sir Arthur Quiller Couch argued that:

> From Anglo-Saxon prose, from Anglo-Saxon poetry, our living poetry and prose have, save linguistically, no deriva-tion . . . whatever the agency – whether through Wyatt, or Spenser, Marlowe or Shakespeare, or Donne, or Milton, or Dryden, or Pope, or Johnson, or even Wordsworth – always our literature has obeyed, however unconsciously, the precept *Antiquam exquisite matrem*, 'seek back to the ancient mother'; always it has recreated itself, kept itself pure and strong, by harking back to bathe in those native – yes, native – Mediterranean springs. (Quiller Couch, 1918, pp.25–6)

The war situation meant that nothing but the purely linguistic connections between the Anglo-Saxon and modern English literature could be acknowledged. Thus by a neat interpretation of history, all significant cultural contact with the 'war-like' Teutons could be denied and our direct descent from the democratic Greeks and Romans reaffirmed.

In his own deployment of this rhetorical strategy De Quincey was using elements from previously articulated discourses of patriotism involving language, since Junius had derived Anglo-Saxon from Greek, and G.W. Lemon in his etymological dictionary of 1783 had also held that 'the groundwork of our modern English tongue is Greek' (Lemon, 1783, p.v). And it was in the political realm that such analogies were to prove most durable. For Lemon the linguistic connection between writers in English and the Greek and Latin poets meant that English-speakers 'naturally' shared the classical precepts of freedom and debate. Thus, he argued, 'as England is the *land of liberty*, so is her *language* the voice of freedom'. It follows from this that:

> Others then may admire the flimsiness of the French, the neatness of the Italian, the gravity of the Spanish, nay even the native hoarseness and roughness of the Saxon, High Dutch, Belgic and Teutonic tongues; but the purity and dignity, and all the high graceful majesty, which appears at present in our *modern English tongue*, will certainly recommend it to our most diligent researches.   (*Ibid.*, pp.6–7)

There is a clear tone of pride in these words but we may find too a sense of anxiety: not simply an anxiety about a neglected area of knowledge but anxiety about the contemporary historical situation. The louder the praise for the 'liberty', 'freedom', 'purity', 'dignity' and 'high graceful majesty' of the language, the more one might be led to ask why such clamour is necessary. And it is to that question, the problem of how the contemporary historical situation influenced the appearance of the cultural field now known as 'the history of the language' that we have finally to turn in this chapter.

De Quincey's critical essay was produced in relation to a crisis that profoundly altered many distinct discourses at particular levels: the crisis of Chartism. Early industrial Britain passed through several crises in the early nineteenth century, but what Stedman-Jones has described as the intricate arrangements of critical moments focused around forces and activities as diverse as Luddism, radical reformism, trade unionism and campaigns for suffrage, was to find its most salient point (and in some senses its breaking point) in the Chartist movement. In 1845 a commentator upon the state of Britain over the past twenty-five years noted that there had been a:

> Coexistence of so much suffering in one part of the people, with so much prosperity in another; of unbounded private wealth, with unceasing public penury . . . of the utmost freedom consistent with order, ever yet existing upon earth, with a degree of discontent which keeps the nation constantly on the verge of insurrection.   (Alison, 1845, p.15)

It was a division that was to be clearly visible in Victorian architecture, in that contrast between the bold, perspicuous glass case of the Great Exhibition and the enormously boastful municipal buildings, and the concealing slums and workhouses. Yet Chartism in its most radical phases appeared to produce a discourse that challenged the rule of capital since as Hobsbawm has argued:

> Marx and Engels rightly pointed out [that] in the 1840s the spectre of communism haunted Europe. If it was relatively less feared in Britain, the spectre of economic breakdown was equally appalling to the Middle Class. (Hobsbawm, 1969, p.77)

And the form of the British ghost was Chartism.

The educationalist James Kay-Shuttleworth (described by Arnold as 'the founder of English popular education'), writing in the period 1839–41 accurately described the shift within discourse brought about by elements of the Chartist movement with their recovery and forging of radical forms of resistance. He asserted that:

> A great change has taken place in the moral and intellectual state of the working-classes. . . . Formerly they considered their poverty and sufferings as inevitable, as far as they

thought about them at all; now, rightly or wrongly, they attribute their sufferings to political causes; they think that by a change in political institutions their condition can be enormously ameliorated.   (Kay-Shuttleworth, 1862, p.229)

Inevitability no longer proved acceptable in the discourses of politics and economics since poverty was now attributed (by the reform movement and its allies) to specific causes in the political sphere and, therefore, changes could be demanded to eradicate those causes. The same writer noted the effects of this discursive shift as he wrote that, 'the Great Chartist petition . . . affords ample evidence of the prevalence of the restless desire for organic changes, and for violent political measures, which pervades the manufacturing districts and which is everyday increasing' (*ibid.*). For Kay-Shuttleworth the contradiction between the older discourse of 'inevitability' and the 'natural' state of affairs, and the new discourse of 'restless desire' and 'violent political measures' could be resolved only in one way: the 'natural laws of trade' had to be reasserted in order to dominate the 'armed political monster', the 'anarchical spirit of the Chartist association'. Which is to say that for this writer at least, struggle within discourse had to take place in order to prevent the outbreak of other forms of struggle.

Chartism was linked to previous forms of radical resistance but was itself a specific form of radicalism as Stedman-Jones has recently argued. Its specificity lay in 'the equation of the people with the working-class' and upon 'a corresponding shift of emphasis upon the relationship between the state and the working-class' (Stedman-Jones, 1983, p.173). In the first instance this class–state relationship was one structured by overt repression with the state figuring as the implement for the political and economic suppression of working-class interests through measures such as the New Poor Law, the Municipal Corporations Act, opposition to factory legislation, attacks upon trade unionism and the extension of the police force. And thus as the same writer argues of this period:

The legislative record, from Peel's introduction of the Metropolitan police to the petering out of the Whig reform

programme in the late 1830s, did indeed signify the most
consequential attempt to dismantle or transform the
decentralised treatment of problems of crime, poverty and
social order characteristic of the eighteenth-century
state.   (*Ibid.*, p.175)

However, by the end of the 1830s 'the state was already
beginning to withdraw from [its] exposed position', and the
harsher, more overt forms of oppression, and the discourses
used to justify it, were displaced by the new discourses of
reform, evolution and gradual development. And coetaneous
with that shift was the recession of the radically threatening
dangers of Chartism. Hobsbawm describes this process as the
most marked emergence within the British social formation
of, 'the characteristic combination of a revolutionary social
base and, at least at one moment – the period of militant
economic liberalism – a sweeping triumph of doctrinaire
ideology, with an apparently traditionalist and slow thinking
institutional superstructure' (Hobsbawm, 1969, p.17). By a
discursive shift in widely varying areas of the social realm (the
political, economic, juridical, and educational in particular),
the dangers threatened by Chartism were to be defused. As
the state took responsibility for measures of reform in distinct
fields (slow-thinking though it was), the radical thrust and
distinctive appeal of the discourse of Chartism was to be
robbed of its critical edge. That is not to say, of course, that
the undemocratic constitution of the British social formation
was fundamentally altered in this period since political,
cultural and economic power was still exclusively exercised.
The alterations were enough, however, according to Stedman-
Jones, to ensure that 'as coherent political language and a
believable political vision, Chartism disintegrated in the early
1840s'.
    One of the most significant of the reforms made in response
to Chartism was the introduction of the most elementary
forms of education after the first state grant for that purpose
in 1833. Kay-Shuttleworth summarised the thinking behind
such an economic and cultural measure thus:

The sole effectual means of preventing the tremendous evils

with which the anarchical spirit of the manufacturing population threatens the whole country is, by giving the working people a good secular education, to enable them to understand the true causes which determine their physical condition and regulate the distribution of wealth among the several classes of society.

Repressive state measures would not, in the view of this observer, bring about the cessation of 'restless desire' or 'violent political measures', and thus education had to fulfil that role. He continued:

Sufficient intelligence and information to appreciate these causes might be diffused by an education which could easily be brought within the reach of the entire population, though it would necessarily comprehend more than the mere mechanical rudiments of knowledge.   (Kay-Shuttleworth, *op. cit.*, p.231)

A 'good secular education' then, to be brought easily 'within the reach of the entire population' and extending beyond the 'useful knowledge' advocated by the Society for the Diffusion of Useful Knowledge in the early nineteenth century, was required as a response to Chartism.[4] This was the case since Chartism had radically affected those terms (and the discourses within which such terms were used) such as state, nation, class, rights and so on, that were of particular importance in political debates. As one of Thomas Paine's critics had alleged against him, the Chartists had brought about what amounted to 'a revolution in language' (Adams, 1793, p.10).

It is in response to the developing cultural and political crisis engendered by Chartism that we can best read De Quincey's essay and, thereby, the appearance of 'the history of the language'. The essay and the cultural project that it heralded can best be seen not as a direct or overt response but as a part of the more general set of responses that attempted to challenge the new discourses that the crisis had created. The new radical discourses of history, involving terms and concepts such as antagonism, rupture and upheaval, were met by an opposed discourse of history that stressed instead terms and concepts such as continuity, solidity and evolutionary progress. There were many aspects to the responses to Chartism (ranging from overt repression to liberal reform), which produced numerous complex effects; but one of the most important of the cultural and educational responses, and one with far-reaching effects, was the institutionalised appearance of the new discipline 'the history of the language'.

De Quincey's appeal had been for 'a moment of learning and patriotism', 'a History of the English language from its earliest rudiments, through all the periods of its growth to its stationary position', and 'an investigation of its gradual rise and progress'. In fact these aims may be taken to encapsulate many of the ends of those who worked in the area of knowledge that was to be known as 'the history of the language'. Patriotic learning was dedicated to the construction of a history of an object that had evolved gradually and continually until it reached its present, great, achieved state. Thus, against those who were to argue that history is contradictory and constituted by antagonistic forces, 'the history of the language' was to be a useful tool in an opposed discursive practice. For example, if the nation was – as a common definition of the nation proposed – nothing but the group of individuals that had always spoken one single and continuously evolving common language, did 'the history of the language' not demonstrate precisely that English was such a language and the English such a nation? For many of the mid-nineteenth-century historians of the language its unbroken existence was undoubted and that in turn therefore entailed that the English nation had itself been a long-standing, continuously evolving entity.

It is certain that historians of the language saw such an equation as unproblematic and thus their work helped solidify the unity of language and nation. G.L. Craik, for example, asserted:

Taking a particular language to mean what has always borne the same name, or been spoken by the same nation or race, which is the common or conventional understanding of the matter, the English may claim to be older than the majority of the tongues in use throughout Europe.   (Craik, 1861, vol. 1, p.30)

Here it is the nation that comes before the language, but the equation is often reversed by such writers with no apparent unease. Moreover the methodological split made by historians of the language between the internal history of the language and its external history reinforced the concept of an organically developing language. The internal history, dealing primarily with syntax and grammar, was the history of an object without historical content since it was often held that the language moved from the synthetic to the analytic state organically and not by dint of historical pressure. The external history of the language dealt with all those features not included under internal history and these were problems such as the importa tion of foreign words, or questions of good and bad taste with regards to usage and so on. The two spheres were held to be unrelated: internal history moved progressively towards formalisation and logic, external history towards those areas of meaning that were most easily perceivable as involving social and historical pressures. Another way of putting it would be to say that according to this scheme the 'essence' of the language and nation (the internal), remains always organically ordered in terms of its development and only the 'accidental' features of language and nation (the external or historical), are constantly open to change.

In concentrating upon the formal continuities of the language (the internal history), 'the history of the language' successfully portrayed its object as having a complex but unified pattern of evolution. As Craik argued, the textual specimens arranged by 'the history of the language' demonstrated continuity and unity in their development:

Of the English language, we have a continuous succession of written remains since the seventh century at least; that is to say, we have an array of specimens of it, from that date, such as that no two of them standing next to one another in the order of time could possibly be pronounced to belong to different languages, but only at most to two successive stages of the same language. They afford us a record of representation of the English language in which there is no gap.   (*Ibid.*)

W.W. Skeat was even more explicit in his arguments for the benefits of the study of 'the history of the language' for the English schoolboy:

> Perhaps the next important step, is that his eyes should be opened to the Unity of English, that in English literature there is an unbroken succession of authors, from the reign of Alfred to that of Victoria, and that the language which we speak *now* is absolutely *one* in its essence, with the language that was spoken in the days when the English first invaded the island and defeated and overwhelmed its British inhabitants.   (Skeat, 1873, p.xii)

Moreover, it was the perception of such unity and continuity that at least partly informed the debates within the 'history of the language' over terms such as 'Anglo-Saxon' or 'Old English'. As one participant in the debates later argued in favour of one of these terms, 'it is certainly an argument in favour of the designation as Old English of what is here called Anglo-Saxon, that it makes prominent the continuity of our speech' (Lounsbury, 1894, p.v).

For De Quincey too natural growth and gradual change were perceptible in both language and nation as, like a 'shallow brook', the English language (and nation) had gradually evolved into a great river. The analogy was developed in the essay as he argued that 'great Rivers as they advance and receive vast tributary influences, change their direction, their character, their very name' (De Quincey, *op. cit.*, p.149). Yet they are nonetheless the same river, developing and increasing in torrential power. The English language and nation may be subjected to historical pressures but essentially (internally) the genius of both remains everlastingly the same. It became the task of the 'history of the language' to trace the development of that genius as it historically evolved. In so doing, of course, it engaged with one of the most crucial tasks for any nation: the figuring of the national past in regard to its critical present.

Conclusion

It has been argued in this chapter that Foucault was correct in analysing the appearance of historicity as the major factor in the shift that took place in linguistic studies (as well as other fields), around the turn of the nineteenth century. However, it has also been argued that his account, and other more coventional accounts, would be reductive if applied to Britain. Comparative philology – 'the study of the history of language' – was not to take root in Britain and instead a distinctive type of concern for the relations between language and history was to appear. The concern for such relations formulated (and in turn was formulated by) a new discourse, one that we now recognise as 'the history of the language'. Moreover, it has been argued that the anxieties and concerns that brought about the new discourse were not simple scholarly worries about the state of British intellectual culture but were of more significant import. Such anxieties were produced at least in part by shifts in the political, economic and cultural discourses of early- and mid-nineteenth-century Britain.

The appearance of 'the history of the language' and much of the work produced within that discourse were specific counter-developments to the discursive shifts produced by the crisis of Chartism and earlier radical movements. Max Müller had claimed that 'in the science of language, languages are not treated as a means; language itself becomes the sole object of enquiry'. However, in so far as British linguistic work was concerned, his claim is inaccurate since British linguists did not pursue language, but *a* language (English). And the specific forms of their enquiry were influenced by concerns other than the linguistic since language *was* to be the means to other ends.

Dickens's view of the philologist in the 1840s is given in *Dombey and Son* in the sketch of Miss Blimber:

There was no light nonsense about Miss Blimber. She kept her hair short and crisp, and wore spectacles. She was dry and sandy with working in the graves of deceased languages. None of your live languages for Miss Blimber. They must be dead – stone dead – and then Miss Blimber dug them up like a ghoul.

However, for the historians of the language in Britain the main concern in language studies was not with 'dead' languages but with the relationship between the English language and past and present history. Historians of the language of this period did not and could not remove themselves from 'social and rhetorical concerns' since their discipline had been produced precisely by such concerns. To exemplify that claim, we shall turn next to an analysis of the texts of one of the most popular and influential of the mid-nineteenth-century linguistic historians, Dean (later Archbishop) Trench.

2

Archbishop Trench's Theory of Language: The Tractatus Theologico-Politicus

The first philologists and linguists were always and everywhere *priests*. History knows no nation whose sacred writings or oral traditions were not to some degree in a language foreign and incomprehensible to the profane. To decipher the mystery of sacred words was the task meant to be carried out by the priest-philologists.
(Vološinov, *Marxism and The Philosophy of Language*, 1930, p.74)

Introduction

In the previous chapter extracts were quoted from historians of the study of language who argue that nineteenth-century language studies in western Europe made a decisive break with all such previous study in their concern with 'historicity'. In their opinion the nineteenth-century study of language took its place alongside other new discourses that were accredited with the status of science. Against this view, however, two principal points were argued: first, that within western Europe British linguistic study evinced a distinct type of concern with history that marks it off from mainstream continental (comparative) philology; second, that this British concern with history marks a continuity with previous British linguistic study in that it continues to be concerned with social and rhetorical issues. In this chapter both lines of argument will be pursued through an examination of the texts of one of the most popular linguists of mid-nineteenth-century Britain, Archbishop Richard Chenevix Trench.

Max Müller had written rather plaintively in a private letter, 'there is nothing left but to avoid all living subjective topics and take refuge in the past' (Müller, 1976, vol. 1, p.21). For others engaged in the study of language in Britain, however, the question was not one of taking refuge in history but of confronting it since the historical study of language was not to be used as a shelter, but as the site of confrontation with 'living subjective topics'. For Archbishop Trench in particular, language was not an object of study *per se* but a medium of study that offered answers to many of the questions posed by contemporary controversies. Therefore this chapter will examine Trench's texts (the major British work on language in the 1850s), in order to demonstrate in further detail how cultural producers working within the new discourse of 'the history of the language' were not concerned simply with language as an object but with language as a means to other ends.

The motto of Trench's earliest linguistic work, *On the Study of Words* (1851), asserted that 'Language is an instrument of knowledge'. If this is taken together with the motto of the radical newspaper *The Poor Man's Guardian*, 'Knowledge is Power', we begin to find new and important links and concerns with and between language, knowledge and power.[1] These links and concerns dominate the study of language in the mid-nineteenth century and by looking at Trench's texts this chapter will outline one presentation of such links and concerns. These texts were produced from within the new discourse of 'the history of the language' and yet they were to range over three crucial nineteenth-century discourses that involved the distribution of knowledge and power: theology, nationalism and social unity. Language was to be an important component in the study of all three.

Trench's four highly influential and popular linguistic texts were written during the 1850s: *On the Study of Words* (1851), *English Past and Present* (1855), *A Select Glossary* (1859), and *On Some Deficiencies in our English Dictionaries* (1860). Although these texts were produced from within 'the history of the language' they are markedly different from most of the early texts in the new field since the early texts had been unsure and still rather defensive and hesitant as to their own status. By the 1850s, however, the new discourse had gained the self-confidence to assert forcefully its independence of both Comparative Philology and the Classics as a new discipline in its own right. Thus if the argument is correct that 'the history of the language' had produced specific effects in the cultural crisis provoked by Chartism, then in the 1850s the new discourse was to be engaged in other discursive struggles.

The 1830s had been a period of bitter strife, antagonism and eventual reform and the following decade was to see the deepest of the nineteenth-century depressions (1841–2) inducing general social anxiety that manifested itself in different forms in specific discourses. Such anxiety was expressed in the discourses of medicine and public hygiene (especially with regard to the dangers of a cholera outbreak), public order (the lingering though largely ineffective appeal of Chartism and the 1848 Revolutions), and populist nationalism (directed largely against the Irish immigrants fleeing the Famine). Social unease then was the order of the day in the early and mid 1840s and yet by the end of the decade, and certainly in the 1850s, such anxieties were to become increasingly muted. The 'age of equipoise', as W.L. Burn described the 1850s (Burn, 1964) saw a significant improvement in the economic state of Britain with a general sense of improvement in living standards and lowering of social tension. The enormous expansion of the railway system is perhaps the best example of economic and social development as it demonstrated both new spending power and the deep social changes that were produced in the creation of a new sense of the national territory and of the relation of its inhabitants to each other. From 1830–50 over 6000 miles of railways were opened in Britain, accompanied by dire warnings of the effects of such unheralded expansion upon the familiar patterns of public and private life (Hobsbawm, 1969, p.110).

It is within this specific historical conjuncture that we can note the further development of 'the history of the language' within which Trench's work was written. The belief in the apparently boundless potential of British industry and empire and the social changes it brought about, gave rise both to a sense of security and to a sense of the new problems that were appearing. Moreover, both the renewed national self-belief and the awareness of the new problems created a cultural conjuncture that had a clear effect on the direction of the development of language studies. Renewed national self-belief led to a sense of the worth of the study of the national language, but the perception of new problems meant that 'the history of the language' again had a specific role in cultural and political debate.

Language as material history

If Liddell really had believed that 'sound theology' and the study of 'dialects and etymology' were distinct then the development of the study of language in the nineteenth century would have proved him wrong. The study of language and the study of theology were not mutually exclusive pursuits in Victorian Britain any more than they had been in the sixteenth century. In the earlier period the study of language had an important role in political and theological controversies as the vernacular was set against the classical languages in order to demonstrate the independence of the English church and nation, and in the nineteenth century, linguistic, theological and political discourses were again to be entwined.

In an important text that dealt (amongst other things) with the newly coined 'philosophy of language', J.W. Donaldson attempted to achieve specific theological objectives. His primary objective was to refute the materialist theory of language proposed by the radical Horne Tooke in his highly influential *EΠEA ΠTEPOENTA or, The Diversions of Purley* (1789–1805), along with the concomitant theory of evolution that proposed progression from barbarity to our present stage.[2] With regard to the latter point, Donaldson clearly thought that the battle was half-won:

> The Philosophy of grammar . . . has already achieved one decisive victory over scepticism, in demonstrating from the organisation of language the impossibility of the hypothesis, maintained by many, of the human invention of language,

and a progression from barbarism to metaphysical perfection. In this point the conclusions of our science are identical with the statements of revelation.   (Donaldson, 1839, p.14)

Writing twenty years before Darwin's troublesome text appeared, Donaldson was able to write confidently of the close connections of language and theology:

> Of the importance of philology, as the method of interpretation, to the theologian it is unnecessary to speak: as far as theology is interpretation or exposition, it is but a branch of philology. We speak here of the effect of theology in establishing the grounds of revelation.   (*Ibid.*, p.13)

The scientist C.K.J. von Bunsen agreed with Donaldson in the matter of the doctrine of 'continuous revelation', according to which revelation was not a single act of God external to history but a continuing historically located process. Such revelatory unfolding for Donaldson could best be seen in that entity which developed historically: language. For Bunsen too, 'language and religion are the two poles of our consciousness, mutually presupposing each other' (Burrow, 1967, p.197). Language and theology then were held to be interlinked, but these writers were all concerned with the comparative philological approach to language (or 'philosophical grammar' as Donaldson called it). The major contribution of Trench was to shift the emphasis in British work towards the study of the English language as a support for theological dogmatism. His method was to use material taken from the novel discourse of 'the history of the language' in order to uncover the hidden historical messages that lay within language.

The concern with the study of language as a means of gaining access to hidden history was evidently a common concern in the later eighteenth century and throughout the nineteenth century. Herder, for example, after developing his doctrine that the origin of language lay with human beings and their sensuous reaction to the sounds of the world, concluded that verbs rather than nouns were the first words. He continued to argue that it followed from this that:

> All the old unpolished languages are replete with this origin,

and in a philosophical dictionary of the orientals every stem word with its family – rightly placed and soundly evolved – would be a chart of the progress of the human spirit, a history of its development, and a complete dictionary of that kind would be a most remarkable sample of the inventive skill of the human soul.   (Herder, 1770, pp.132–3)

Thus by a clear ordering and evolutionary tracing of the verbal stems of the eastern languages the philologist could derive the progress and history of the 'human spirit'. Müller too was to describe language as 'the living and speaking witness of the whole history of our race' (Müller, 1862, p.27), and in the *Transactions of the Philological Society* of 1855 the Rev. John Davies declared that, 'a good philology is one of our best media for determining obscure questions of history'. He continued to assert that, 'its value in this respect is not yet sufficiently acknowledged in England, though well understood by scholars of France and Germany' (Davies, 1855, p.283). Davies's rejoinder notwithstanding, it is clear that the study of language was viewed by many as a possible field for historical discovery. Indeed for some writers language was the most reliable source of historical truths since when historical narratives fell silent, language itself could speak. Donaldson asserted that:

It may seem strange that anything so vague and arbitrary as language should survive all other testimonies, and speak with more definiteness, even in its changed and modern state, than all other monuments however grand and durable. . . . Though we had lost all other history of our country we should be able to tell from our language, composed as it is of a sub-stratum of Low German with deposits of Norman-French and Latin . . . that the bulk of our population was Saxon and that they were overcome and permanently subjected to a body of Norman invaders.   (Donaldson, 1839, p.12)

The very being of language itself demonstrates history since as W. Mathews put it, 'often where history is utterly dumb concerning the past, language speaks' (Mathews, 1882, p.226).

The study of language takes one beyond the narratives of history to a closer examination of the material of the narrative: the words of which it is composed. From this perspective therefore one should rather trust the history *in* words rather than the historical narratives constructed *by* words. For example, if a historical narrative were to contain the following proposition: 'on debating the point, a parliament of the British people would come to a consensus as to the Germanic genius of the English tongue', then the very material from which it is composed would betray the falsity of the proposition. The words of French etymological stock would stand as intrinsic counter-evidence to the claim. In this respect, the close attention paid to words by the philologists bears a resemblance to Freud's methodology a little later since it is evident that both the philologists and Freud paid strict attention to the possibility of words betraying false histories.[3] In this respect too the analogy becomes more interesting when philologists begin to think of language as the unconscious autobiography of the nation and the dictionary of a language as the conscious, narrated autobiography. In any case for all such viewpoints language is the key to history:

> The study of language, therefore, in its wider range may be used as a sure means of ascertaining the stock to which any nation belonged, and of tracing the changes of population and government which it has undergone. (Donaldson, 1839, p.12)

The metaphors used by students of language are themselves indicators of the way in which language was viewed as the metaphors of linguistic 'strata' and 'deposits' indicate the close connections between the study of language and geology in this period. Language (like geological phenomena) offers proof of historical occurrences that is definite, durable and yet at the same time lies before us every minute, as surely as the ground upon which we walk. Indeed its very omnipresence served as a hindrance to its study since as Müller asserted, 'the gravel of our walks hardly seemed to deserve a scientific treatment, and the language which every ploughboy can speak could not be raised without an effort to the dignity of a scientific problem' (Müller, 1862, pp.26–7). The linkage of the study of language and geology became a commonplace as language was consistently compared to an enormous collection of fossils, bones or rock formations. Craik described 'our earliest English' as a 'fossil' and a 'skeleton' from which we could build a picture or construct a history (Craik, 1861, vol. 1, p.vi). And the comparison was often more explicit as in the President of The Philological Society A.J. Ellis's declaration that:

> Dialectal speech is of the utmost importance to a proper conception of the historical development of English pronunciation, just as an examination of the existing remains of those zoological genera which descend from one geological period to another, serves to show the real development of life on our globe.   (Ellis, 1869, Pt. IV, p.1090)

Or in Whitney's comment on the 'noteworthy and often remarked similarity [that] exists between the facts and methods of geology and those of linguistic study' (Whitney, 1867, p.47). For Donaldson the science of language was:

> indeed perfectly analogous to Geology; they both present us with a set of deposits in a present state of amalgamation which may however be easily discriminated, and we may by an allowable chain of reasoning in either case deduce from the *present* the *former* condition, and determine by what courses and in what manner the superposition or amalgamation has taken place.   (Donaldson, 1839, p.12)

Language became a geological site to be dug over by scientists in order to force it to give up its historical secrets and it was this perspective that led Latham to argue for the study of language on the grounds that:

> In this respect, with its arguments from effect to cause, from the later to the earlier, from the known to the unknown, it has exactly the same method of Geology – that typically palaeontological science. At the same time, like geology, comparative philology is a history. It is a record of events

in sequence, just like a common history of Greece or Rome. It covers more ground, and it goes over greater space: but this is a question of degree rather than kind. It is a material history.   (Lathan, 1862, p.750)

Language then is constituted by history and is a medium that could not hide its message even if it tried to do so since a false history of 'the English people' would be given away by the words in which it was written. Words exhibited history in their existence not in their relational arrangements. This lent linguists a special significance to their work since it meant that their object of study was the receptacle of the history of the human race. It followed that any particular language such as English was likewise the vehicle for the history of a portion of that race: the English-speaking nation. It was for reasons such as these that language was to be venerated as holding beneath its surface the treasures of history. Müller argued the point in a way that managed to invoke history, theology and an idealist form of politics. He argued that the study of language was to be undertaken since, 'there are chronicles below its surface, there are sermons in every word. Language has been called sacred ground because it is the deposit of thought' (Müller, 1862, pp.2–3).

The historical theology of language

Language became a holy geological site in which to dig, to go beneath its surface in order to discover the historical strata it holds. It was to be explored in order to discover its regular formations and its xenoliths (in classical terms its analogies and anomalies) since both would be instructive. This doctrine is best exemplified in the theologico-political investigations of Trench since for Trench language was to be dug over in order to make it render its innermost secrets: its hidden moral and political truths. The fundamental axiom of his archaeology was that, 'not in books only . . . nor yet in connected oral discourse, but often also in words connected [singly] there are boundless stores of moral and historical truth' (Trench, 1851, p.1). According to Trench's theory it is not only in constructed narratives (written or spoken), that historical and moral truths can be found for they can more reliably be discovered often in a single word and its derivations. This stress on a single word is of interest in that it is only the diachronic perspective that is stressed and already in this early work there is a privileging of the paradigmatic associations of a single word over the syntagmatic relations between words, as metaphor attracted more interest than metonym and unit more than narrative. Pre-empting Saussure's model (and Jakobson's development of it), linguists were working practically along one of the lines that such later linguists were to theorise. In fact it is generally correct to argue that the largest part of British work on language in the nineteenth century was undertaken along the diachronic (paradigmatic and metaphoric) axis, as it was later to be formulated by Saussure. Though it is also true to argue that towards the end of the century there was a fair amount of rather more theoretical and synchronic work undertaken by linguists such as Sweet. Despite this belated theoretical work, however, it is still a valid generalisation to argue that the type of work under discussion here falls under the first of the two branches of philology outlined by Donaldson. He made precisely such an important distinction when he argued that:

> Under the name philology we include the two great branches of a scientific enquiry into the principles of language: the theory of the origin and formation of words, which is generally called the philosophy of language; and – the method of language, or, as it is more normally termed, logic or dialectic, which treats of the formation of sentences. (Donaldson, 1839, p.5)

The distinctions between the two branches of linguistic study were perhaps even more clearly illustrated in Lothair Butcher's essay 'On Political Terms':

> Every political term, however, has a twofold connexion with other languages, one I may call vertical, the other horizontal, one by means of its roots with the underlying strata; the other, with the surrounding vegetation, by runners and wall-roots.   (Butcher, 1858, p.51)

Pre-empting Saussure's use of the spatial metaphor Butcher indicates the distinct areas of linguistic interest: one concerns itself with digging below the surface to discover roots and the other with the relations between the units. For these British linguists the first of these areas was to predominate and the interest was to be in etymology rather than syntax, words rather than sentences, and signs rather than structures. Diachrony was to hold sway since, as Müller summarised the thinking of many such linguists, 'biographies of words are perhaps the most useful definitions which it is in our power to give' (Müller, 1889, p.32). Trench also took language to be a repository of sacred truths and it thus followed that individual words were to be investigated in order to uncover such truths. As Professor of the Exegesis of the New Testament he concentrated upon the 'boundless stores of moral truth in language' since words, he argued:

> do not hold themselves neutral in the great conflict between good and evil, light and darkness, which is dividing the world . . . they receive from us the impressions of our good and evil, which again they are active further to propagate amongst us.   (Trench, 1851, p.55)

Language for this writer was both ἔργον and ἐνέργεια, finished work and continuing operation, and this in turn meant that lessons are to be learnt from words in order to put other lessons into practice. Thus in Trench's work language became the means to ascertain the moral state of humanity:

> Is man of divine birth and stock? Coming from God, and when he fulfills the law and intention of his creation, returning to him again? We need no more than his language to prove it. . . . But has man fallen and deeply fallen from the height of his original creation? We need no more than his language to prove it.   (*Ibid.*, p.26)

Language was to be a 'moral barometer' (*ibid.*, p.59) in which the forms of words had the role of carefully graded vessels and their meanings, which were derived from history itself, were the substances contained in the vessels, their level indicating the morality of the word and its users. Particular forms and meanings exhibited different scores on the historico-moral scale since words 'embody facts of history or convictions of the moral sense' and even 'so far as that moral sense may be perverted, they will bear witness and keep a record of that perversion' (*ibid.*, p.5).

For this theologian language was to be the medium by which the original perfection and consequent debasement of humanity could be proved. He argued that since, 'God having impressed in language such a seal of truth on language that men are continually uttering deeper things than they know' (*ibid.*, p.8). And given the further point that 'we can always reduce the different meanings which a word has to some point from which they all immediately or mediately, proceed, [as] no word has primarily more than one meaning', then it follows that it is possible to dig deeply into the history of a word to discover its original truth (as sealed by God) and the path of its consequent degeneration (as caused by the post-lapsarian imperfection of humanity). Words were thus placed in the categories of 'children of light' and 'children of this world' and both were to be investigated thoroughly by the linguist. It was necessary to excavate both types of word since not only did language offer witness to morality and righteousness, it was also the case that, 'not less, where a perversion of the moral sense has found place, words preserve oftentimes a record of this perversion' (*ibid.*, p.9). Anomalies can suggest as much as analogies, xenoliths can be as instructive as the rocks you expect to find, and sinners can be as interesting as the righteous.

Digging deeply into language is one way of describing the study of etymology and it was this study that was the key to Trench's methodology. His task, as he saw it, was to discover (or rediscover) moral truth and to recover what he called, 'the witnesses to God's truth, the falling in of our words with his unchangeable word: for these are the true uses of the word while the others are only its abuses' (*ibid.*, pp.38–9). In this doctrine he echoes Herder's doctrine that the language of a nation is a study 'in the aberrations of human passion and fantasy' in the same way as is its mythology. For Herder as for Trench:

Every family of words is a tangled underbrush around a sensuous central idea, around a central rock, still bearing traces of the impression received by the inventor from this dryad. Feelings are interwoven into it: what moves is alive; what sounds speaks; and since it sounds for or against you, it is friend or foe: god or goddess, acting from passion as you are. (Herder, *op. cit.*, p.134)

Words according to Trench were indeed friends or foes and thus morally good or evil:

There are also words which bear the slime on them of the serpent's trail; and the uses of words, which imply moral evil – I say not upon their parts who now employ them in the senses which they have acquired, but on theirs from whom little by little they received their deflection and were warped from their original rectitude. (Trench, 1851, pp.41–2)

The etymology of 'etymology', once examined, proclaims the presuppositions behind such a method. 'Etymology' derives from the Greek (ἔτυμος, λόγος) bearing the translation of the true (real, actual, authentic) word (meaning, thought). It is the search for the original *etymon*: the radically 'true' meaning of a word beyond which there is no history since at that juncture we have reached the point of the creation of semantic value. The point at which word and world link up. Or if not word then part of a word since the etymologists were often attempting to split the *etymon* and so in the beginning was not *logos* but the *stoicheion* (στοιχεῖον) bearing the translation of letter of the alphabet as well as primary body or element. Therefore the aim of the etymologist was to return to that origin in order to recover the beginnings of history. Such etymology was the search for the original act of semantic creation, no matter if that act is held to have been undertaken by the first 'name-givers' (the 'legislators') as held in *Cratylus*; or by the act of naming undertaken by Adam once God had bestowed the gift of reason and speech. Moreover the search is, in effect, the quest for the linguistic state at which truth was transparent in words: the state at which words had their unique meaning by dint of referring to one single object in the world. At such a point, as Trench acknowledges, truth is wholly unproblematic since it is not contextually dependent but a question of simple (true or false) pictorial use. That, for writers such as Trench, was the original seal of truth upon language that human history had broken. Before the fall human history did not exist, but once the fall had taken place the history of the pains of labour and labour pains began. For Trench and others that history was recorded in language.

In the beginning was the Word with its purity assured; but not long after came the words exchanged between Adam and Eve that were to mark the beginnings of the 'impure' language. Trench was not, however, the first to hold the doctrine of original purity followed by human debasement since the doctrine can be traced in a text as early as the Platonic dialogue *Cratylus*. In the dialogue Socrates asserts that 'the Gods must clearly be supposed to call things by their right and natural names' whereas human beings cannot be trusted to do the same:

> (soc.)   Yes, my dear friend; but then you know that the original names have been long ago buried and disguised by people sticking on and stripping off letters for the sake of euphony, and twisting them and bedizening them in all sorts of ways: and time too may have had a share in the change. Take for example, the word κάτοπτρον; why is the letter ϱ inserted? This must surely be the addition of someone who cares nothing about the truth, but thinks only of putting the mouth into shape. And the additions are often such that at last no human being can possibly make out the original meaning of the word. Another example is the word σφίγξ, σφιγγός which ought properly to be φίγξ, φιγγός, and there are other examples.

According to such a view of language it is clear that human beings debase language and the remedy for such errors is etymology as it permits the possibility of a return to the original and thus true meaning.

In fact this desire for the perfectly 'transparent' language can properly be described as one of the metaphysical problems that emerges consistently in the history of western thought. The seventeenth century, for example, saw a number of schemes designed to make signification unambiguous and pure, perhaps the most important being Bishop Wilkins's *Essay Towards a Real Character and a Philosophical Language* (1688). Ironically, however, it was in the work of one of the most avowedly anti-theological philosophers of the twentieth century that this problem was most clearly addressed in the modern period. Bertrand Russell's philosophical quest in 'The Philosophy of Logical Atomism' (1918) was to work out the basis for the 'logically perfect language' and he summarised the task by arguing that 'in a logically perfect language, there will be one word and no more for every simple object. . . . A language of that sort . . . will show at a glance the logical structure of the facts asserted or denied' (Russell, 1918, p.58). Russell's 'logically perfect language' was to be expressed in the form of symbolic notation and was therefore to go one step beyond Trench's etymological work since it aimed to escape the historically laden nature of the words of the common language. The aim was to produce a language that would be uniaccentual and radically synchronic. However, though the emphases of their accounts (and their ultimate aims) differed, there is a common methodological purpose to their work in one respect. They both sought a means to guarantee the status of language as the vehicle of truth and clarity by paring it down to its original (Trench) or logical (Russell) constituents.

A few examples will illustrate Trench's theologico-linguistic method. 'Tribulation' he notes:

> is derived from the Latin 'tribulum', that word signifying the threshing instrument or roller, by which the Romans separated the corn from the husks; and 'tribulatio' in its primary significance was the act of this separation. But some Latin writer of the Christian church appropriated the word and image for the setting forth of a higher truth.   (Trench, 1851, p.6)

The 'higher' truth, and thus the moral content of the word, was the principle that the means for separating the solid and true from the poor and trivial in human affairs is tribulation. Another example was the word 'pain', which was a very useful word for a Victorian moralist to excavate. 'Pain', Trench wrote:

> is the correlative of sin, [in] that it is *punishment*; and to this the word 'pain' which there can be no reasonable doubt is derived from 'poena' bears continual witness. Pain *is* punishment, so does the word itself declare no less than the conscience of everyone that is suffering it.   (*Ibid.*, p.36)

Just how unreliable such etymological beliefs were is demonstrated by the fact that the Archbishop died as a result of a long illness stemming from a fall on a ship whilst crossing the Irish Channel in which he sustained two fractured knees.

Trench worked within the field of 'the history of the language' in order to achieve particular purposes since from his perspective there was no question that language could be an object in itself. In his work 'the history of the language' was important in that it became a discourse that could be used on the side of theology in the fierce disputes that broke out in the decade of Darwin's *Origin of Species* (1859). Language had become a crucial focal point of interest as the 'instrument of knowledge' and the next section will show how Trench's work extended beyond the theological and into the social sphere.

Language: the political unconscious

Throughout Europe in the nineteenth century there were significant political developments brought about by the appearance of modern nations that knew themselves and demanded recognition from others for the first time. In these cultural and political shifts language was to play an important role since it was a primary means of creating or bestowing nationhood as it was the ideal medium for signalling inclusion and exclusion. As Pedersen described it, in nineteenth-century Europe 'national awakening and the beginnings of linguistic science go hand in hand' (Pedersen, 1931, p.43) and for many

of the newly formed nations the writing of a grammar book
or the compilation of a dictionary were declarations of political
intent. Evidently this equation of linguistic and national
identity is linked to the concept of history being impressed in
language since if, as Müller had declared, language is 'the
living and speaking witness of the whole history of human
beings', then it followed that *a* language would be the living
and speaking witness of a unified, collective group of such
beings; or in other words a nation. In fact Müller commented
upon the political role that the study of language had played
when he asserted that 'in modern times the science of language
has been called in to settle some of the most perplexing social
and political questions'. Its role had been to act in favour of
'nations and languages against dynasties and treaties' (Müller,
1861, p.12). To put his argument in more ideological terms,
language had acted in favour of the organic and natural
against the social and historical.

The conception that a language reflected the national
character was held firmly in this period. G.F. Graham, for
example, defined a language as:

> the outward expression of the tendencies, turn of mind, and
> habits of thought of some one nation, and the best criterion
> of their intellect and feelings. If this explanation be admitted,
> it will naturally follow that the connection between a people
> and their language is so close, that the one may be judged
> of by the other; and that the language is a lasting monument
> of the nature and character of the people.   (Graham, 1869,
> p.ix)

It also followed that a language is crucial to the unity of the
nation since as G.P. Marsh noted:

> It is evident therefore that unity of speech is essential to
> the unity of a people. Community of language is a stronger
> bond than identity of religion or government, and contempo-
> raneous nations of one speech, however formally separated
> by differences of creed or of political organisation, are
> essentially one in culture, one in tendency, one in
> influence.   (Marsh, 1860, p.221)

These assertions were clearly indebted to such romantic conceptions of language and nationality as those of Diderot, who described the vocabulary of any particular language as a 'faithful and authoritative record of the knowledge of that people', or Von Humboldt, who held that 'language is the outward appearance of the intellect of nations'. However, what is important for us is not that such beliefs were repetitious but that it was deemed necessary to repeat them with reference to the English language. This is in fact rather puzzling since the English were not a people whose nationhood was forged in the nineteenth century, and not a people eager to establish their independence from a foreign imperial power. The historical situation was just the opposite in fact. So then why were these claims being made? The answer lies in the important point that the construction of a national identity is not settled at one point and then fixed for ever (as most of the nineteenth-century commentators would have argued), but a constant process of change and development determined among other things by the political purposes that such constructions were to serve. In this sense nationality is never achieved (in the French sense of *achever*, to complete or finish), but always in the process of being forged. And it is this that explains the processive repetition of claims for the unity of language and nation in Britain during this period. The specific characteristics of a particular nationality are not immutably fixed but historically variable, and thus the self-image of the English people, and of course the very idea that there was 'an English people', would not have been the same in the 1650s and the 1850s. Constructions of national identity are motivated in particular ways with specific ends in view, and it is from this perspective that Trench's linguistic nationalism will be considered here.

Trench was a follower of the doctrine that a language has within itself the history of a nation. He wrote that any particular language is, 'full of instruction, because it is the embodiment, the incarnation if I may so speak, of the feelings and thoughts and experiences of a nation (Trench, 1851, pp.21–2). In precisely the same way that God impressed morality upon words, the nation impresses its history upon its language, and once viewed in this light the study of the

English language became crucially important since it was viewed as a sacred repository for the national truths of history. The language became a focal point for national unity and this led Trench to argue that, 'it is of course our English tongue, out of which mainly we should seek to draw some of the hid treasure which it contains . . . we cannot employ ourselves better. There is nothing that will more help to form an English heart in ourselves and others' (*ibid.*, p.24). The reason for such advocacy is that the English language is the site of national history and therefore the perfect pedagogical tool:

> We could scarcely have a lesson on the growth of our English tongue, we could scarcely follow upon one of its significant words, without having unawares a lesson in English history as well, without not merely falling upon some curious fact illustrative of our national life, but learning also how the great heart which is beating at the centre of that life, was gradually being shaped and moulded.   (*Ibid.*)

As with the nation itself, the language is subject not to individual but to collective direction since it is the vessel of all the past experiences of those who comprise the nation. It follows therefore that it is also the vessel for all future experience. In this argument Trench reworks Burke's theory of the social order, in which 'society' is 'indeed a contract' between its past, present and future members. For the conservative Burke, society:

> ought not to be considered as nothing better than a partnership agreement in a trade of pepper and coffee, callico and tobacco, or some such other low concern, to be taken up for a little temporary interest, and to be dissolved by the fancy of the parties. It is to be looked upon with other reverence; because it is not a partnership in things subservient only to the gross animal existence of a temporary and perishable nature. . . . As the ends of such a partnership cannot be obtained in many generations, it becomes a partnership not only between those who are living, but between those who are living, those who are dead, and those who are to be born.   (Burke, 1790, pp.194–5)

The contract is neither animal, temporary, nor perishable. And it is interesting since these were precisely the qualities possessed by language for Trench. It was on these grounds that both he and other writers cited the English language as that force which created a non-material, non-perishable ideological bond between all English citizens. One example of such thinking is given by F.J. Furnivall, the first editor of an important cultural project closely linked to 'the history of the language', the *Early English Texts Society*. Furnivall saw his work as fulfilling this type of social contract when he characterised it as paying off 'a sort of debt to the past generations' (Murray, 1979, p.90).

It is important to stress that once viewed in this light the English language was accorded a crucial role in cultural and political debate. Whenever political and cultural crisis threatened the English language was offered as evidence of the underlying or unconscious unity that held all together despite superficial differences. In this sense language became the political unconscious of the nation since if nothing else there could at least be agreement that 'we' (the unifying pronoun) all speak 'the same language' and therefore all share 'the same background' historically and culturally. Language bears testimony to the 'great historic changes . . . whereof it may well happen that the speakers have never heard' (Trench, 1851, p.13) and so is precisely the political unconscious of its speakers. This theoretical tenet is encapsulated in Müller's outline of the task of historical linguistics:

> What I call an historical definition is an account of those very changes which take place in the meaning of a word, so long as it is left to the silent and unconscious influences which proceed from the vast community of the speakers of one and the same language.   (Müller, 1889, p.32)

The project of maintaining the English language as a focal point of national unity is a major factor in another of Trench's works, *English Past and Present* (1855). This work, written and published during the Crimean War, was addressed to those who have 'the duty in general of living lives worthy of those who have England for their native country and English for their native tongue' (Trench, 1855, p.vi). Its aim was to teach students moral respect and thereby 'to lead such through a more intimate knowledge of [English] into a greater love of [England]'. It is in this work that one can best see the realisation of De Quincey's double-edged project of 'learning and patriotism' since for Trench and other linguists the English language and nation had one thing in common: their greatness. The more the English nation extended the boundaries of its empire, the more the English language was praised as a superior language and subjected to extensive study. And, as a corollary, the more the unified English people were praised as all sharing in this sense of superiority. That such a sense of confidence and superiority in the English language was widespread is demonstrated in that it was even promulgated by some who were not English. Trench quotes Jacob Grimm as having written that English, 'may with all right be called a world language, and like the English people appears destined hereafter to prevail with a sway more extensive even than its present over all the portions of the globe' (ibid., p.28). Appeals to nationalist pride were consistently conducted through appeals to, and notifications of, the strength of the English language since as Trench asked rhetorically, 'what can more clearly point out [our ancestors'] native land and ours as having fulfilled a glorious past, as being destined for a glorious future, than that they should have acquired for themselves and for those who came after them a clear, a strong, a harmonious, a noble language' (ibid., p.2). The 'glorious future' of the 'strong' language was to be ensured by the spread of the empire since just as the imperialists were to conquer new areas and peoples the language was also to gain victories. Guest asserted prophetically that, 'if, instead of looking to the past, we speculate on the future, our language will hardly sink in our estimate of its importance. Before another century has gone by, it will, at the present rate of increase, be spoken by hundreds of millions'. English was not merely to be the language of the conquerors since it too was to have conquests and like the other institutions exported with the imperialists the language was to be an instrument for civilising wild and barbarous peoples. Guest continued to praise the imperial language:

> That language, too, is rapidly becoming the great medium of civilisation, the language of law and literature to the Hindoo, of commerce to the African, of religion to the scattered islands of the Pacific. The range of its influence, even at the present day, is greater than ever was that of the Greek, the Latin, or the Arabic; and the circle widens daily.   (Guest, 1838, p.703)

Like the other great empires the British Empire bestowed upon its citizens the greatest gift of all, the language of civilisation. Thus English was most worthy of study precisely because it is in the position of 'bearing most directly on the happiness of mankind'.

For many linguists English had become the 'world language' by dint of extra-linguistic factors and for Marsh these were:

> circumstances in the position and the external relations of the English language, which recommend to its earnest study and cultivation. I refer, of course, to the commanding political influence, the widespread territory, and the commercial importance of the two great mother countries whose vernacular it is.

For this writer these were the reasons that:

> English is emphatically the language of commerce, of civilisation, of social and religious freedom, of progressive intelligence, and of an active catholic philanthropy; and beyond any tongue ever used by man, it is of right the cosmopolite speech.   (Marsh, 1860, p.23)

However, for other writers English had become the language most directly bearing upon the happiness of mankind by dint of its internal characteristics. E. Higginson, in what was to become something of commonplace, assigned specific characteristics to particular languages and thus Greek and Latin were the languages of oratory, French the language of conversation, Italian the language of song, and German the language of metaphysics and theology. However:

> For all the various and combined purposes of a language

. . . for all the mixed uses of speech between man and man, and from man in aspiration to the one above him, we sincerely believe that there is not, nor ever was, a language comparable to the English. The strength, sweetness and flexibility of the tongue [recommend it].   (Higginson, 1864, p.207)

Arguments linking the superiority of the English race and language were also deployed and one commentator held that the past mixture of races upon the territory of Britain had created, 'a people, who, by their impetuous but enduring courage, by their active and persevering enterprise, have made themselves successively the dominant race of the world' (Davies, 1857, p.93). Just as the admixture of races had created a noble people so the mixture of languages had created a noble language fit for such a people and thus the Rev. W.W. Skeat declared that England was, 'a modern nation which is fit to lead the world, especially in the very matter of language' (Skeat, 1895, p.415). 'Fit to lead the world' reflects the confidence of the Victorian linguists with regard to their object of study since in the 'matter of language' the English language was viewed as the great exhibit of the empire. Like the empire itself the language subjugated all other contenders to its own rule and power since as far as claims for the status of a world language went in the competition of languages, there simply was none to compete with English. An article by T. Watts in the 1850 *Transactions of the Philological Society* made the position clear when he argued that, 'at present, the prospects of the English language are the most splendid the world has ever seen. It is spreading in each of the quarters of the globe by fashion, by emigration, and by conquest' (Watts, 1850, p.212). Allowing for such expansion Watts looks forward to the time when 'the world is circled by the accents of Shakespeare and Milton', a point at which all the world's writing and speech would be in English. This led the same writer to view the different peoples of the world as the sites of experimentation to be conducted by linguistic scientists:

It will be a splendid and novel experiment in modern society, if a language becomes so predominant over all

others as to reduce them in comparison to the proportion
of provincial dialects.   (*Ibid.*, p.214)

The vehicle of such experimentation was to be imperialism
since the language of the empire was to be the means both of
exercising power and of announcing the global encirclement
enacted by the imperialists:

> The sun never sets on the British dominions; the roll of the
> British drum encircles the globe with a belt of sound; and
> the familiar utterances of English speech are heard on every
> continent and island, in every sea and ocean, in the
> world.   (Meiklejohn, 1891, p.6)

For another linguist the imperial language was not merely an
instrument of domination but itself a dominating power, male,
teutonic and all conquering:

> We do not want to discard the rich furniture of words which
> we have inherited from our French and classic eras; but we
> wish to wear them as trophies, as the historic blazon of a
> great career, for the demarcation and amplification of an
> imperial language whose thews and sinews and vital
> energies are essentially English.   (Earle, 1901, p.63)

The English language had achieved and conquered much and
thus became a crucial focal point of rallying calls for national
unity. Pride in the language was accompanied by pride in the
nation and both were set against the anxieties and disturbances
of equipoise that were produced by the wars of the 1850s.

Language and social unity

The English language and its study in the discourse of 'the
history of the language' were foci of calls for national self-
acknowledgement and thus organising forces for national
identification. However, within the nation itself these discursive realms were to be important factors in the debates around
other 'living subjective topics'. The superiority of the English

language was not only used to delineate the superiority of its speakers in relation to other national groups but was also to be used in cultural and political debates within Britain to argue for social unity. The language and its history were to be media for the self-images of Victorian society in that both the language and Victorian society itself were praised as liberal, unified and morally virtuous.

Trench issued such an appeal for the recognition of a parallelism between liberal institutions and a liberal language. He proclaimed that, 'we may trace, I think, as was to be expected, a certain conformity between the genius of our institutions and that of our language' (Trench, 1855, p.43). Therefore just as 'it is in the very character of our institutions to repel none, but rather to afford a shelter and a refuge to all, from whatever quarter they come', then likewise the English language had formerly received foreign words and idioms. No language, he argued, 'has thrown open its arms wider, with a greater confidence, a confidence justified by experience, that it could make truly its own, assimilate and subdue to itself, whatever it thought good to receive into its bosom' (*ibid.*). Such 'non-native' words had, in the revealing words of Kington-Oliphant, 'been admitted to the right of English citizenship' (Kington-Oliphant, 1873, p.19). Not all linguists, however, agreed with this estimation of the entry of foreign words into the language since for some writers such words were a sign of degeneration. A leading article in the *Leeds Mercury* entitled 'English for the English', for example, argued that a 'serious assault upon the purity of the English language' was taking place. For the leader-writer the introduction of foreign terms was 'a vicious kind of slang utterly unworthy to be called a language' and he argued that 'if some kind of stand is not made against this invasion, pure English will soon only exist in the works of our dead authors'. He declared, 'we think therefore that the interests of morality as well as those of pure taste concur in calling upon those who have influence with the public to set their faces against this vicious English' (*Leeds Mercury*, 12 November 1863). Such sentiments, however, largely contradicted the self-image of the age in this regard since it was usually constructed around the 'liberality' of the language. In fact this type of rhetorical ploy was a repetition of claims heard at the end of the eighteenth century. The elocutionist John Walker declared in 1774, for example, that the English, 'far from excluding foreign words that are happier than their own, . . . embrace with eagerness every expression from every language that promises a nearer acquaintance with the human mind' (Walker, 1774, p.26). The nineteenth-century appraisal of the language in such terms is perhaps best summed up by Meiklejohn:

> The English language, like the English people, is always ready to offer hospitality to all peaceful foreigners – words or human beings – that will land and settle within her coasts. And the tendency at the present time is not only to give a hearty welcome to newcomers from other lands, but to call back old words and old phrases that had been allowed to drop out of existence.   (Meiklejohn, 1891, p.279)

The liberal English therefore, one writer commented in the last year of the Great Irish Famine, must study their language sacramentally since:

> The English tongue is worthy of our holiest and never ceasing devotion. It will bear to future ages the sentiments of a free, generous and singularly energetic race of men. It carries with it the cherished and sanctified institutions of its native soil.   (Harrison, 1848, p.378)

English language and liberty were also concatenated a little later in the century in Skeat's ditty to James Murray on the completion of volume 1 of the *N/OED*. It ran:

> Wherever the English speech has spread
> And the Union Jack flies free,
> The news will be gratefully, proudly read
> That you've conquered your ABC.
>   (Murray, 1979, p.273)

One peculiarly English institution of the type specified by Harrison was the gentleman's club since the word 'club', Trench claimed, is purely English and gives evidence of how a single word can reflect the national characteristics of a people. He argued that:

> It is singularly characteristic of the social and political life of England as distinguished from that of the other European nations, that to it alone the word 'club' belongs. . . . In no country where there was not extreme personal freedom could they have sprung up; and as little in any where man did not know how to use this freedom with moderation and self-restraint, could they have been long endured.   (Trench, 1855, p.58)

Given that England was held to be the land of liberality, freedom and moderation, it followed that along with the process of welcoming foreign words it also fell to the English to export the language of democracy and tolerance to other countries in order to attempt to give them free and democratic political traditions. As Kington-Oliphant put this version of the white man's burden, 'to make amends for all this borrowing, England supplies foreigners (too long enslaved) with her own staple – namely the diction of free political life' (Kington-Oliphant, 1873, p.339). For Trench England and its institutions were almost Utopian:

> Peace, Freedom, Happiness, have loved to wait
> On the fair islands, fenced by circling seas;
> And ever of such favoured spots as these
> Have the wise dreamers dreamed, who would create
> That perfect model of a happy state,
> Which the world never saw. Oceana,
> Utopia such, and Plato's isle that lay
> Westward of Gade and the Great Sea's gate.
> Dreams are they all, which yet have helped to make
> That underneath fair polities we dwell,
> Though marred in part by envy, faction, hate –
> Dreams which are dear, dear England, for thy sake,
> Who art indeed that sea-girt citadel
> And nearest image of that perfect state.
>   (Trench, 1865, p.84)

England was almost perfect but not quite so since despite

living under 'fair polities', there were still those who disturbed the equilibrium and unity of the 'happy state' with their 'envy, faction and hate'. The crisis of the 1830s and early 1840s was not to be forgotten easily and despite the easing of social tension within Britain in the 1850s there was still a deep awareness of the divided nation. It was such division that the discourses constructed around the English language attempted to help heal as constant appeals were made to the socially unifying character of the language both nationally and intra-nationally. Thus, the grammar of the language might be difficult to understand and eccentric in its relation to the universal laws of the German philologists, but the language, at least for one commentator of the time:

> is like the English constitution . . . and perhaps also the English Church, full of inconsistencies and anomalies, yet flourishing in defiance of theory. It is like the English nation, the most oddly governed in the world, but withal the most loyal, orderly, and free.   (Swayne, 1862, p.368)

The socially unifying tendency to which end many of the discourses around the language were deployed is particularly evident in the cultural responses made to the two major foreign affairs crises of the 1850s: the Crimean War (1854–6) and the Indian Mutiny (1857). The Mutiny, the only occasion in the nineteenth century when a native army trained by Europeans rose against its masters, was a 'fearfully savage war' as one officer recalled in his memoirs (Smart, 1874, p.50). The savagery of the campaign combined with the losses of the Crimean War (reported for the first time by professional war-correspondents) to produce significant unrest in British society and it was to that unrest that Trench directed his linguistic studies. His appeal for the recognition of the parallel strengths of the nation and language became more evidently an appeal for social unity and gained particular intensity in *English Past and Present* precisely because it was written during that time of national crisis provoked by the Crimean War. In justifying the type of work in which he was engaged, he asserted that the study of English was vitally important, 'especially at the present. For these are times which naturally rouse into liveliest

activity all our latent affections for the land of our birth'
(Trench, 1855, p.1). The war itself became a force that
mobilised attempts at social unification since:

> It is one of the compensations, indeed the greatest of all,
> for the wastefulness, the woe, the cruel losses of war, that
> it causes a people to know itself as a people; and leads each
> one to esteem and prize most that which he has in common
> with his countrymen, and not now any longer these things
> which separate and divide him from them.   (*Ibid.*)

Identity rather than difference was to be the order of the day,
which meant that the formative stress was to be laid upon
Englishness rather than economic and cultural status. It was
important that the sense of unity engendered by the crisis
should be maintained and again one of the ways of ensuring
that was to encourage pride in the language. As if to summarise
the point Trench asked, 'and the love of our language, what
is it in fact but the love of our country expressing itself in one
particular direction?' (*ibid.*).

In fact the linking of language and nation and its social
effect had often been pursued in British linguistic study. Swift
had compared the correction, improvement and ascertainment
of the language to the preservation of the 'civil or religious
constitution', and Johnson continued in the same vein in his
'Preface' to his *Dictionary* when he argued that 'tongues, like
governments, have a natural tendency to degeneration: we
have long preserved our constitution, let us make some
struggles for our language'. Ingram later defended the utility
of Anglo-Saxon literature on the grounds of its importance to
'the statesman, the patriot, and the scholar', and De Quincey
called for a monument to 'learning and patriotism'. Trench's
appeal, however, was distinct in that he called not just for
national self-awareness but for social unity too. He demanded
recognition of that which British citizens have 'in common
with their countrymen' and a banishment of any remembrance
of 'those things which separate and divide' them from their
fellow citizens. In effect he was exemplifying the theory of the
nation set forward by Ernest Renan in which it was argued
that:

Or l'essence d'une nation est que tous les individus aient beaucoup des choses en commun, et aussi que tous aient oublié bien des choses.   (Renan, 1947, vol. I, p.892) [Now the essence of a nation is that all its individual members have many things in common, and also that they have all forgotten a good deal.]

For both Renan and Trench, national and social unity was to be brought about by the foregrounding of specific discourses and the elimination of others: a form of selective amnesia in which the unifying features of the language were to be set over and against its divisive features.

Such overt use of language for specific cultural and political ends was not confined to Archbishop Trench since other linguists were likewise influenced by the historical context in which they wrote. For example one of the hundreds of nineteenth-century orthographic reformers argued that imperialist expansion had brought about the need for new types of linguistic research. He argued in particular that it had made the introduction of spelling reform imperative since:

The circumstances of the time seemed to require a more perfect alphabet. Military expeditions and the yearly increasing cycle of missionary or commercial enterprise, have brought us into contact with nations with whom it must alike be our interest and our duty to cultivate the most intimate relations. The defects of our present alphabet oppose very serious obstacles to the acquisition of a new language, and thereby increase the difficulties which stand in the way of a more cordial intercourse between ourselves and distant races.   (*Trans. Phil. Soc.*, 1842–44, 215)

The Crimean War in particular was to have its effect in producing a specific form of linguistic work. A letter from Sir Charles Trevelyan, on behalf of the government, to Max Müller, dated 20 March 1854, demonstrates that the study of language was not, despite Müller's claims, an autonomous discipline in this respect. Trevelyan wrote to Müller of various actions taken by the government to facilitate the success of the Crimean campaign though evidently he thought them insufficient and recommended a further measure:

> But something more than this ought to be attempted. We cannot tell how far and how long this remarkable intervention of the Western nations in Eastern affairs may lead us; and I know, from my Indian experience, that a knowledge of the native languages is an indispensable preliminary to understanding and taking an interest in native races, as well as to acquiring their good will and gaining influence over them. Without it, officers charged with important public affairs, feeling themselves at the mercy of a class of interpreters whose moral character is often of a very questionable kind, live in a state of chronic irritation with the natives, which is extremely adverse both to the satisfactory transaction of business, and to the still more important object of giving to the people of the country a just impression of the character and intentions of our nation.
>
> It is, therefore, extremely desirable that the attention of all our young officers who are, or are likely to be, employed in the East, not only in the Commissariat, but also in the military and naval services, should be directed to the study of the languages which are spoken in the northern division of the Turkish empire, and the adjoining provinces of Russia.   (Müller, 1854, p.iv)

In the light of this Trevelyan directed Müller to produce a simple text book for officers which was to include a guide to 'the language of the Tartar population of the Crimea, and of the leading tribes of the Circassians, including that of the redoubtable Shamil'. Hence the direction of linguistic study was advanced in a specific field (Müller had often complained of the difficulties of starting oriental language studies at Oxford), and the book had to be produced rapidly since 'every part of his great effort, including this important literary adjunct, is under war pressure'. Müller responded to Trevelyan's request by producing his work *On the Languages of the Seat of War in the East* in 1854, and his justification for the book was couched in similar militaristic and utilitarian terms to those used by Trevelyan. He wrote:

The great desideratum during the present war will no doubt, be a knowledge of Turkish. Most officers will probably be satisfied if they are able to speak by interjections and gestures, and succeed in making a Turk understand that they want a horse, or provisions, or directions for the road in a country not advanced to signposts. This can be learned from dialogues, and even without a knowledge of the Turkish alphabet. (*Ibid.*, p.144)

However, although this basic communication was satisfactory more was evidently required and therefore Müller's work was to provide further instruction for the officers:

The necessity, however, of being able to converse with the people in the East, will soon be felt; and although interpreters, ready to offer their services for any transactions, political or commercial, will not be wanting, yet it is hardly necessary to say, with the experience of so many foreign campaigns before us, how much an officer's discharge of his duties will benefit by a knowledge of the languages of the people among whom he and his soldiers are, perhaps for years, to be quartered, and on whose good will and ready co-operation so much of the success of an expeditionary army must always depend. (*Ibid.*, p.1)

In fact Müller's work had already been slightly preceded by that of Dr L. Loewe who had composed his *Dictionary of the Circassian Language* in 1853. This work was presented to the Philological Society and recommended for printing by the society on the grounds that there was as yet no proper dictionary of that language, and 'one would be of great service to our officers in the war with Russian, as we should certainly have to act with the Schmaze or Circassian tribes' (Loewe, 1853, p.212).

Neither Müller's text nor that of Loewe is directly related to the study of 'the history of the language' in England yet they demonstrate, along with the works of Trench, how the study of language in England was markedly influenced by political exigencies. The expressed aims of texts such as Trench's *English Past and Present*, Müller's *On the Languages of the Seat of War in the East,* and Loewe's *Dictionary,* make it impossible to agree with Müller's claim (made at the end of the 1850s), that language was 'the sole object of enquiry' for linguists. On the contrary, language became a means to specific political and cultural ends.

Trench and the appeal for English studies

The concern for national and social unity centred around a sense of unease about the contemporary political scene together with reflections upon the national past. The most striking example of this concern at this period was the set of varying attempts to come to terms with the historical writing of the national past and to evaluate the political and cultural heritage of the nation. The appearance of 'the history of the language' as an area of knowledge in the 1830s and 1840s is one such attempt. Another closely linked attempt at ordering and evaluating the cultural heritage of the nation was signalled by the appearance of appeals for the institutionalised study of 'English studies' (or more usually 'English language and literature') in the 1850s. Thus this will be a convenient place at which to begin an analysis of this development to which we shall return briefly later.

The study of the vernacular language and literature at the beginning of the nineteenth century was effectively proscribed in the major public schools as a result of the important 1805 Leeds Grammar School Case. The endowment that had enabled the setting-up of Leeds Grammar School was to have been deployed by the school in the early nineteenth century for the teaching of modern subjects. This was proposed since its advocates held that 'the Town of Leeds and its neighbourhood had of late years increased very much in trade and population . . . and, the learning of *French* and other modern living languages was to become a matter of great utility to the Merchants of Leeds' (Lawson and Silver, 1973, p.252). However, the application to use the endowment to this end was refused by the Lord Chancellor, Lord Eldon, who used Johnson's definition of a grammar school in its strictest sense as a basis for his judgement. He took it to be a school 'for teaching grammatically the learned languages' (*ibid.*). The wide-ranging effect of this case was to enshrine the classical languages and literatures in the grammar and public schools as the main subject of the curriculum at the expense of 'modern subjects (including English). And in fact this demotion of English was so comprehensive that James Murray was to claim in the 1860s that the English Master at Marlborough ranked lower than the Dancing Master in terms of superiority[4] (Murray, 1979, p.71).

After the first state grant for education was bestowed in 1833, however, the increasing enlargement of state education throughout the nineteenth century made the position of classics as the core subject of the educational curriculum increasingly untenable, though it was not to relax its grip for more than a century after the first education grant. Before widespread educational opportunity was made available it was clear that classical study was of central importance since, in the words of a later education report:

> Greek would enable a clergyman to read the New Testament in the original, Latin would qualify a barrister to study Roman law, or a doctor to write his prescriptions; Mathematics was essential for the soldier, sailor or engineer. But for English there seemed no call.   (Newbolt, 1921, p.197)

Yet the advances made in the struggle for universal education rendered the classics open to attack for their inaccessibility and the elitism they engendered. And English studies sprang from the fissure created between the expanding number of those to be educated and the difficulty of educating them with the prevailing methods and curricula.

Various forces combined to call for English studies and these have been fully explored in Baldick's *The Social Mission of English Criticism* (Baldick, 1983). First, there was a growing need for middle-level bureaucrats and administrators in the mid-nineteenth century, to be employed in the task of imperial expansion. The growing numbers meant that recruitment would have to tap a larger section of the population than had previously been the case and this in turn encouraged the mid-Victorian belief in competition, with exams being designated in various fields to attract the 'strongest' candidates. The 'payment by results' system ordained by the Newcastle Commission (1858–61) was one example of this procedure; but more significant for the development of English studies was the opening of the Civil Service to competitive examinations in English language and literature as recommended by the report of Trevelyan and Northcote, *The Organisation of the Permanent Civil Service*, in 1853. The impetus this development gave to the study of English language and literature can be seen in the appearance of texts such as A.H. Keane's *Handbook of the English Language* (1875). The Preface makes clear the basis of the text:

> The History of the English Language, as distinct from that of its literature, constitutes a separate division of the English Department at the Civil Service and other Government Examinations. An effort has been made in the following pages to throw into as small a space as possible all such matter as is needed to meet the requirements of that single head.   (Keane, 1875, p.xiii)

The amount of specialised work required for such a paper is evinced by the first question on the 1858 English language paper:

> Give a distinct account of the constitution of the English language, in respect both of the vocabulary and grammar, at each of the following dates: in the tenth century, when it was still what is usually called Saxon or Anglo-Saxon by modern philologists, in the twelfth century to the fourteenth century; in the sixteenth and eighteenth centuries; noting carefully the difference between each stage of its progress, and the preceding one, and assigning the cause or causes of the change.   (*Ibid.*, pp.xiii–xiv)

Not the least surprising aspect of the paper is that the examiners felt that there were other things that could be examined after the first question. The detail of the knowledge required for this type of question would clearly necessitate intensive study within a highly specialised field and such a demand both reflected and influenced the development of English studies within educational institutions.

A second reason for the development of English studies was the growth of the various movements for universal education at both basic and advanced levels. Women and the working class of both sexes, it was held, would not be able to manage the intellectual demands of the classics and therefore in the Mechanics Institutes, the Working Men's Colleges (of which there were over 1000 in 1851), the University Extension Lectures, and all of the ever-expanding and numerous developments made by women for their education, practically all the academic teaching was concentrated around English language and literature. In fact James Murray accredited the women's movement directly for the appearance of English studies at Oxford in the nineteenth century when he argued that 'but for the movement to let women share in the advantages of a university education, it is doubtful whether the nineteenth century would have witnessed the establishment of a School of English Language and Literature at Oxford' (Murray, 1900, p.31). The logic of Murray's argument was that if women had not gained access to university education then no one in the universities would have admitted the need for such a subject since for university men the classics were requisite. The basis of the argument for English studies was of course that women could not suffer the discipline and rigour of the classics and therefore needed an easier subject such as English. It was in precisely such terms that Skeat argued the need for English when he wrote that:

> In fact it is one of the very great advantages of such an excellent subject as the English language and literature that, with a little supervision and management, it can easily be adapted for female students, who at least in some cases from my own experience, take a keen and intelligent interest in it and reap much benefit therefrom.   (Skeat, 1873, p.viii)

In his text that dealt with 'Questions for Examination in English Literature', Skeat followed his distinctions practically by setting different levels of paper for 'boys, senior students and ladies'. And in a similar vein Kingsley later argued that

'English literature is the best, perhaps the only, teacher of English history, to women especially' (Wilson, 1905, p.176).

As the study of English language and literature developed in the universities there were criticisms that 'Anglo-Saxon is abandoned to ladies and foreigners' (Wyld, 1913, p.167). The early provisions for women's education in particular were met with outright hostility as this *Punch* poem of the 1870s illustrates:

> The woman of the future! She'll be deeply read that's
>   certain,
> With all the education gained at Newnham or at
>   Girton;
> Or if she turns to Classic tomes, a literary roamer,
> She'll give you bits of Horace, or sonorous lines from
>   Homer.
>   . . .
> O pedants of these later days, who go on undiscerning
> To overload a woman's mind and cram our girls with
>   learning,
> You'll make a women half a man, the souls of parents
>   vexing
> To find that all the gentle sex this process is unsexing.
>   (Quoted in Granville-Barker, 1929, p.114)

Clearly the right of women to read classic tomes, or of Lady Macbeth's desire to unsex herself, was in the opinion of *Punch* a right that could only produce disastrous consequences and the language of the piece demonstrates the anxious fears held in regard to educated women. History ('the woman of the future'), education ('deeply read') and gender ('our girls') are brought together in a formula that reveals the deep disquiet and fear of the male *Punch*: educated women might, like Lady Macbeth, decide to throw off their gender roles and the 'gentle sex' begin to question such stereotyping.

One of the most interesting features of Trench's work in relation to the position of English language and literature in education was his early and determined advocacy of its centrality. As with most other contestants in the debate of the period, Trench's appeal for the development of English studies was closely linked to its political and cultural context. In effect Trench pre-empted Mathew Arnold in his call for a new cultural programme in the latter half of the mid-Victorian period. In a frequently used rhetorical ploy of this period, industrial sophistication (and all its barbarities) threatened to displace Sophocles (and Hellenism) and thus Arnold envisaged a programme that attempted the use of a specific form of culture as a remedy to the general philistinism of industrial capitalism. However, other cultural commentators such as Trench saw this remedy as clearly limited in its application and thus they argued for the use of English language and literature as the best vehicle for reform. Although only second best, English studies (the 'poor man's Classics') presented the best option available since:

> In the present condition of education in England . . . the number of those enjoying the inestimable advantages, mental and moral, which more than any other languages the Latin and Greek supply, must ever be growing smaller.   (Trench, 1859, p.vi)

Trench continued:

> It becomes therefore a duty to seek elsewhere the best substitutes within reach for that formation of the discipline which these languages would better than any other have afforded. And I believe, when these two are set aside, our own language and literature will furnish the best substitutes.   (*Ibid.*)

Such beliefs rapidly became the site of fierce contestation with John Earle (one of the strongest supporters of the study of English) declaring that 'in subtle ways of its own, English language gives a man surer hold of his distant possessions . . . for him there is ready access to the national fountain of poetry' (Earle, 1871, p.viii). The direct political and social aspects of this shift were outlined by W. Johnson in 1868 as he argued for English studies and against the classics on precisely the same grounds as Trench and later, as we shall see, the Newbolt Commissioners:

It can be no abstract advantage, with the present political
prospects of this country, and indeed of Europe, that any
education should retain an exclusive or class character. . . .
Any training which tends to keep up distinctions, whether
real or fictitious, must injure [our] community.   (Farrar,
1868, pp.383–4)

Having specified the content of the core curriculum Trench
went on to specify the methods of study to be adopted in the
study of English language and literature. He recommended
'the decomposition, word by word, of small portions of our
best poetry and prose', 'a decomposition, followed by a
reconstruction, of some small portions of great English Classics', and a 'close examination . . . of the words employed' in
such texts. This early form of close, practical criticism was to
be geared towards tracing the changes which the words had
undergone, showing 'the exact road by which a word has
travelled' (Trench, 1859, p.vi). In a return to his earlier
concerns he argued that the study of literature had to be
conducted through the medium of 'the history of the language'
and indeed one might extend this and argue that English
literature as an academic discipline was produced from within
the discourse of 'the history of the language'. In creating 'the
history of the language' linguistic historians such as Trench
had simultaneously created a parallel study: the history of the
literature. Language thus became no longer an object in itself
but the medium for the exploration of a new object which was
to become institutionalised in various forms as 'English
literature'.

Conclusion

This chapter has concentrated upon the texts of Trench in
order to demonstrate the highly political concerns of much of
the mid-nineteenth-century work on language in Britain.
Across a number of different fields, ranging from theology to
the construction of the national identity and social unity, work
on the English language was used to gain specific ends. It has
also been argued that Trench's work was not isolated in this

respect but in fact part of a larger trend that asserted a desire to 'know language' and yet continued to treat it as an instrument for the acquisition of other forms of knowledge. Of course this is not to argue that other British linguists did not engage in wide-ranging and voluminous research in the comparative scientific mode. Texts such as Latham's *Elements of Comparative Philology* (1862), or Sayce's *Introduction to the Science of Language* (1890), bear witness to the gradual (though never comprehensive) progress made in that field in Britain. However, the remainder of this text will concentrate upon the first of these trends as it was evinced in the new academic study that was to be institutionalised in the universities, colleges and schools: English language and literature. It is to the increasing interest in the history of that set of writings that we now call English literature, along with the interest taken in various forms of the spoken language and their political significance, that we shall next turn.

3

The Standard Language: the Literary Language

The victory of one reigning language (dialect) over the others, the supplanting of languages, their enslavement, the process of illuminating them with the True Word, the incorporation of barbarians and lower social strata into a unitary language of culture and truth, the canonisation of ideological systems, philology with its methods of studying and teaching dead languages, languages that were by that very fact 'unities', Indo-European linguistics with its focus of attention, directed away from language plurality to a single proto-language – all this determined the content and power of the category of 'unitary language' in linguistic and stylistic thought.

(M.M. Bakhtin, *The Dialogic Imagination*, p.271)

Introduction

The term 'standard' has a complex recorded history in that it demonstrates at least two major senses amongst the variety of its uses. First, there is the sense of 'standard' as a military or naval ensign, defined in the *OED* as 'a flag, sculptured figure or other conspicuous object, raised on a pole to indicate the rallying point of an army (or fleet) . . . the distinctive ensign of a king, great noble, or commander, or of a nation or city'. The function of this 'standard' was to act as an authoritative focal point, as a marker and constructor of authority around which could be grouped armies, fleets, nations and cities. Thus the 'standard' would be a focus of unity and under it would be all those who recognised its authority. In this sense the 'standard' is intertwined with crucial concepts of commonality, unity and therefore, at least in part, uniformity.

The second sense is distinct from though related to the first. In the second sense 'standard' signifies an exemplar of measure or weight:

> The authorized exemplar of a unit of measure or weight, for example, a measuring rod of unit length; a vessel of unit capacity, or a mass of metal of unit weight, preserved in the custody of public affairs as a permanent evidence of the legally prescribed magnitude of the unit. *Original Standard*: the standard to which others are copies, and to which the ultimate appeal has to be made.

The function of 'standard' in this sense is derived from the authority described in the first sense since a 'standard' here has a clearly marked role within an order of evaluation derived from its use in phrases such as the 'standards of the Exchequer', 'the King's Standard', and 'Standards of Commerce'. A 'standard' in this sense is no longer simply a marker *for* an authority external to it but becomes an authority *in itself*. Moreover 'standard' in this second sense further extends the concepts of commonality and uniformity that were described in the first and it now indicates the means of gaining agreement on fundamental questions in particular areas of knowledge. The 'standard' here is to be used in processes of evaluation and comparison in order to gain agreement by the use of a specific uniform and communally accepted code (twelve inches to the foot, sixty minutes to the hour and so on).

There are important concepts involved in both these uses of the term 'standard' since across both definitions the 'standard' involves questions of authority, commonality and evaluation. The next two chapters will attempt to explore how those concepts are deployed in uses of the terms 'standard English' or 'the standard language' in British linguistic studies of the nineteenth and early twentieth centuries. Let us begin, however, by looking at the term 'standard' in relation to its use by writers in the seventeenth and eighteenth centuries and attempt to relate such uses to nineteenth- and twentieth-century developments.

Maintaining standards

The major seventeenth-century British philosopher John Locke opened Book III of his *Essay Concerning Human Understanding* with the following:

> God designed Man for a sociable Creature, made him with not only an inclination, and under a necessity to have fellowship with those of his own kind; but furnished him also with Language, which was to be the great Instrument, and Common Tye of Society. (Locke, 1690, p.402)

Human beings are gifted, according to Locke, with a predisposition to associate and to use language to bind them one to another. Here then language was a 'standard' in our first sense since it served as a 'common tye' or instrument of unity. However, the second sense of 'standard' was far more popular in the fields of discourse concerned with language that existed in the eighteenth century and this referred to a linguistic value to be reached and one that could be communally recognised.

Swift, one of Locke's near-contemporaries, had issued his *Proposal* in order to meet the possibility of refining the language 'to a certain standard' and then fixing it for ever. His emphasis on refining the language to a particular state and then making that state an authority in itself, a 'standard' to guide all other usage, became a dominant theme in much eighteenth-century linguistic theorising. Lord Chesterfield, for example, followed Swift in calling for a process of 'purifying, and finally fixing our language' (Chesterfield, 1777, p.166) and also held that the language could be refined to a 'standard' which could then act as an exemplar. He commented that he 'had long lamented that we had no lawful standard of our language set up, for those to repair to, who might chuse to speak and write grammatically and correctly' (*ibid.*). There was as yet, however, no standard and so he argued, 'I cannot help

thinking it a sort of disgrace to our nation, that hitherto we
have had no such standard of our language' (*ibid.* p.167).
Since the language had not been refined to its optimum
'standard' the linguistic authorities containing the 'standard
language' were not to be found either:

> But a grammar and a dictionary and a history of our
> language through its several stages were still wanting at
> home, and importunately called for abroad . . . learners
> were discouraged by finding no standard to resort to and
> consequently thought it incapable of any.   (*Ibid.* p.169)

Despite the absence of any official codification there was a
continuing insistence in the eighteenth century on the value
of a certain set of texts that approached a 'standard' to be
matched: the King James translation of the Scriptures. The
eighteenth-century grammarian Bishop Lowth, for example,
held that 'the Vulgar Translation of the Bible . . . is the best
standard of our language' (Lowth, 1762, p.89). The use of
language in the scriptures was reckoned to have at least a
dual authority as it functioned as both an exemplar of linguistic
style and of religious faith and this opinion was to become
a commonplace in the eighteenth century, as when Lord
Monboddo described the language of the Bible as 'the standard
of our language as well as of our faith' (Monboddo, 1792, vol.
1, p.479). Such beliefs also carried into the nineteenth-century
discourses upon the English language in declarations such as
that:

> The English Bible is practically the standard of our lan-
> guage. It has been, more than any other influence, the
> means of teaching the English language, and maintaining it
> comparatively unchanged for 250 years. No academy or
> authoritative dictionary or grammar could have produced
> so general a standard of appeal, or given such uniform
> instruction throughout the nation. (Higginson, 1864, p.192)

One of the most interesting points of Higginson's argument
is that both senses of the term 'standard' are used in it. He
argues that the Bible is the 'standard of our language' in the

sense that it is a standard 'to which the ultimate appeal has to be made'. And he also argues that the Bible is the 'standard' in the sense that it acts as a unifying force, a way of encouraging people to unite around a set of particular values.

What is of particular interest for our argument in the quotations cited is that there is often a running together of both senses of the term 'standard'. Sometimes it appears to mean a value which has to be met and other times it appears to mean a uniform practice. What is likewise of interest is the conflation of written and spoken language. Does 'standard' when used of language refer to a level that has to be met in written language, or a uniform set of practices of writing? Or does it mean a level that has to be met in the spoken language, or a uniform set of ways of speaking? Such problems are in fact highly difficult to disentangle and an attempt will be made to unravel the complexities by studying the use of the term 'standard language' in the context of nineteenth- and twentieth-century language studies. However, before moving to an examination of such usage a brief examination will be made of a major difficulty facing many nineteenth-century linguists working in Britain: what is a language and where do we find it? This was accompanied by a more specific difficulty facing those working within the historical study of the language at this period: what is the English language and where is it to be found?

Finding a language: where to look and what to look for

It is a commonly held view that Ferdinand de Saussure launched the discipline of general linguistics through the theories encapsulated in the posthumous *Course in General Linguistics* first published in 1916. Central to the launching of the new discipline, it is generally argued, was Saussure's radical distinction between *langue* and *parole*. That is, the distinction between the linguistic structure that exists as a Durkheimian 'social fact' and the usage that the structure facilitates which is individual and contextual. In fact Saussure's role as the founding father of this type of linguistic study is open to challenge since at least some of his central concepts had been formulated elsewhere previously, yet there can be no doubt that they had never been gathered together, nor in such a creative manner, as they were in his text. His distinction between *langue* and *parole* was one of the most important since in drawing it Saussure was attempting to resolve a central methodological problem faced by linguists, which was the problem of deciding what exactly it was that they were supposed to study. To the problematic question that had troubled linguists throughout the nineteenth century – 'what is a language?' Saussure's *langue–parole* distinction was an innovative and enabling advance. In view of the difficulties of studying the linguistic heterogeneity presented in usage, Saussure's solution of relegating it to second place was both welcome and massively creative.

Linguistic diversity had created many problems for nine-teenth-century linguists since variation meant uncertainty with regard to boundaries. One such problem was that of distinguishing between a dialect and a language and it was one that proved difficult to resolve. One writer exposed the problem in asserting that 'if the question is asked, what is a dialect? No scientific or adequate definition can be given. For all practical purposes this will suffice. A language is a big dialect, and a dialect is a little language' (Meiklejohn, 1891, p.7). The problem of variation, however, was not to be solved so easily. One of Max Müller's most implacable opponents, the American linguist W. Dwight Whitney, commented (and in this was followed by Saussure) that 'in a true and defensible sense, every individual speaks a language different from every other' (Whitney, 1875, p.154). Every speaker has individual quirks and peculiarities in pronunciation, the comprehension and use of terms, and the 'grammaticality' of their discourse since:

> The form of each one's conceptions, represented by his use of words, is different from any other person's; all his individuality of character, of knowledge, education, feeling, enters into this difference. (*Ibid.*)

As a social being each subject and their language is constituted differently and in addition to these idiolectal differences there are also other forms of variation since, 'every separate part of a great country of one speech has its local form, more or less strongly marked . . . every class, however constituted, has its dialectic differences: so, especially the classes determined by occupation' (*ibid.*). The nineteenth-century linguists were clearly well aware of these differences in language use that have become the staple diet of modern socio-linguistics. Yet there is an apparent internal contradiction in Whitney's argument. Each speaker, he claims, as an individual subject has a particular form of speech influenced by geographical and social positioning (region, class, gender, age). Yet each speaker, he insists, shares in the 'one speech' that exists in a 'great country' and this appears to contradict the principle of diversity since individual speakers are held to speak their own language and the 'one speech' of the country. It is, of course, at this point that resort has to be made to Saussure's distinction since it is only by means of the *langue-parole* distinction that uniformity and diversity can be held in balance.

This distinction was not, however, plucked out of the air in an act of intellectual genius by Saussure since linguists had used a similar distinction in the nineteenth century precisely to attempt to solve the problem of distinguishing between a dialect and a language. Whitney himself had commented upon the elusiveness of 'a language' when he argued that 'no one can define, in the proper sense of that term, a language; for it is a great concrete institution, a body of usages prevailing in a certain community, and, it can only be shown and described' (*ibid.*, p.157). In a pre-emption of the terms of Wittgenstein's doctrine of 'saying and showing', Whitney asserts that language is beyond definition. However, he does maintain that one can show what 'a language' is simply by pointing to 'a body of usages' that prevail in 'a certain community'. yet this too appears problematically indeterminate in that it is still unclear as to what is to count as a token of the language. Is it any usage within 'a certain community'? Or is certain usage to be preferred on the grounds that it 'prevails' over others? Moreover, appealing to the body of usages, in a certain community, is further complicated if the boundaries of the community itself are set according to the language. That is, if the English nation were to be defined as all those native

English speakers born in England, as it often was, then it appears rather circular to define English as the language of the English nation. However, Whitney went on to specify with more precision where language lay:

> You have it in its dictionary, you have it in its grammar; as, also in the material and usages which never get into either dictionary or grammar; and you can trace the geographical limits within which it is used in all its varieties. (*Ibid.*)

Yet questions still appear to be being begged here since a language is said to be found in a dictionary or grammar but it is also in a supplementary way elsewhere: in other 'material and usages' that are ex-lexicographic. Moreover, tracing a language within its 'geographical limits' appears even more difficult conceptually since how does one know when one has crossed a 'geographical limit' with regard to language? How does one know in a specific area whether a particular usage belongs to a 'variety' of the language or if it 'properly' belongs to another language? Where are the limits of a language to be drawn?

For the nineteenth-century linguists such problems were enormously difficult in their methodological implications though in fact many linguists ignored them. However, for those concerned with the problem one way around it was to begin negatively, with the definition of a dialect. In his important text *English Dialects* Skeat proposed the following:

> According to the New English Dictionary, the oldest sense, in English, of the word *dialect* was simply 'a manner of speaking' or 'phraseology', in accordance with its derivation from the Greek *dialectos*, a discourse or way of speaking; from the verb *dialegesthai*, to discourse or converse.   (Skeat, 1912, p.1)

Such a definition was in itself not particularly precise or useful since it could equally well have been applied to a language and therefore Skeat continued to specify and narrow the definition:

> The modern meaning is somewhat more precise. In relation

to a language such as English, it is used in a special sense to signify 'a local variety of speech differing from the standard or literary language'. (*Ibid.*)

This was a crucial distinction since within it the 'local variety of speech' is contrasted with the 'standard or literary language'. 'Standard' or 'literary' become synonymous here and serve to contrast with the dialect along two axes. First, the dialectal form is spoken as opposed to the written standard. And second, the dialect is a local form rather than the standard (universal) literary form. The sense of 'standard' here is clearly that which refers to uniformity and thus the 'standard language' in this use indicates the literary language as used uniformly over the cultural, political and geographical territory of the nation. Hence the theoretical and methodological problems faced by linguists when considering 'a language' were to be met by the concept of the 'standard language'. In a sense we might argue that this use of the 'standard language' is the equivalent of Saussure's langue in the *langue-parole* distinction.

The standard language: the uniform language?

In this sense then the 'standard language', used synonymously by Hermann Paul with 'the common language', was a sort of meta-language. It is a form of language in any particular national geographic territory which lies beyond all the variability of usage in offering unity and coherence to what otherwise appears diverse and disunited. It is the literary form of the language that is to be used and recognised all over the national territory.

Historians of the language first perceived what they took to be a 'standard' form of the English language in this sense in the collection of texts that remained from the Old English period. Within those texts the linguists specified a group that exhibited a form of the language that was taken as the 'standard', the West Saxon. For example the early linguistic historian Kemble held that for the study of Old English:

As, in giving any account of what in grammatical parlance

we call dialects or variations, we necessarily assume a fixed
standard from which to measure deflections, we shall take
the West Saxon dialect as that standard. (Kemble, 1845,
p. 130)

Interestingly, it is a 'dialect' that is specified here as the
original form that becomes recognised as the 'standard' by
which we can measure deviation. And later the Wrights
followed this lead and asserted in their *Old English Grammar*
that:

There can hardly be any doubt that all practical teachers
of the subject will agree that it is better and easier for the
student to take early West-Saxon as the standard for Old
English and to group around it the chief deviations of the
other dialects.   (Wright, 1908, p.viii)

If such was the case for the Old English period then the
linguistic historians argued that after the Norman Conquest
there was no 'standard language' in England for a long time.
John Earle argued on this point that the conquest had
engendered 'the destruction of the standard language [which]
reduced English to a divided and dialectal condition' (Earle,
1876, p.15) The West Saxon was displaced and linguistic
'anarchy' prevailed since as another linguist writing in the
1870s put it, 'in our island there was no acknowledged
standard of national speech; ever since 1120 each shire had
spoken that which was right in its own eyes' (Kington-
Oliphant, 1873, p.154). According to this argument both the
spoken and written forms had lost their standards and disunity
prevailed. Later, however, in the fourteenth and fifteenth
centuries, there emerged (according to the linguistic historians) a new 'standard language' which was to be the
uniform literary language of the whole kingdom which was
discussed extensively by Skeat in his *English Dialects*. He
divided later medieval Britain into three distinct dialectal
areas, Northern, Midland and Southern (with a further
sub-division of the Midland into the Eastern and Western
Midland). He commented on the earlier history:

Between all these [forms] there was a long contention for

supremacy. In very early days, the Northern took the lead, but its literature was practically destroyed by the Danes, and it never afterwards attained to anything higher than a second place. From the time of Alfred, the standard language of literature was the Southern and it kept the lead till long after the Conquest.   (Skeat, 1912, p.37)

He then revised the dating of the fall of the 'Southern dialect' and went on to argue that in the Middle English period the Midland dialect:

Began in the thirteenth century to assume an important position, which in the fourteenth century became dominant and supreme, exalted as it was by the genius of Chaucer. Its use was really founded on practical convenience. It was intermediate between the other two [Northern and Southern], and could be more or less comprehended by the Northerner and the Southerner, though these could hardly understand each other.   (*Ibid.*)

From the fourteenth century there was, as far as the linguistic historians were concerned, a common language or, as Alexander Gil confusingly described it in his *Logonomia* (1619), a 'communis dialectus'. This 'common dialect' became the perceived standard literary language of the nation for the linguistic historians and just as Dante was credited with the formation of a national Italian language from the regional Tuscan form, various writers were credited with the standardising of the English language. A.H. Keane compared King Alfred's work with that of Dante, Boccaccio and Petrarch in the formation of 'the standard literary model' (Keane, 1875, p.37); Marsh chose Chaucer (a generally accepted figure) as 'eminently the creator of our literary dialects' (Marsh, 1860, p.22); and Kington-Oliphant unusually specified Robert of Brunne:

Strange it is that Dante should have been compiling his *Inferno*, which settled the course of the Italian literature for ever, in the self-same years that Robert of Brunne was compiling the earliest pattern of well-formed English. (Kington-Oliphant, 1873, p.211)

In any case, whoever derived credit for its formation it is clear that the linguistic historians had perceived the appearance and development of a uniform literary form. In the words of the *OED* editor James Murray:

> By the close of the fifteenth century, when England settled down from the Wars of the Roses, and the great collusions of populations and dialects by which they were accompanied, there was thus but one standard language acknowledged. (Murray, 1872, p.45)

Herman Paul argued that the geographic and cultural territory of Britain had been linguistically unified by this 'common language', and this was predictably the case since according to his theory 'in all modern civilised countries, we find side by side with manifold dialectic ramifications a widely diffused and generally recognised common language' (Paul, 1890, p.475).

Thus the development of the 'standard' written language was perceived by the linguistic historians as having taken place in the medieval period. However, to argue that such a 'standard' exists is not to say that it is actively used by the nationals whose 'standard' it is, since the 'standard' could exist amongst a small group, but not amongst the illiterate mass of the population. And in fact by definition the true commonality of the 'standard' written language could only be established with the gaining of mass literacy. To illustrate that point we may consider the late-nineteenth-century declaration of Thomas Elworthy in the preface to his study of *The Dialect of West Somerset*:

> The Education Act has forced the knowledge of the three Rs upon the population, and thereby an acquaintance in all parts of the country with the same literary form of English, which it has been the aim and object of all elementary teachers to make their pupils consider to be the only correct one. The result is already becoming manifest. . . . There is one written language understood by all, while the inhabitants of distant parts may be quite unintelligible to each other *viva voce*. (Elworthy, 1876, p.xliii)

Elworthy's estimate of literacy amongst the British population may well have been over-optimistic, although according to the educational historians Lawson and Silver literacy rates in 1840 were around 66 per cent for men and 50 per cent for women and had reached 97 per cent for both sexes by the end of the century (Lawson and Silver, 1973, p.259). What is beyond dispute is the existence of a common or 'standard' literary language throughout the complete territory. And yet what should also be beyond dispute is the relatively novel appreciation of such an achievement since Olivia Smith, for example, in her work *The Politics of Language 1791–1819*, cites Tory pamphleteers in the late eighteenth and early nineteenth centuries who attempted to prevent the spread of what may be called 'national literacy' (and thereby political awareness and the possibility of certain forms of national awareness) by employing a dialectal form of English in their political pamphlets. Smith cites as an example of such work a pamphlet entitled '*A Wurd or Two of Good Counsel to about Half a Duzzan Diffrant Sortes a Fokes* (Birmingham, 1791). Of course another way of viewing this political project would be to argue that it is a literary construction of what are taken to be popular modes of speech. In that case it would be an early instance of the populist literary-political style so clearly marked in the tabloid press.

The problem of the construction of a national literary language was addressed in nineteenth-century Italy since at the time of unification in 1861 most Italians used one of a large number of dialects (or 'small languages'). Only a small minority used 'Italian' which was the dialect of medieval Florence that had been adopted as the 'standard literary language' by educated minorities in the sixteenth century for its cultural prestige. In the light of such a situation, the Italian political theorist (and historical linguist) Antonio Gramsci argued in the early twentieth century that 'it is rational to collaborate practically and willingly to welcome everything that may serve to create a common national language, the non-existence of which creates friction particularly in the popular masses' (Gramsci, 1985, p.182). For Italian radicals the existence of the national language and the consequent unity it brought was a useful tool in eradicating merely local disputes. In Britain, however, the standard literary language was not a form around which radical struggle was to be focused, though it was promulgated and acknowledged in various cultural modes for specific ends.

The standard language: the central form

Within British linguistic research there was an increasing acknowledgement of and interest in the 'standard' form of the language. The 'standard' form was held to be the central and uniform literary form around which were grouped distinct sub-varieties (dialects), and thus it was held to be the form common to all literary pieces not tainted by the merely provincial. Latham, for example, demonstrated that linguists had to distinguish carefully between the different forms in their research when he argued that his own 'limited researches in our dialects have all been made with one object; *viz* that of determining the amount of direct Scandinavian, not in the standard, but in the provincial English' (Latham, 1841, p.73). It is clear that Latham considered there to be a very clear distinction between the 'standard' and the provincial forms, and another linguist, Derwent Coleridge, reinforced this view in an early critical article on the plan of the Philological Society to publish a *New English Dictionary*. In the article he argued for the inclusion of 'provincial' or dialect words in the Dictionary on the grounds that:

> It is merely stated that since the Reformation, there has been a standard language to which the provincial (country?) dialects do not conform. . . The question is not whether a dialectic word belongs to the standard currency of the language, but whether on other grounds it deserves to be recorded.   (Coleridge, 1860–1, p.164)

What is at stake here is not the existence of a standard literary language, which is indisputably to be recorded in the dictionary, but whether non-standard literary forms (those of 'provincial dialects') are to find their way in. In fact the distinctive points of Coleridge's argument were to be embodied in the development of a wholly new area of interest. The new discourse of 'the history of the language' produced new types of cultural producers in the Victorian period and within that discourse there emerged distinctive fields of knowledge and interest. There was that area of interest concerned with the history of the 'standard' language which was to be the focus for the construction of the *New/Oxford English Dictionary* published between 1888 and 1933. And there was also that area of interest concerned with the history of English dialects that was to produce the *English Dialect Dictionary* published between 1898 and 1905. The fields were clearly related and in terms of both the theoretical hierarchy and the practical relationship of the *N/OED* to the *EDD*, the relationship was to take the form of dominance and centrality opposed to subservience and eccentricity. Just as the 'standard' literary language was held to be central and the dialects peripheral theoretically, the *N/OED* was considered the major project and the *EDD* a much more secondary task in terms of practical production.

The English Dialect Society (EDS) was set up in 1873 with the aim of organising the collection of words that were not to be counted as 'standard' and the specific goals of the society were:

1. To bring together all those who have made a study of the Provincial Dialects of England, or who are interested in the subject of Provincial English;
2. To combine the labours of collectors of Provincial English words by providing a common centre to which they may be sent, so as to gather material for a general record of all such words;
3. To reprint various useful Glossaries that have appeared in scarce or inconvenient volumes;
4. To publish (subject to proper revision) such collections of Provincial English words as exist at present only in *MS*;
5. To supply references to sources of information which may be of material assistance to word-collectors, students, and all who have a general or particular interest in the subject.   (English Dialect Society, 1874)

The task in hand was indeed an urgent one and Aldis Wright

described it as being 'the *last* chance of saving the fast-fading relics of those forms of archaic English which have lingered on in country places (Wright, 1870, p.271). The urgency of appeals of this type, and in particular that of A.J. Ellis in his important appeal of 1871, brought about the formation of the EDS. Ellis had appealed for work on the dialects in order that the scope of linguistic research should be exhaustive since he argued that it was highly desirable that 'a complete account of our existing English language should occupy the attention of our ENGLISH DIALECT SOCIETY' (Ellis, 1869–89, pt III, p.xii). Thus if the *N/OED* was to supply the codification of the 'standard language' then the *English Dialect Dictionary* was to complete the account by the codification of the dialects.

One view of the relation of the 'standard' literary language to that of the dialects is spelt out by James Murray in his Romanes Lecture of 1900 by means of an interesting analogy. He argued that 'the relation of Latin to, say, the Romanic of Provence was like that of literary English to Lancashire or Somerset dialect' (Murray, 1900, p.8). This is a remarkable analogy in that if the comparison is followed through, it reverses the chronological relationship of the 'standard' literary language to the dialects and in this Murray's account was at sharp odds with the prevailing linguistic thought in the mid-century. Max Müller, opposing Murray's view, stressed the primacy of the dialects precisely at the expense of the literary language and argued that:

> What we are accustomed to call languages, the literary idioms . . . must be considered as artificial, rather than as natural forms of speech. The real and natural life of language is in its dialects . . . in spite of the tyranny exercised by the classical or literary idioms.   (Müller, 1862, p.49)

In an analogy that harked back to the German Romantic concern with the national language of the Volk, he continued to argue that just 'as political history ought to be more than a chronicle of royal dynasties, so the historian of the language ought never to lose sight of these lower and popular strata of speech from which those original dynasties sprang and by which alone they are supported' (*ibid.*, pp.51–2).

However, in spite of Müller's theory of 'dialectal regeneration', the latter half of the nineteenth century saw the full development of interest in the 'standard' language at the expense of the dialects (though it is true to say that Müller's theory did gain partial acceptance even amongst those working on the *N/OED*). The emergence of a consolidated body of labour working on the history of the 'standard' literary language was a result of the process of recognising what James Halliwell called the 'essential distinction between the language of literature and that of the natives of a country' (Halliwell, 1847, vol. 1, p.xi). Even dialectal poets were to recognise the theoretical distinction since William Barnes published his *Poems of Rural Life* in the Dorset dialect (1844–62) but he also published two further editions of the *Poems* in 'National English' (1846) and 'Common English' (1868). Not long after this it is clear that the 'standard' literary language had become the main focus of attention for linguists in Britain. A.J. Ellis, author of a major historical work upon pronunciation and dialectal speech-forms, argued in the 11th Presidential Address to the Philological Society that 'there is no doubt that the received literary English, such as I am using at the present time, is considered the English language pure and simple, and the other forms used in England are considered to be its dialects' (*Trans. Phil. Soc.* 1882–4, pp.21–2). This was the 1880s and it is clear that at this stage the 'standard' literary language had become equitable with the English language 'pure and simple'. In order to understand how that equation became possible it will be necessary to go back in history in order to trace the discursive processes and theoretical work by which it was facilitated.

The Oxford English Dictionary: the theoretical source of the standard literary language

The Rev. R. Morris was able to write confidently of the history of the literary language in 1876 when he asserted that 'our present Standard English was originally a local dialect which, under favourable circumstances not afforded to others, rose to the condition of a literary language' (*Trans. Phil. Soc.*, 1875–

1876, p.284). Fifty years later, at precisely the moment of the completion of the *N/OED* project, the Wrights pronounced in their *Elementary Historical New English Grammar* that 'what may reasonably be termed a standard literary language has existed since the early part of the fifteenth century, that is, some time before the end of the Middle English period' (Wright, 1924, p.1). It was argued earlier that the discourse of 'the history of the language' had produced a new object whose study was to dominate much of the nineteenth-century linguistic work in Britain. In this section this analysis will be continued by sketching the process by which 'the history of the language' produced a text whose central concern was the history of the standard literary language.

Early work on the earlier periods of English usage was disparate in that it had no unifying subject under which it fell. Yet by the mid-nineteenth century such work had been unified in the new study of language in England and its concerns had been set out. One effect of this unification was the enormous expansion of the range of the new study since rather than simply desiring to research particular periods or areas of the language it now wanted to research all periods and all areas. The new science wanted to totalise the English language by synthesising it as a whole and thus began by analysing component parts of the language in order to fit them back with more understanding into the historical totality. This theoretical aim had serious implications for the methods of the new study since it meant that its range had to be all-inclusive. It meant that the historians of the language had to work on an extremely large corpus, which is to say that their project, in the words of one of those who undertook the task, was 'systematically to read and extract English literature' (Murray, 1900, p.46). One linguist of the period specified the change that the new discourse had brought about in the form of this desire for all-inclusiveness: 'I well remember', he wrote, 'the Grimms being sternly upbraided for having – with a just appreciation of reality not always discernible in their dictionary – actually quoted a word from the advertising columns of a Berlin newspaper, not yet extinct' (Butcher, 1858, p.46). The Grimms had clearly stepped outside the bounds of permissible interest by quoting from a newspaper and, what is more, from a newspaper not yet extinct. However, such a breadth of scope had by the latter half of the century become a theoretical and methodological necessity. Writing on 'Political Philology' Butcher again exemplified the point as he argued that 'in order to discover and observe the genesis of new words or meanings . . . one not only has to read scientific works, but to watch speeches, pamphlets, newspapers, even fly sheets' (*ibid*). Evidently 'the history of the language' had produced a new object of study, new methods and new aims. However, within this new discourse it is clear that there was to be a gradual narrowing of scope as specific forms (dialects) were to be given less prestige than the central form (the standard literary language). This narrowing was perceptible in the realisation of De Quincey's call for work upon a 'monument of learning and patriotism' which was to become the text of *The New/Oxford English Dictionary*. And the construction of that text was to ensure the durability of 'the history of the language' both as an academic discipline and as the predominant form of linguistic research in Britain. Moreover, it was both to give cultural centrality to the new discourse and to give it forms of coherence and organisation that were to dictate the form of its end result.

The concept of a 'standard' literary language was crucial to the *N/OED* project since without it the task could not proceed. The 'standard' literary language gave to the *N/OED* precisely the narrowing in scope that was requisite and thus it will be necessary to examine the emergence and consolidation of the 'standard' literary language as the core of the *N/OED* project. In order to do this it will be necessary to examine the *Proposal for the Publication of a New English Dictionary* (1858), the rules drawn up for the editing of the *Dictionary*, the *Canones Lexicographici* (1860), and the *Preface* to Vol. 1 of the *Dictionary* (1888). In 1857 the Philological Society passed a resolution at the behest of Archbishop Trench that the society form a committee (the 'Unregistered Words Committee') for the collection of words not registered in the dictionaries of Johnson and Richardson, with the aim of publishing a supplement to these texts. As the work progressed, however, it became clear that the scale of the project had been underestimated (as it was until its completion), and thus it was further proposed that, 'instead of the Supplement to the standard English Dictionaries . . . a New Dictionary of the English Language should be prepared under the authority of the Philological Society' (*Proposal*, 1858, pp.7–8). Such was the inception of the project that was to be launched in terms of De Quincey's original appeal as the aim was to collect materials, 'for a Dictionary which, by the completeness of its vocabulary and by the application of the historical method to the life and use of words, might be worthy of the English language and English scholarship' (Preface, 1888, p.v). The project was to supersede the 'Standard English Dictionaries' by the construction of an exhaustive dictionary of the 'standard' literary language as the familiar texts were to be replaced by a text whose breadth, historical basis, and general excellence was novel.

The proposal for the new dictionary aimed at realising the project so boldly announced by De Quincey and yet if it was De Quincey who signalled the emergence of a new discourse and new cultural producers, then it was the dictionary text itself that was to organise and give credit to the newly formed cultural work. The *Proposal* intended:

> To enlist the sympathies of the public on behalf of the work, and to bring, as far as possible, the scattered learning and energy which exists plentifully enough in this country, if it can be effectually reached and addressed, to bear upon a common, and we may add national, project.   (*Ibid.*)

Calls for such a collaborative project of this kind were not, in fact, confined to the nineteenth century since in Chesterfield's letter to *The World* of 25 November 1754, he noted that 'many people have imagined that so extensive a work would have been best performed by a number of persons, who should have taken their several departments of examining, sifting, winnowing, . . . purifying and finally fixing our language, by incorporating their respective funds into one joint stock'. However, in order to begin their nineteenth-century project the Philological Society set up two committees, 'the one Literary and Historical' and 'the other Etymological'. The two committees were to work within the plan outlined in the

Proposal which consisted of five main points. These were: (i) that the lexicon should be exhaustive (containing 'every word in the literature of the language it professes to illustrate'), since the lexicographer was not to be an 'arbiter of style'; (ii) following from (i), to 'admit as authorities all English books'; (iii) to set the historical limits of possible quotation and thus to define the historical limits of 'English'; (iv) within those limits to treat each word according to the 'historical principle', that is, to trace the development of the 'sense' and the history of its appearances in the language; (v) to settle the etymological origins of the word and to show its cognate history.

The methodological and theoretical implications of these five points are extremely interesting and in order to derive the clearest significance from them they will be treated in reverse order. First, point (v), the etymology of words. The proposal follows Müller's dictum that 'every word in our dictionaries is derived from roots' and thus specifies that the comprehensive lexicographer has to dig beneath the surface of the words in order to expose the roots. The dictionary, however, was to provide two sets of roots, two etymologies, and these are what we may call the internal and the external. First there is the attempt to settle 'the proximate origins of each word' within 'the English language' which in effect means to give its first recorded use in a form that is to be counted as 'English'. Second, the attempt to demonstrate its cognate history: to 'exhibit several of its affinities with the related languages for the sake of comparison'. As a further development of this second etymological aim the 'comparative anatomy' of the word was to include 'that language which seems to present the radical element contained in the word in its oldest form'. Thus as well as the exposition of the root of the word within 'English' and the affinities of the word with other forms in other languages the etymology has even greater aims: to derive the non-English *etymon* of the English *etymon*, to derive the root of the root, origin of the origin. It is clear that this aim holds important considerations concerning both the nature of a word and linguistic history. First, there is the presupposition that a word remains the same – although its form and meaning change – as a sort of Platonic form that maintains its purity and unity beyond all accidental changes. This allows for the possibility of searching for the radical element of the word in its oldest form which may bear little (if any) relation to its contemporary form. This would then open the possibility of etymology to a remarkable extent since who but a linguistic historian of some sort would imagine that 'padas' and 'foot' are related or, more importantly, even conceivably the 'same' word? Such is the legacy of the appearance of historicity. And related to this point is the presupposition that we could find the 'oldest form' by consulting the historical hierarchy of languages. Beginning (of course) with the oldest language, we look for the oldest form of the word by consulting the linguistic laws that were held to govern language and which enable us to predict what to look for in the word stock. When we find our form we are then at the point of the origin of the word, the *etumos logos*. The objection to this presuppositon would not be that we could never find the *etymon* of a particular word – since we might do this by chance or even by consulting the linguistic laws – the point would be that we would never be sure absolutely that we had found the *etymon* since there is always the open possibility that an older form might appear, or even that the historical hierarchy of languages could be disrupted (as it had been in the late eighteenth century). The point is that the temptation to talk of origins here obscures the restriction that the philologists worked within. It is only possible to discuss etymology and origins with the constant reminder that it is an 'origin' only from within a particularly limited set of materials, and a set that always lies open to the possibility of disruption.

The presuppositions of point (v) are underpinned by those of point (iv). In this case there is the belief that a form is born and can die as a word. An infinite number of forms is potentially possible but only a limited number are realised as words, and thus the past realisation of certain forms as words is exhibited in their appearance in writing. Therefore, the *Proposal* argued, care will be taken 'to fix as accurately as possible, by means of appropriate quotations, the epoch of the appearance of each word in the language, and in the case of archaisms and obsolete words, of their disappearance also' (*Proposal*, p.4). However, it is not simply their existence that needs to be noted, not simply a task of issuing 'as accurately as possible' their birth certificate and notification of their deaths. The linguist also needs to narrate the history of their life by constructing the 'Biographies of Words'. The linguist is obliged to show 'the development of the sense or various senses of each word from its etymology and from each other, so as to bring into clear light the common thread which unites all together' (*ibid.*). Despite changes in both form and sense a word can be traced as a single coherent unit by means of the laws that will account for formal change and by a tracing of 'the common thread which unites' all senses together. In the words of the Preface, that is, by a 'logical and historical view' of words in which the historical point of view was to trace the word through its formal variation and the logical point of view was to trace its semantic changes. In this sense then again the historical variation of a word ceases to be a problem as the word becomes an essential unity and is an atom that lies beyond, and is unchanged by, history.

Point (iii) likewise depends upon point (iv). If point (iv) holds that it is possible to ascertain the limits (the birth and death) of each word, then it is clear that the very limits of the language too will have to be fixed. If such limitation is not undertaken then the history produced would be that of a linguistic form, not a word in a language. In order for the word to come into being the limits of its existence have to be marked and thus the language too has to have its own being delimited. Point (iii) continued to assert that:

> The limits of quotation in point of time are next to be fixed. We have decided to commence with the commencement of English, or, more strictly speaking, with that definite appearance of an English type of language, distinct from the preceding semi-Saxon, which took place around the end of the reign of Henry III.   (*Proposal*, p.3)

Such a break was widely recognised since Bosworth earlier had terminated the Anglo-Saxon language with the reign of Henry III (1258) on the grounds that 'what was written after this period has generally so great a resemblance to our present language, that it may evidently be called English' (Bosworth,

1838, p.xviii). What is of interest in the limitation given in the *Proposal* is the revision of the definition of the term English: 'the commencement of English, or more strictly speaking, with that definite appearance of an English type of language, distinct from the preceding semi-Saxon'. The limit to English is to be drawn around the period 1250 and yet the limit is not to be taken as the commencement of the English language but as that of 'an English type of language', a form held to be distinct from the preceding semi-Saxon but not yet English. Such a revision indicates the self-consciousness of the dictionary-makers and the precision for which they strove, although such precision has not prevented the appearance and development of the popular idea that the English language began at AD 1000, AD 1100, AD 1250 or any other point. The lexicographers, however, were aware of the arbitrariness of the boundary they were proposing as demonstrated by their declaration that, 'of course, this, like every other line of demarcation, is hard to draw and occasions a few apparent incongruities' (*Proposal*, p.4). In fact any attempt to delimit the language on almost any grounds, which leads inevitably to the question of what was, or had been, 'in' the language and what was 'out', had its attendant difficulties. The *General Explanations* to Volume 1 argued on this point that 'the language presents yet another undefined frontier, when it is viewed in relation to time'. And this problem was evidently one that caused linguists many difficulties. In 1861 Craik wrote of the difficulties of delimiting English literature and language when he argued that:

> If the history of a national literature is to have any proper unity, it can rarely embrace the language in its entire extent. If it should attempt to do so, it would really be the history not of one but of several literatures.

Restrictions and selectivity had to be introduced since:

> In some cases it might even be made a question when it was that the language properly began, at what point of the unbroken thread which undoubtedly connects every form of human speech with a succession of preceding forms out

of which it has sprung, we are to say that an old language has died and a new one come into existence.

The problems of continuity and discontinuity were marked since even in the 'same' language variation will occur historically:

> At any rate, even when a language is admitted to be the same, it not infrequently differs as much in two of its stages as if it were two languages. We have a conspicuous example of this in our own English. We may be said to have the language before us in complete continuity from the seventh century; but the English of the earliest portions of this long space of time, or what is commonly called Anglo-Saxon, is no more intelligible to an Englishman of the present day who has not made it a special study than is German or Dutch.   (Craik, 1861, vol. 1, pp.v–vi)

The interesting thing to notice here is how close Craik comes to arguing for the existence of different languages rather than for the existence of stages of the 'same' language. Variation appears to argue logically for a distinction between languages and yet this conclusion is prefaced by the conditional 'as if'. 'English', for the linguistic historian, was an organically developing and continuous entity and thus forms such as Anglo-Saxon were to be counted as an earlier form of English, not a distinct language theoretically separate from it.

In fact the arbitrary 'line of demarcation' was even more 'hard to draw' than it at first seemed. The *General Explanations* referred to this point of difficulty when it specified that:

> The present work aims at exhibiting the history of signification of the English words now in use, or known to have been in use since the middle of the twelfth century. This date has been adopted as the only natural halting place short of going back to the beginning, so as to include the entire Old English or 'Anglo-Saxon' Vocabulary. . . Hence we exclude all words that had become obsolete by 1150. But to words actually included this date has no application; their history is exhibited from their first appearance, however early.   (*Explanations*, p.xviii)

Although there is a clear confidence here in regard to the knowledge of the 'beginning' of English, the dictionary does not in fact attempt to start its record at that point. Instead the cut-off point is to be at the 'only natural halting place', which is given as the mid-twelfth century. However, for any form that is accredited with the status of 'English word' (i.e. not a form that appears in the language existing before the mid-twelfth century but disappears thereafter), its history will not be terminated at 'the only natural halting place'. For any form given the status of 'English word' through inclusion in the dictionary, its history will be extended beyond the primary limit of 'the English language' and even its history in pre-, or Old, English will be recorded. And for all 'words' given in the dictionary their history is to be periodised thus:

> The periods into which a language may, for philological purposes, be most conveniently divided, are three: 1. From its rise, cir.1250, to the Reformation – of which the appearance of the first printed translation of the Bible in 1526 may be taken as the beginning.
> 2. From the Reformation to Milton (1526–1674, the date of Milton's death).
> 3. From Milton to our day.   (*Proposal*, p.5)

Thus the limits of 'the history of the language' had been formally circumscribed and once its structure had been ascertained the 'history of the language' could now be written and its contents filled in.

The contents of the dictionary were to be 'English words now in use, or known to have been in use since the middle of the twelfth century'. The problem for the lexicographers was to establish and determine the English words now in use, and with more difficulty the words 'known to have been in use' since the twelfth century. How, it could be asked, were lexicographers to establish which words had been in use since the middle of the twelfth century? The answer to the problem lay in ascertaining precisely the sense of the word 'known' in the phrase 'known to have been in use'. The lexicographers did not seek an exhaustive account of, for example, mid-twelfth-century English since, as with etymology, there was no possibility of recognising when one had reached the limits of descriptions required for the term 'exhaustive' to make sense. Instead the lexicographers were content to 'know' that particular words had been in use at a particular period because they had the evidence of such use, and this is made clear in point (i) of the *Proposal*:

> We may begin by asserting that, according to our view, the first requirement of every lexicon is that it should contain *every word occurring in the literature of the language it professes to illustrate.*   (*Proposal*, p.2)

That is, the lexicographers had a carefully ordered and historically arranged canon of English literature to consult. Or rather, given that none as yet existed they rapidly constructed such a canon. Academic literary history and the *N/OED* project are necessarily closely related in the latter half of the nineteenth century; necessarily since they were often the same historians working on the same material for only slightly different ends in both fields.

As point (ii) of the *Proposal* indicates the lexicographers were concerned with one form of the language alone. This is borne out by the quotation that was later to serve as an illustration under the entry 'Standard Language' (though ironically there was no such entry in the original *N/OED* and it appeared only in the 1933 supplement), which was taken from the 1858 *Proposal*:

> As soon as a standard language has been formed, which in England was the case after the Reformation, the lexicographer is bound to deal with that alone.   (*Proposal*, p.3)

In fact 'the history of the language' and the lexicographers who worked within the new discourse in some senses did more to theorise and delineate the standard literary language than any other influence. Their project and the discourse within which they worked did, in a certain sense, create the 'standard literary language' since their work demanded it. They needed the 'standard literary language' as a concept since it offered a set of delimitations that were essentially required for the project to be able to function since it delimited both the period they had to cover and the material they were to consider. There are many references to 'Standard' in relation to 'English' or 'language' before this date even in the *Proceedings of the Philological Society*, yet the familiar and recognised use of the term 'Standard English' with the sense of an authorised, delimited and uniform literary form of the language is a product of the linguistic problems and labours of the 1850s and 1860s.

The historical location of the 'standard language' was to be post-Reformation and its material location was to be 'literature' since it had been specified that a lexicon should contain 'every word occurring in the literature of the language it professes to illustrate'. Thus the lexicographers were to 'admit as authorities all English books, except such as are devoted to purely scientific subjects, as treatises on electricity, mathematics, etc. and works written subsequently to the Reformation for the purpose of illustrating provincial dialects' (*Proposal*, p.3). All words, as specified in the *Canones*, that are to be found 'in works of general literature as opposed to purely technical or scientific treatises' (*Canones*, 1858, pt. II, no. 3) are to be recorded.

The placing of texts upon scientific subjects and post-Reformation dialect texts outside the bounds of the 'standard

language' seems puzzling. It is the more so since the *General Explanations* to Vol. 1 of the *Dictionary* offers more than the recording of all literary words. In the *Explanations* Murray wrote of recording the 'common words' of the language, 'some of them only literary, some of them only colloquial, the great majority at once literary and colloquial'. Murray's broader view was illustrated by means of the diagram above.

This impression of the project as being more than the record of literary words, a record of 'all the common words of speech and literature', is furthered by the assertion in the *Canones Lexicographici* that:

> This Dictionary shall record, under certain limitations, the existence of every word in the language for which sufficient authority, whether printed or oral, can be adduced, shall investigate its history and derivations, and shall determine as far as possible, fully and precisely, its several meanings and its appropriate usage, illustrated by quotations. (*Canones*, p.3)

It appears from such a declaration that the colloquial, the common words of speech, and even words with sufficient oral authority would be recorded. However, if the project had proceeded with such aims then its termination (long delayed in any case), would have been surely placed in doubt. The task of recording 'every word' in the language and treating it according to the 'historical principle' would have become gargantuan and, moreover, it would again have raised the question of who is to decide upon the matter of 'oral authority' not merely in the present, but even more contentiously in past centuries. The task was not in fact to be so ambitious and was to keep itself within literary boundaries since the 'certain limitations' that are mentioned above became the limits of the 'standard' literary language. The Preface to Vol. 1 made this quite clear:

> It was resolved to begin at the beginning, and extract anew typical quotations for the use of words, from all the great English writers of all ages, and from all the writers on special subjects whose works might illustrate the history of

words employed in special senses, from all writers before the sixteenth century, and from as many as possible of the more important writers of later times.   (Preface, p.5)

Although it appears from the structure of the *N/OED* that the history of the words was compiled and then supported by literary evidence — the illustration of 'the facts by a series of quotations ranging from the first known occurrence to the latest' – this impression is not in fact accurate. Although it appears that the vocabulary and history of the language came first and the literature second it was precisely the opposite case. Before a history of the language could be constructed the written records of the language had to be consulted. This had to be the case since as the *General Explanations* made clear;

> The vocabulary of the past times is known to us solely from its preservation in written records; [and] the extent of our knowledge of it depends entirely upon the completeness of the records, and the completeness of our acquaintance with them.   (*Explanations*, p.xviii)

In a precise sense, literature had to come before the language since without written records there could be no history of the language.

The shifting emphases of the term 'literature' have been traced by a number of cultural historians, notably Raymond Williams in *Keywords* and other texts. Yet the appearance of 'literature' as a novel academic field of study was also acknowledged by many of the Victorian linguists and a number of them were engaged on behalf of English literature in the struggle for English studies at the universities. Richard Morris, editor of *Specimens of Early English* 'selected from the chief English authors 1250–1400', argued that 'an intimate and thorough acquaintance with a language is only to be acquired by an attentive study of its literature' (Morris, 1867, p.v). Craik made the point more clearly when he asserted that 'in tracing . . . the history of the English literature and of the English language together, we shall be obliged to look at the language principally, or almost exclusively, as we find it employed in the service of the literature' (Craik, 1861, p.1).

For Morris the tracing of the history of the language through studying its literature stood on at least a par with the comparative method:

> Each language has a history of its own, and it may be made to tell us its own *life*, so to speak, if we set the right way to work about it.

There are two ways of devising such an autobiography:

> The first mode is by comparing one language with stems that are well known to us. The second is by studying the literature of a language in order of time, or chronologically, beginning with the very oldest books, and coming down to the latest and newest.   (Morris, 1875, p.1)

This second mode, the new discipline, was to herald a new form of literary criticism concerned neither with censure nor taste but with a new sense of examination and evaluation. This new sense was linked to the process of examining closely the very material of which literature was formed, language itself. The 'close reading' of texts and the 'practical criticism' bestowed upon them are in fact methodologically linked to this early 'scrutiny' of words and again this recalls Trench's work in this regard. Earle claimed a long pedigree for such linguistic criticism when he argued that:

> From the very dawn of literary education, it has been the most universal aim of teacher and of student to ascertain the variable meaning of words in the standards of literature. The whole pedigree of the Latin Dictionary has been devoted to this more than to any other end. Johnson was the first to take in hand this task for English. Since his day there has been no great effort of the kind until now in the New English Dictionary under the editorship of Dr Murray.   (Earle, 1890, p.138)

Agreeing with Earle on the underdeveloped state of English criticism in this sense Skeat commented that 'it must be further observed that the critical study of our best authors is almost a new thing; that there are many words yet unexplained, allusions not yet understood (Skeat, 1873, p.xiii). Thus both the formation of English literature as a set of canonical texts that needed to be read, and a closely scrutineering approach to such texts, was emerging from within the discourse of 'the history of the language' since, as Murray described it, the project of the *N/OED* was precisely 'systematically to read and extract English literature'. An alternative description of the project was that given by F.J. Furnivall when he stated that 'the notion was to strain all English literature through a sieve, as it were and so to catch the first appearance of every word as it came into the language, and its last appearance before it died out' (Benzie, 1983, p.91). The new discourse had produced from its own requirements 'English literature', an ordered literary history, and a method for approaching the texts. The *Proposal* had divided the language according to literary markers (the printing of the first translation of the Bible, the death of Milton and so on) and more significantly had outlined a 'list of the printed literature of England belonging to the period 1250–1526' (and later periods) consisting of over 500 individual texts and collections of texts, along with recommendations for the mode of reading them.

The canon of English literature had been set down in this way in order to conquer a problem posed to the linguistic historians. This was the fact that:

> The excessive rarity of most of the books themselves, which form our authorities . . . will exclude nearly all who cannot read them in the British Museum or the Bodleian, or some other large library, where alone they are to be found. Many poems and other pieces, a collation of which would be invaluable for such a work as this, still lie hid in M.S.   (*Proposal*, p.9)

The reason for the marked appearance of the canon of English literature at this period was quite simply its previous non-existence and the need for it that had been produced by the work of the linguistic historians. The editions that were available, primarily those of small printing clubs such as the Roxburgh and Abbotsford, were too expensive to enable widespread access. Thus, the *Proposal* proclaimed optimistically that 'we cannot but express an earnest hope that those who are qualified to assist us in this portion of our task . . . will not hesitate to come forward at once' (*Proposal*, p.7). The task of providing easy access to the previously inaccessible canon was fulfilled by volunteer workers in societies such as the Early English Text Society (EETS). According to Sweet, the founder of the *EETS*, James Furnivall, discovered:

> That our earliest authors had not been sufficiently exploited, and that many highly important *MSS* had been incorrectly printed and insufficiently glossed, and many more had not been printed at all. . . . Having made this all-important discovery, he promptly applied the right remedy by founding the EETS, which has entirely altered the situation by giving us accurate texts and useful glossaries. (Munro, 1901, p.177)

And Furnivall himself described the role of the EETS as 'the bringing to light of the whole of the hidden springs of the noble literature that England calls its own' (Furnivall, 1867, p.1). The EETS and others founded by Furnivall such as the New Shakespeare Society (1873), the Browning Society (1881), the Shelley Society (1886), and the Wyclif Society (1881), produced, in a material sense, this new academic field ('English literature') as a widely available and recognisable set of texts. And their motives were closely linked to De Quincey's call for a 'monument of learning and patriotism'. The 7th Report, in February 1871, of the EETS work made the position clear. It quoted Professor Selley's comments in the 1868 Report to the effect that:

> 'Classical studies may make a man intellectual, but the study of the native literature has a moral effect as well. *It is the true ground and foundation of patriotism* . . . I call that man uncivilised who is not connected with the past through the state in which he lives'. . . . The committee again declare that they take no lower ground for the Society's work than this. Not dilettante Antiquarianism, but duty to England is the motive of the Society's workers. (EETS, 1871, pp.1–2)

Once again the study of the language, and thus by derivation the study of the literature, of England had been explicitly linked to moral and political concerns.

Conclusion

In this chapter the development of particular types of interest within the work carried out on language in the nineteenth century has been traced. By examining the problems faced by linguists in relation to the problem of delineating a language and a dialect an attempt has been made to demonstrate the distinction drawn between a local spoken form (dialect) and the uniform literary form (standard language). Following from this it has been demonstrated how the concept of the 'standard literary language' was used by many nineteenth-century British linguists as referring to the central, historically validated, and uniform form of the written language. Further, after having considered this material, the historical development of this concept has been retraced by considering its evolution in the *New/Oxford English Dictionary* project and a few of the implications of the new concept for the study of English literature have been suggested.

It was argued then that the term 'standard language' emerges from the difficulties and problems faced by nineteenth-century linguists and in particular the lexicographers of the late nineteenth century working on the new dictionary. However, this sense of the term 'standard' was not the only use that it had when concatenated with 'language'. As this chapter began by pointing out, 'standard' can have the sense both of uniformity and of a level of excellence to be met. The next chapter will consider another use of the term 'standard English' that differs from that outlined in this chapter. It is to the political and discursive meanings and implications of that distinct use that we turn next.

4

The Standard Language: the Language of the Literate

It has largely influenced the local dialects, for the children hear a form of it from the teachers in their schools, servants hear it from their masters, tradesmen from their customers – everyone hears it in the parish church.

(H. Wyld, *The Growth Of English*, 1907, p.48)

Another standard

The term 'standard language' achieved at least one clear use in the mid-nineteenth century in that it indicated the uniform and commonly accepted national literary language upon which linguistic historians and lexicographers worked. Such a sense had in fact been indicated in the work of the eighteenth-century grammarian Priestley a century earlier when he had argued that 'the English and the Scotch, had the Kingdoms continued separate, might have been distinct languages, having two different standards of writing' (Priestley, 1762, p.139). However, the cultural and political conjunction of the two kingdoms that culminated in the 1707 Act of Union meant that there had emerged a single standard of writing throughout the whole national territory which was to be traced later by the nineteenth-century linguistic historians.

There was another use of the term 'standard' in relation to language, however, and this sense of the term was applied to the spoken rather than the written language. It can be found again in the work of Priestley as he wrote of variation in the Greek language:

All the different modes of speaking, like all other modes, might have grown into disrepute, and, by degrees, out of use, giving place to one as a standard, had particular circumstances contributed to recommend and enforce it. (*Ibid.*, p.136)

In the Greek community, however, this single standard spoken language has not appeared since:

In Greece every seperate [sic] community looking upon itself as in no respect inferior to its neighbours in point of antiquity, dignity, intelligence, or any other qualifications; and being constantly rivals for power, wealth and influence, would no more submit to receive the laws of language from another than laws of government.   (*Ibid.*, p.137)

In this usage there is clearly a distinct sense to the word 'standard' in that it refers to a single form of speech that will replace diversity and variation. Such a cultural transformation would involve enormous cultural and political problems, and these are noted by Priestley in his estimation that issues such as the historical background and self-esteem of a community, as well as more overtly economic matters, would militate against such a piece of linguistic legislation. The laws of language are like the laws of government or politics in this respect in that they are both difficult to impose.[1]

By the end of the eighteenth century in Britain it was precisely such a cultural transformation that was being called for and one that had in fact already begun. In this period the process of imposing one spoken form as a 'standard' and thus devaluing others was under way, and evidence of the emergence of attitudes towards such a 'standard' form of speech is attested by the large number of texts that start to appear for the purposes of elocution training. John Walker, one such elocution master, wrote that 'our shops swarm with books whose titles announce a standard for pronunciation' (Walker, 1774, p.22) Though when consulted, he reported, they prove to consist mainly of 'a barbarous orthography and a corrupt pronunciation'. These texts often made enormous claims and Thomas Sheridan's *British Education. Or, the Source of the Disorders of Great Britain* (1756), for example, claimed to be:

An Essay Toward Proving that the Immorality, Ignorance and False Trust, which so Generally Prevail, are the Natural and Necessary Consequences of the Present Defective System of Education. With an Attempt to show that a Revival of the Art of Speaking and the Study of our Own Language might contribute in A Great Measure to the Cure of Those Evils.   (Sheridan, 1756)

Most of these texts were not quite as ambitious as this and restricted their aims to a prescription of particular uses and styles. Yet the sheer bulk of the work was enormous: to take Walker himself as an example, he produced *A General Idea of a Pronouncing Dictionary of the English Language* (1774), a *Dictionary of the English Language Answering At Once The Purposes of Rhyming, Speaking and Pronouncing* (1775), *Exercises for Improvement in Elocution: Being Extracts from the Best Authors For the Use of Those Who Study The Art of Reading and Speaking in Public* (1777), and the *Critical Dictionary and Expositor of the English Language* (1791). Such works were highly prescriptive and often made clear their attempt to construct a 'standard', as in James Buchanan's attempt to produce an *Essay Towards Establishing a Standard for an Elegant and Uniform Pronunciation of the English Language* (1767). And embodied within these texts themselves is a clear historical signal as to the contemporary anxieties in the British social formation that centred around language. It was clear that the language, or at least the spoken language you used (accent, tone, style and vocabulary), were laden with social significance. To make a mistake was not simply a grammatical error but a social faux-pas.

A notable exception to the prevailing fashion in the study of language was Priestley's work. Rather than attempting to set up a standard which would count as the form to be emulated Priestley attacked the theory that lay behind such an idea. He argued that:

> In modern and living languages, it is absurd to pretend to set up the composition of any person or persons whatsoever as the standard of writing, or their conversation as the invariable rule of speaking. . . . The general prevailing custom, where ever it happens to be, can be the only standard for the time it prevails.   (Priestley, 1762, p.184)

His work was, however, contradicted by many other texts that aimed to guide language-users in their writing and speech by prescribing particular forms and usages and proscribing others. In fact Priestley had classical guidance for citing 'usage' as the standard to be followed since Quintilian (one of the most frequently quoted references in eighteenth-century linguistic text books) had likewise done so when he had argued that 'usage however is the surest pilot in speaking, and we should treat language as currency minted with the public stamp' (Quintilian, Book I, v. 72–vi. 4). This apparently concurs with Priestley's anti-prescriptive stance and yet this concurrence is merely superficial since Quintilian's own linguistic views were prescriptive. He argues in the *Institutio Oratoria* that 'language is based on reason, antiquity, authority, and usage': 'reason' from analogy and etymology, 'antiquity' from the 'sanctity' of the past, 'authority' from 'orators' and 'historians'. He continues to define what he means to signify by 'usage' by arguing that, 'if it be defined merely as the practice of the majority, we shall have a very dangerous rule affecting not merely style but life as well, a far more serious matter. For where is so much good to be found that what is right should please the majority?' He then specifies the activities of the 'majority' that persuade him of its essential degradation:

> The practices of depilation, of dressing the hair in tiers, or of drinking to excess at the baths, although they may have thrust their way into society, cannot claim the support of usage, since there is something to blame in all of them (although we have usage on our side when we bathe or have our hair cut or take our meals together).

'Usage' then is not simply the practices and activities that take place in society but refers only to those practices and activities which are morally blameless. Thus an essential theoretical and practical distinction needs to be drawn and the case is similar for language:

> So too in speech we must not accept as a rule of language words and phrases that have become a vicious habit with a number of persons. To say nothing of the uneducated, we are all of us well aware that whole theatres and the entire crowd of spectators will often commit *barbarisms* in the cries which they utter as one man. I will therefore define usage in speech as the agreed practice of educated men, just as where our way of life is concerned I should define it as the agreed practice of all good men.   (*Ibid.*, Book I, vi. 42–5)

Quintilian's exclusion of the 'barbarisms' of the uneducated or the mob and his preference for the language agreed between educated men (as seen in their practice) were generally followed by the eighteenth-century prescriptivists. They too drew linguistic distinctions based on social grounds or on the basis of educational status and they too prescribed one form and proscribed others.

In the nineteenth century, however, historians of the study of language assert that such crude preferences were replaced by 'historical' and 'scientific' work such as the tracing of the 'standard' literary language and the construction of a canon of English literature. The 'social and rhetorical concerns of the eighteenth century', it is argued, were replaced by the objectivity and neutrality of the nineteenth century. The aim of this chapter will be to show by an analysis of the term 'standard English' in particular debates, that the nineteenth century did not drop the cultural project of imposing a particular form of speech as the 'standard' to which others had to rise. In fact the opposite was true.

'The higher instrument': a standard for speech

One phrase that became increasingly current in the nineteenth century was 'the Queen's English', a phrase originally formed by analogy with phrases such as the 'King's Coin' or the 'King's Standard' and first recorded in Thomas Wilson's *The Arte of Rhetorique* (1553). The phrase had originally been used to refer to particular uses that Wilson had objected to and that he had referred to as 'counterfeiting the King's English', and it was to become familiar in the more popular linguistic text books of the nineteenth century. For example, Henry Alford, the Dean of Canterbury, published his *Plea For the Queen's English* which (like Wilson's first use) appealed against 'abuses' of speech. In his popular text (the second edition alone ran to 10,000), Alford offered this definition of 'the Queen's English'.

> It is, so to speak, this land's great highway of thought and speech and seeing that the Sovereign in this realm is the person round whom all our common interests gather, the source of our civil duties and centre of our civil rights, the Queen's English is not an unmeaning phrase, but one which may serve to teach us some profitable lessons with regard to our language, its use and abuse.   (Alford, 1864, p.2)

The Queen's English does not refer to the idiolect of any particular sovereign but to a recognised and institutionalised form of the language. Like the sovereign herself the Queen's English is symbolic in that it is that which unites all English speakers since it is the medium in which 'all our common interests gather'. It unites all native English speakers by giving them rights of citizenship and demanding from them civil duties, and this linkage of language and citizenship was later to become a key theme in cultural and political debates in the early twentieth century. The Queen's English clearly marks out certain speakers as English citizens and demands in return an allegiance to the language. Moreover, the Queen's English, like the sovereign herself, has to be protected from abuse and it has to be cared for and protected in order to safeguard both it and our ability to think and speak.

Although not the sovereign's idiolect, neither was the Queen's English the language of all British speakers. It was not, to use Herman Paul's words, 'the entire sum of the products of linguistic activity of the entire sum of individuals in their reciprocal relations'. Instead it was specified as a particular form of English which was taken to be the usage of particular speakers marked by specific characteristics. A clear example of the relational nature of the Queen's English is given by F.T. Elworthy's comments upon the 'pronunciation, intonation and those finer shades of local peculiarity which mark divergences from the Queen's English almost more than the words used' (Elworthy, 1875, p.4). According to this account the Queen's English is specified as a form that is not local in its deployment and thus can be recognised in contradistinction to purely local 'peculiar' forms. Moreover it is clearly held to have its own unique forms of pronunciation, intonation and lexicon that differentiate it from the local forms. This form is that in which all traces of locality are supposedly eradicated and it is the form which again offers a simple definitive answer to the problem of distinguishing dialects and dialectal speakers. It offers the solution to that problem in asserting that a dialect is a form of the spoken language that deviates from the Queen's English and a dialect speaker is a speaker who uses this variant form. Such speakers will betray by their vocabulary, as well as their 'pronunciation, intonation and those finer shades of local peculiarity', their social or geographical origins. However, although it proved popular in many of the text books produced in the nineteenth century to deal with questions of taste and decorum in language, fashion, literature and much else besides, the phrase the 'Queen's English' was to be superseded by another, more culturally and ideologically loaded phrase that centred around the ambiguous term 'standard'.

In an updated version of Walker's *Pronouncing Dictionaries* published in 1836, B. Smart offered 'principles of Remedy for Defects of Utterance'. He argued that before:

> anything is said respecting the several defects which rank under the foregoing denomination [Vulgar and Rustic, Provincial and Foreign Habits] it may be as well to consider what is that dialect from which they all deviate.   (Smart, 1836, p.xl)

Smart continues to specify the form according to which all

other forms can be evaluated and from which all other forms deviate:

> The dialect then, which we have here in view, is not that which belongs exclusively to one place, – not even to London; for the mere Cockney, even though tolerably educated, has his peculiarities as well as the mere Scotchman or Irishman; but the common standard dialect is that in which all marks of a particular place of birth and residence are lost and nothing appears to indicate any other habits of intercourse than with the well-bred and well-informed, wherever they may be found.   (*Ibid.*)

Clearly then the 'standard dialect' is that which conceals the birthplace and habitation of the speaker but more interesting than this is the social significance ascribed to it. This form bears within it the mark of a specific social class since it is the language of the 'well-bred' and 'well-informed'. What is remarkable here is not simply the early example of a form which is defined in terms of neutrality (geographically non-specific) although its constituency is socially specific, but the continuity with the eighteenth-century theorists' definitions of the 'usage' to which the 'good' speaker should aspire.[2] The form specified is not simply a definition of the 'common' language but a 'standard' to be reached. Moreover, even if the 'standard' is not reached it is important that the 'good' speaker should attempt to emulate it since:

> It may be that a person cannot altogether reach this standard; but if he reach it very nearly, all the object of a complete uniformity may be gained. A person needs not blush because he cannot help betraying that he is a Scotchman or an Irishman; but it may nevertheless be an object of ambition to prove that his circle of intercourse has extended much beyond his native place.   (*Ibid.*)

Thus the 'standard dialect' becomes a social marker to be acquired by a speaker in order to allow the speaker to speak without difficulty or embarrassment. 'Indulgence' can be allowed to foreigners for their lack of complete acquisition of the 'standard' spoken form, 'but a rustic or cockney dialect meets not the same quarter; or a man displaying either the one or the other, must have a large portion of natural talent or acquired science who can overcome the prejudice it creates' (*ibid.*). In these quotations then we can find a new sense of the term 'standard' emerging in reference to language. This sense was related to the sense of 'standard' as signifying a level of excellence to be reached and a quality to be emulated rather than to a sense of uniformity since in fact the new 'standard' was neither 'common' nor 'uniform' but socially restricted. It was a level that had to be reached in order to gain social acceptance since without it, who can overcome the prejudice it creates?

This sense of the 'standard language' as a form of speech from which others deviated was to be increasingly deployed in linguistic debates. Latham, for example, warned against taking examples of dialectal speech from Chaucer and Shakespeare as veracious since in such cases, he argued, 'an imitation of a dialect may be so lax as to let its only merit consist in a deviation from the standard idiom' (Latham, 1841, p.76). Latham's comment points up several problems since 'a deviation from the standard idiom' will clearly be marked as dialectal, though whether it reflects any actual dialect is a matter of empirical research. Added to this are the further methodological problems of whether the deviation itself was a standard dialectal form from which other deviations are in turn to be marked as 'idiolectal'. And then whether the idiolect has a standard form from which deviations are to be marked as 'stylistic' or 'contextual' and so on. These are precisely the sort of problems that were later to face Saussure and his followers in modern linguistics. However, Latham's theoretical point is of more concern at the moment since it is clear that what he calls the 'standard mode of speech', or the 'standard idiom', is to be taken as the primary or central spoken form according to which all other spoken forms can be evaluated. Here again we see the process by which this 'standard idiom' becomes equatable with the language itself, as it displaces other forms and appears as the culturally hegemonic spoken form. For at least one writer such an equation between the 'standard mode of speech' and 'the English language' *per se* was valid as Richard Garnett, writing on 'English Dialects', argued that:

> We consider it superfluous to discuss the causes of dialects in the abstract, or to attempt to establish a clear and positive distinction between the vaguely employed terms *dialect* and *language*. . . . Within the English pale the matter is sufficiently clear; all agree in calling our standard form of speech the English language, and all provincial variations from it – at least all that assume a distinct specific character – dialects.   (Garnett, 1859, p.42)

An analogy can be made here, using Garnett's own terms, between this process of elavating the 'standard form' to hegemonic status 'within the English pale' and the erection of the 'English pale' itself. The 'pale', used most commonly in the phrase 'beyond the pale', referred to that part of Ireland that had fallen under British rule and cultural influence. One early example of such usage is given in the sixteenth century by Andrew Boorde in 1547 when he asserted that Ireland was 'devyded in ii parte, one is the Englysh pale, and the other, the wyld Irysh'. The bases of the division were related to language and power since as Olden pointed out in 1892, 'the pale was not a definite territory, it merely meant the district in which the King's writ ran, and in which the Irish parliament exercised authority' (Olden, 1892, p.7). The 'pale' then was that area of Ireland in which the English language and English rule had been imposed and beyond that primarily linguistic boundary lay the 'wyld Irysh'. Within Britain, however, within the boundaries of English language and law – Garnett is claiming – there is another kind of boundary or measure of language since the 'standard form of speech' is that which enables one to mark off the English language from its 'wyld' dialects. Moreover, the 'standard forms of speech' can also help to mark out those who are beyond the social pale and thus to mark out, in Smart's words, those of 'vulgar and rustic, provincial and foreign habits'.

Later in the century the 'distinct specific character' of both standard English speech and dialectal speech was to be evaluated primarily according to pronunciation rather than to any lexical characteristics and this is a clear line of continuity with the eighteenth-century concerns. Henry Sweet (usually taken as Shaw's model for Henry Higgins in *Pygmalion*, though it is also claimed that it was Daniel Jones[3]) explained anomalies in his account of 'The History of *Th* in English' by claiming that 'these anomalies may, however, be mere provincialisms of late adoption into the standard pronunciation' (Sweet, 1868–9, p.140). This concept of a particular standard form of pronunciation was taken up most significantly in the voluminous work of the most prodigious of all the nineteenth-century phoneticians, A.J. Ellis. Ellis expounded the idea of 'the theoretically received pronunciation of literary English' (Ellis, 1869–89, pt. I, p.13) and this was an idea that was to gain enormous currency in discourses relating to language and society. Ellis proposed the theoretical existence of two phenomena: first, the nationally recognisable written form of English (the standard literary English), and second, a 'received pronunciation' of that form (standard spoken English). Ellis outlined further the concept that later became known as the abbreviated 'R.P.' when he asserted that 'in the present day we may, however, recognise a received pronunciation all over the country, not widely differing in any particular locality, and admitting a certain degree of variety' (*ibid.*, p.23). Within this term there are again important distinctions to be made since 'R.P.' is not 'received' all over the country if by this it is meant that all linguistic subjects hear it constantly. There would clearly be large geographic and social territories that would not hear such pronunciation. However, this is not the sense of 'received' that is at work here as it is rather that sense of the term that signifies 'generally adopted, accepted, approved as true or good, chiefly of opinions, customs, etc.', as in the phrases 'received opinion' or 'received wisdom'. Rather than the 'common' form of the spoken language, 'R.P.' is that particular form that is counted as 'generally adopted, accepted, approved as true or good'. It is not clear who has made such evaluations or even the basis for describing them as 'general', yet there is a clear argument here for a form of the spoken language that is counted (at least amongst certain quarters) as a superior form. In this sense, 'R.P.' is linked to the terms 'received English', 'received standard' and 'received standard English' that were to gain currency in the late-nineteenth century.

Ellis made it quite clear that 'R.P.' was not received everywhere in the same way since it was not 'standard' in the sense of bearing a uniform set of features:

> There will not be any approach to uniformity of speech sounds at any one time, but there will be a kind of mean, the general utterance of the more thoughtful or more respected persons of mature age, round which the other sounds seem to hover, and which, like the averages of the mathematician, not agreeing precisely with any, may for the purposes of science be assumed to represent all and be called the language of the district at the epoch assigned. (*Ibid.*, p.18)

Ellis makes clear in this extract the fact that 'R.P.' is a theoretical fiction in that it does not reflect actual usage but is a 'kind of mean', 'an average' representing 'the general utterance' of a specific group that is marked by certain qualifying characteristics. Thus it is not an attempt to impose uniformity but an attempt to select the representative features in order 'for the purposes of science' to represent all speakers and to count it as 'the language'. However, the crucial shift in the argument here is that which passes from 'the general utterance of the more thoughtful or more respected persons of mature age' through an economy which equates such utterance with the discourse of 'all' and can therefore allow such usage to be described as 'the language'. This shift moves from a particular form of the language to the language itself and, of course, the standard spoken form (the average utterance of the mature, respected, thoughtful persons) must by definition exclude certain usage since it does not 'agree precisely with any'. In short it approximates to a mean of mature, respected and thoughtful utterance, is grounded upon the exclusion of all other usage, and is then cited as 'the language'.

Henry Sweet also followed Ellis's definition of 'a standard of spoken English' as 'the theoretically received pronunciation of literary English'. Sweet asserted that:

After London English had become the official and literary language of the whole kingdom, it was natural that some dialect in its spoken form should become the general speech of the educated classes, and that as centralisation increased, it should preponderate more and more over the local dialects.   (Sweet, 1890, pp.v–vi)

The word 'natural' is interesting here as it masks two separate historical processes in which the elevation of one particular form to cultural hegemony amongst a certain class and then the consequent widening of such hegemony are marked as natural, self-regulating and perhaps inevitable processes. This means of course that the historical and social shifts and developments that lie behind such processes disappear from sight. However, even within their own terms this 'natural' process had not been completed for Sweet (and for Ellis) since a standard speech form, they noted, was not spoken and received everywhere:

The unity of spoken English is still imperfect: it is still liable to be influenced by local dialects – in London itself by the cockney dialect, in Edinburgh by the Lothian Scotch dialect and so on . . . it changes from generation to generation, and is not absolutely uniform even among speakers of the same generation, living in the same place and having the same social standing.   (*Ibid.*, pp.vi–viii)

Variation in fact appears to dominate the 'standard' since local, diachronic and idiolectal variation all militate against the achievement of the 'perfection' of 'spoken English'. However, empirical variation did not prevent Sweet (as it had not Ellis) from using the term 'standard English' as though there were a uniform, recognisable and standard spoken form of speech. Indeed Sweet is quoted as one of the authorities for its use in the *N/OED* entry under 'Standard' in the 1933 Supplement where the definition of 'Standard English' is:

applied to a variety of the speech of a country which, by reason of its cultural status and currency, is held to represent the best form of that speech. *Standard English*: that form of the English language which is spoken (with modifications, individual or local), by the generality of the cultured people in Great Britain.

The illustration is from Sweet's *The Sounds of English* (1908) which argued that: 'Standard English, like Standard French, is now a class dialect more than a local dialect: it is the language of the educated all over Great Britain' (Sweet, 1908, p.7). Unlike the standard literary language the standard spoken form could not be regarded as uniform linguistic practice. Variation dominated spoken usage ('modifications, individual or local'), and this meant that the standard spoken language could only be defined extra-linguistically. That is, it could be defined coherently only in terms of the social characteristics of its speakers.

The lower instruments of speech: the spoken dialects

If there was (at least theoretically) a spoken standard then there must also have been, as a logical corollary, non-standard forms of speech and within the discourse of the study of language in nineteenth-century Britain these non-standard spoken forms were described as the dialects. Although the comparative philologists had a specific use for this term, the dialects for most British linguists were (as in Garnett's account cited earlier), deviations from a standard mode of speech. Whitney classified the dialects as, 'deviations from a former standard of speech which have hithero acquired only a partial currency, within the limits of a class or district; or they are retentions of a former standard, which the generality of good speakers have now abandoned' (Whitney, 1875, p.156). Here the basis of the definition is that the dialect is a variant form, a partial form (socially or geographically), or a form that is not spoken by 'good speakers'. However, in a later text Whitney offers a definition based on the criterion of intelligibility when writing on the 'peculiarities' of different regions:

When these peculiarities amount to so much that they begin to interfere a little with our understanding the persons who have them, we say that such persons speak a DIALECT of ENGLISH, rather than English itself.   (Whitney, 1877, p.3)

Skeat on the other hand defined the spoken dialects in relation to the 'standard or literary language' when he argued that it is 'a local variety of speech differing from the standard or literary language'. If Skeat meant the 'or' in this phrase to suggest an alternative (either the standard spoken or the standard literary language) then he is drawing up two possible modes of dialectal variation: first, variation from the pronunciation and other verbal qualities of the standard spoken language; and second, variation from the literary language that could only take place in terms of lexical items or orthography. In fact it is the second possibility which is supported by a further definition in which Skeat describes a dialect as 'a provincial method of speech to which the man who has been educated to use the language of books is unaccustomed' (Skeat, 1912, p.1). Not all writers took the view that dialects were deviations from the literary language however, though all held that they were in some sense related to it. Wright, for example, claimed that:

> Among common errors still prevailing in the minds of educated people, one error which dies very hard is the theory that a dialect is an arbitrary distortion of the mother tongue, a wilful mispronunciation of the sounds, and disregard for the syntax of a standard language.   (Wright, 1913, p.xix)

This led her to argue for a strong interest to be taken in dialects on the grounds that the dialects exemplify the as yet unconscious but newly emerging 'laws of language' even more clearly than the standard language. And thus she argued that, 'dialect speaking people obey sound-laws and grammatical rules even more faithfully than we [educated people] do, because theirs is a more natural and unconscious obedience' (ibid., p.iii).

This interest in the dialects was shared by a number of literary figures, including George Eliot who commented that her 'rendering of dialect, both in words and spelling, was constantly checked by the artistic duty of being generally intelligible', particularly in *Adam Bede* and *Silas Marner*. However, she wrote to the secretary of the English Dialect Society asserting that although:

> It is a just demand that art should keep clear of such specialities as would make it a puzzle for the larger part of its public; still, one is not bound to respect the lazy obtuseness or snobbish ignorance of people who do not care to know more of their native tongue than the vocabulary of the drawing room and the newspaper.   (Eliot, 1877, p.viii)

Such interest in dialectal forms was to play a significant though never central role in British work on the spoken language. There were two principal reasons for such interest. The first was the idea (already cited by Wright) that the spoken dialects could be 'purer' than the standard literary language since they were unaffected by such factors as education, printing or elocution masters. For example, the early Anglo-Saxonist Bosworth argued that the 'provincial dialects' merited close study since, 'in these dialects, then, remnants of the Anglo-Saxon tongue may be found, in its least altered, most corrupt and therefore its purest state' (Bosworth, 1838, p.xxvi). A similar argument was used by the dialect poet Barnes who argued that 'the provincial dialects are not jargons but true and good forms of Teutonic speech' (Barnes, 1862, pp.xvii–xviii). Moreover, as a corollary to his interest in 'received pronunciation', A.J. Ellis also cultivated an interest in the 'Natural English Pronunciation':

> By 'natural', as distinguished from 'educated', English pronunciation, is meant a pronunciation which has been handed down historically, or has changed organically, without the interference of orthoepists, classical theorists, literary fancies, fashionable heresies and so forth, in short 'untamed' English everywhere, from the lowest vulgarity ... to the mere provinciality.   (Ellis, 1869–89, pt IV, pp.1243–4)

Thus the 'wyld Englysh' also had its own special interest

for the linguistic historians. After considering 'our artificial literary speech', by which we take him to be referring to the standard spoken form, Ellis proposed a study of 'uneducated or natural or organic local speech known as English dialectal pronunciation'. The reason for such research, he argued, was that:

> Dialectal speech is of the utmost importance to a proper conception of the historical development of English pronunciation, just as an examination of the existing remains of those zoological genera which descend from one geological period to another, serves to show the real development of life on our globe. (*Ibid.*, pp.1089–90)

For John Peile too such research was vital and when commenting on dialectal speakers he argued that 'these words which they use, and the sounds with which they pronounce them, are remnants of the form of English originally spoken in the province, and not merely spoken, but written in books which are of the greatest literary importance' (Peile, 1877, p.14). For a complete 'history of the language' the spoken dialects had to be taken into account as well as the standard literary language since as the same writer argued, 'for the advancement of knowledge among the literate, let the dialects be at least first studied'.

The second reason for the interest in dialects was the widespread belief that they were disappearing in the late nineteenth century and that they would soon be eradicated. Barnes thought it necessary to proffer an apology for composing his poetry in 'a fast-outwearing speech form' which, he feared, might seem 'as idle as writing one's name in snow on a spring day' (Barnes, 1869, p.iii). And A.J. Ellis composed an orthographic system for the recording of dialects – Glossic – that was to be used to set down those speech patterns that were held to be disappearing. In the notice to Pt.III of his mammoth work on *Early English Pronunciation*, Ellis advises his dialect-collectors on the recording of 'genuine' dialects:

> No pronunciation should be recorded which has not been heard from some speaker who uses it naturally and habit-

ually. The older peasantry and children who have not been at school preserve the dialectic sounds most purely. But the present facilities of communication are rapidly destroying all traces of our older dialectic English. Market women, who attend large towns, have generally a mixed style of speech. The daughters of peasants and small farmers, on becoming domestic servants, learn a new language, and corrupt the genuine Doric of their parents. (Ellis, 1869–89, pt III, p.vi)

Skeat outlined the same fears and argued in an introduction to one of the Dialect Society's publications that it seemed worth while 'before our dialects shall die out to make one final collection, of as comprehensive a character as possible, of all the material that can be useful for a complete Provincial English Dictionary' (Skeat, 1876, p.v). The reasons for the fears concerning the eradication of the dialects were frequently cited and Ellis, giving one of the most often attributed causes, blamed 'the present exterminating influence of school boards and railways'. In the same manner Elworthy reported that 'it is said that dialects are disappearing, that railways, telegraphs, machinery and steam will soon sweep clean out of the land the last trace of Briton, Saxon and Dane' (Elworthy, 1875–6, p.4). Later he noted (though with reservations) the 'process of levelling [of] quaint words and local idioms which board schools in every parish will surely accelerate'. For other linguists such as W.H. Cope the introduction of Universal Elementary Education after 1870 was a notable culprit of eradication since:

However great the advantages of the present advanced education of the middle and lower classes, the operation of National and Board Schools is fast effacing all distinctive language in the people of this country; and in another generation or two, it will probably disappear altogether. (Cope, 1883, p.v)

Eradication for Thomas Lounsbury was the result of 'the whole tremendous machinery of education' (Lounsbury, 1894, p.479), and for Peile it was attributable to 'literary English which is taught at school, and this by degrees drives out the provincial English which is spoken at home; and due perhaps most of all to the railroad which levels all local peculiarities' (Peile, 1877, p.15). Perhaps the best summation of these opinions is that of the folklorist Elizabeth Wright as she asserted that 'with the spread of education, and the ever-increasing means of rapid locomotion throughout the length and breadth of the land, the area where pure dialects are spoken is lessening year by year'. This, she argued, is not surprising:

> when one looks at the placards announcing in large letters the extraordinarily cheap day trips offered by the Great Western or the Midland Railway, or sees hoardings decorated with garish posters portraying the arid sands and cloudless skies of Blackpool or Morecambe.   (Wright, 1913, p.1)

The growth of paid holidays, as one of many factors, clearly boosted the domestic tourist industry and this had a marked effect on cultural patterns in Britain. As a later illustration of the point we could take Blackpool where, after the illuminations became a permanent feature in 1925, the tourist trade was to boom. Over 7 million overnight visitors (principally drawn from the working class) a year by the late 1930s and over half-a-million visitors in 50,000 motor vehicles and 700 trains on the Bank Holiday Monday of August 1937 (Stevenson, 1984, p.393). Clearly such developments were to leave their mark upon the national cultural patterns and nowhere more so, it was felt, than in the spoken language of the inhabitants of Britain. Universal education and increasing geographic mobility were perceived as the most direct and principal causes of dialect eradication at least until the arrival of a national broadcasting system. The commixture of dialect speakers would lead (as the linguistic historians likewise argued when describing the process by which the standard literary dialect was founded) to the foundation of a common spoken language, a form of the language that would serve as a lingua franca in order that all the mutually unintelligible dialect speakers (gathered in resorts like Blackpool) would be able to understand each other.

Although Ellis defended the study of the dialects when he argued that, 'we know nothing of the actual relations of the thoughts of a people, constituting their real logic and grammar, until we know how the illiterate express themselves', he also argued that the eradication of the dialects was a positive force:

> Of course it would be absurd for those possessing the higher instrument to descend to this lower one, and for the advance of our people, dialects must be extinguished – as Carthage for the advance of Rome.   (Ellis, 1869–89, pt. IV, p.1248)

In the same work he argued for the imposition of a phonetic system of spelling and a 'standard pronunciation' on the grounds that:

> Recognising the extreme importance of facilitating inter-course between man and man, we should feel no doubt, and allow no sentimental regrets to interfere with the establishment of something approaching to a general system of pronouncing, by means of a general system of indicating our pronunciation in writing, as far as our own widespread language extends.   (*Ibid.*, pt II, p.630)

The dialects, the 'lower' forms of language, were to be replaced by the 'higher' form of standard spoken English and the reason for such eradication was that the dialects, or at least non-standard forms, were viewed as socially divisive. If language, in Locke's words, was to be 'the great instrument and common Tye of Society', then it was clear that many late-nineteenth-century linguists saw the dialects as instruments for undoing the social bonds that should exist. Language for one such linguist was a Lockean instrument for the 'transferring the idea conceived in the mind to other agencies, to communicate with his fellow-men'. However, the same writer went on to argue that given the divided state of society and the 'higher' and 'lower' forms of language, the fact that 'the language of the uneducated should be unintelligble to the educated is again a thing to be expected' (Lyson, 1868, p.45). And this was used as an argument in favour of a standard spoken form of the language. Such comments were later to take on particular force, as will be shown in the concluding chapters of this text, and the perceived division was so enormous that Galsworthy, in his function as President of the English Society, was later to comment that 'there is perhaps no greater divide of society than the differences in viva-voce expression' (Galsworthy, 1924, p.8).

The standard spoken language: whose language?

Given the various problems associated with dialectal usage it is clear that there was a general perception among linguists of a need for a standard spoken language that could unite rather than divide. However, even if such a vigorous project of language-planning had been undertaken, what was meant by the standard spoken language by linguists in this period could not (at least not by their own definition) have served such a purpose. As outlined earlier, the standard spoken language was not defined primarily by a set of uniform linguistic characteristics but by the social characteristics of its speakers. It will be the aim here to demonstrate the specific nature of such characteristics.

The concept of a standard pronunciation had been influential in the late eighteenth century and a continuing interest in this concept was noted by Ellis:

> For at least a century, since Buchanan published his 'Essay towards establishing a *standard* for an *elegant* and uniform pronunciation of the English language *throughout the British dominions* as practised by the *most learned* and *polite* speakers' in 1766, and probably for many years previously, there prevailed, and apparently there still prevails, a belief that it is possible to erect a standard of pronunciation which should be acknowledged and followed throughout the countries where English is spoken as a native tongue, and that in fact that standard already exists, and is the norm unconsciously followed by persons who, by rank or education, have most right to establish the custom of speech.   (Ellis, 1869–89, pt. II, p.624)

Ellis was sceptical of such a project though interested in its aims. His scepticism stemmed from the 'unreliable' orthography which in no way reflected the sounds of speech and his interest lay in the possibility of setting up a phonetic alphabet that could allow the possibility of creating a standard. Thus he wrote that:

> At present there is *no* standard of pronunciation. There are many ways of pronouncing English *correctly*, that is, according to the usage of large numbers of persons of either sex in different parts of the country, who have received a superior education. All attempts to found a standard of pronunciation on our approximate standard of orthography are futile. The only chance of attaining to a standard of pronunciation is by the introduction of phonetic spelling. (*Ibid.*, p.630)

He argued then that no standard was at present possible for technical reasons but that 'correct' pronunciation was. It was the pronunciation of those in receipt of a 'superior education' that was being deemed 'correct' and in this Ellis reflected the overwhelming attitude of most nineteenth-century (and eighteenth-century) linguists. Smart, for example, took as his model of propriety for his pronouncing dictionary 'the usage of the well-educated in the British metropolis' (Smart, 1836, p.xi), and Guest had specified 'the prevailing dialect' as the language of 'the Englishman of education' (Guest, 1838, p.75). Moreover, Ellis himself described 'R.P.' as 'the educated pronunciation of the metropolis, of the court, of the pulpit, and the bar' (Ellis, 1869–89, p.23).

Towards the end of the century such distinctions were to be elevated into a theoretical principle in the study of language. In writing of the formation of a 'common language' Herman Paul argued that:

> As a rule we find the language of some district or town looked on as the model. But considering that in every case in which a real-common language has developed, in however narrow an area, appreciable differences exist between the different classes of the population, the capacity to serve as a model must be restricted to the educated classes of the district in question.   (Paul, 1880, p.477)

This is an interesting argument in that it asserts that the language of the educated 'must' be the only language that can be taken as a model (perhaps because of its *intrinsic* superiority to the language of other classes). The fact that historical factors (i.e. that the language taken as the model has a rule been the language of the educated) indicate a certain pattern is taken as proof that the pattern is inevitable (i.e. that only the language of the educated classes can be the model for the common language). For Sweet educated usage was the only form to be noted in his *New English Grammar* (1891) and thus he ascertains the term 'English' as used in the title in the following way: 'by which we understand the English of the present time as spoken, written and understood by educated people' (Sweet, 1891, pt. I, p.212). This equation also held good for J.H. Staples, an Ulster dialectician who asserted: 'when I use English as referring to pronunciation in these pages, I mean that of the average Southern Englishman, when speaking carefully in lecture-room, pulpit, stage, or platform' (Staples, 1898, p.358). Educated usage was to become a kind of 'standard' in itself and one that did not have to be taught grammatically since educated usage was not a matter of grammatical training but of unconscious imbibing. As one linguist of the period claimed:

> Take the case of an English child, brought up in an educated household. At an early age such a child would speak good English though he had never learnt grammar. . . . On the other hand, a child brought up in an ignorant household would speak bad English, would make mistakes in pronunciation or use wrong forms of expression. Without any grammatical training in either case, these children would speak correctly or incorrectly, would pick up good English or bad English.   (West, 1893, p.30)

The means by which such processes occur were not at all conscious since 'good' or 'bad' English arose, 'through the influence of the people with whom they come into contact. . . . We learn to speak and write correctly by mixing with educated persons and reading well-written books' (*ibid.*). The significance of this assertion lies in the commingling of various discourses and the oppositions set up within them: the process of learning (educated versus ignorant) is equated with the relations that hold in discourse (correct speech and writing versus mistakes in pronunciation and forms of expression), which in turn is supported by the discourse of morality ('good' and 'correct' versus 'bad' and 'incorrect').

It is clear from such arguments that distinctive linguistic forms were being 'ascertained' and 'fixed' along with their moral and social significance and this is a process that will be explored further in later chapters. For the period under consideration, however, Whitney's comments may serve as a convenient summation:

> Then there is also that difference between what we call 'good English' and 'bad English'. By 'good English' we mean those words and those meanings of them and those ways of putting them together, which are used by the best speakers, the people of best education; everything which such people do not use, or use in another way, is bad English. Thus bad English is simply that which is not approved and accepted by good and careful speakers. (Whitney, 1877, p.3)

Although there is a clear specification of a lexicon, a set of significations for the units of the lexicon, and a syntax for conjoining the units, it is nonetheless true that the crux of the definition of good English does not lie in any linguistic features. It lies rather with the delimitation of the class of its speakers: 'the best speakers, the people of best education'. All other English is, by means of a simple binary definition, bad English since it is not the English of the good and careful. In cases of doubt or difficulty the speaker had to be particularly cautious since:

> In order to learn to speak English with accuracy and precision, we have but one rule to follow – to pay strict attention to usage. The authority of usage, the usage of civilised persons, is in all disputed points paramount. (Sedgwick, 1868, p.97)

As in the eighteenth century, 'usage' was not to mean 'common usage' or uniform usage, or the usage of the majority; the 'usage' to be followed was that of 'civilised persons'.

It is clear from this that the 'standard' spoken language did not refer to a common or uniform usage but to a particular spoken form belonging to a specific group which was to be taken as a standard to be emulated and as an authoritative exemplar to be consulted in times of doubt. The educated and the civilised are the 'best speakers' and their language is a crucial signifier of their social status. Thus:

> All are not gentlemen by birth; but all may be gentlemen in openness, in modesty of language, in attracting no man's attention by singularities . . . for it is this, in matter of speech and style which is the sure mark of good taste and good breeding.   (Alford, 1864, p.281)

Questions of 'gentlemanliness', 'style', 'taste', 'good breeding' were at stake in the debate concerning 'standard' spoken English and, more importantly, these questions were entangled in the web of social signification that clustered around the question of class. The 'educated' and the 'civilised' came, of course, from the ruling class:

> It is not easy to fix a standard of pronunciation. At one time the stage, then the bar, and later still the pulpit, have been considered as authorities in this matter. But all these are now rejected, and the conversation of the highest classes in London society is now looked upon as the standard of English pronunciation.   (Graham, 1869, p.156)

There is a revealing glide in this quotation in that the text moves from an initial difficulty to a firm conclusion since in using the present tense to say that 'it *is* not easy to fix a standard of pronunciation' the text suggests that the problem remains. However, it is clear that difficulties in fact lie in the past rather than the present since in the past various attempts were made to 'fix a standard' (stage, bar, pulpit), but 'all these are now rejected'. And these had been rejected since a different answer to the problem had been reached and the difficulty had now been superseded: now 'the conversation of the highest classes in London society' is taken as the standard.

By the late nineteenth century such a view had become a commonplace since according to one writer, 'in saying that the standard of pronunciation is and must be mere usage, the usage of those who are of the highest social culture and position, I am merely uttering a truism' (White, 1880, p.88). It therefore followed that the role of English grammar, in the opinion of many writers on language of the period, was to implement the teaching of the 'standard'. In grammar, for example, Earle commented that:

> The student learns the standard usage of the language, he is shamed out of any little inelegant phrases he may have picked up at home, he is guaranteed against solecisms, he is taught not to say 'I is a good boy' or 'It is me' or 'Give it to I', or 'Handsome is as Handsome does', and he is instructed how contrary to reason is a Double Negative. (Earle, 1890, p.45)

Such instruction, however, was held to be largely ineffective since education made no more than a superficial impression upon the speakers of the non- (or sub-) standard language. Uneducated debasers of the language there were and uneducated debasers of the language there always would be:

> Whatever may be the recognised standard of pronunciation, there will always be a refined and vulgar mode of speech – one adopted by the cultivated and well-informed, and the other used by the rude and illiterate. (Graham, 1869, p.159)

Clearly the threat of dialect eradication thought to be posed by universal education was not perceived in all quarters since for some it was the moral character of the rude and illiterate that prevented 'standardisation'. Moreover, this reflected a common perception within conservative educational thinking that certain groups should not and indeed could not be educated 'beyond their station'. And this way of thinking is likewise mirrored in a pamphlet on the elementary schools published by the National Union of Teachers which asserted that, 'six million children are in the Public Elementary Schools of England and Wales. They are the children of the workers, to be themselves England's workers a few years hence' (Lawson and Silver, 1973, p.318). In itself this was a realistic appraisal since working-class children did and do on the whole take working-class jobs, and this pointed up the fact that education could not overcome the divided nature of class society, although a little later it was to be given precisely such a task in Britain. In linguistic terms this meant that the public elementary schools would produce vulgar-speaking illiterates (as they were perceived), and the private fee-paying schools would produce educated speakers of 'good' English (as it was perceived). The first were the 'sub-standard' speakers of the language, the second its 'standard' speakers.

Sub-standard English: the fatal letters

If standard English was defined as the language of the educated class of British society then it was also the case that a non- or sub-standard variety was ascribed to the uneducated and the poor. In defending his dialect poetry Barnes argued that 'the poor must speak their mother tongue till they can speak another, and they do not find it so easy as some may deem it, even with the little help of the village school, to learn to speak well and without misuse of words, our Latinized English' (Barnes, 1844, p.iv). When he 'translated' the Queen's speech to the Parliament of 1863 into the dialect of Dorset, Barnes argued that material 'usually given in the language of hard words, as the poor call them' could be 'translated' into a more comprehensible form; that is, into 'their own homely speech, and therefore could be given them in plain English' (Barnes, 1863, p.10). This sense of a clearly distinct form of the language spoken by the uneducated also appeared in Ellis's work when he wrote of 'the illiterate peasant, speaking a language entirely imitative, unfixed by any theoretic orthography, untramelled by any pedant's fancies' (Ellis, 1869–89, pt IV, p.317). Ellis was caught in a double bind here since if sub-standard speakers were exposed to education they lost their linguistic purity, and yet if they were not the sub-standard forms could not be recorded by the people who actually used them. It was, he argued, 'as yet extremely difficult to ascertain the sounds used in our dialects, because those who possess the practical knowledge find themselves unable to communicate it on paper with the accuracy required for the present purpose. In fact most of them have to learn the meaning and use of alphabetic writing' (*ibid.*, p.1246). 'Sub-standard' usage was tantalisingly not able to be recorded perfectly since as many dialectologists noted, only its speakers were able to distinguish and identify particular words or sounds and yet the 'sub-standard' speakers only used 'sub-standard' language and therefore could not be trusted to convey the meaning into 'educated usage'. An even bolder formulation of the distinction between educated and uneducated usage was proposed by Whitney. He argued that:

> The highly cultivated have a diction which is not in all parts at the command of the vulgar; they have hosts of names for objects and ideas of educated knowledge . . . and yet more especially, the uncultivated have current in their dialect a host of inaccuracies, offences against the correctness of speech, as ungrammatical forms, mis-pronunciations, burdens of application, slang words, vulgarities.
> (Whitney, 1875, p.155)

Again, as with Ellis, there is a clear notion in this argument of two levels of discourse that are simply parallel since the one is defined over and against the other in a structured arrangement but the two can never meet. The one is precisely defined as what the other is not and the differences between them are both their structuring principle and that which carries their discursive and social power. The discourse of 'educated' language and knowledge is different from *and* barred to the vulgar: 'good' is opposed to 'bad' and linguistic propriety opposed to the inaccurate, incorrect, ungrammatical, mis-pronounced, mistaken form of speech.

The language of the poor and uneducated was viewed as deviant and defective and thus Smart was able to count remedies for 'defects of utterance' such as 'psellimus haesitans' (stammering) along with remedies for such 'defects of utterance' as Cockney accents, 'rustic utterance', 'Hibernian brogue', and 'vulgar' and 'provincial' habits. He also commented upon such grave defects as 'those vulgarisms as the substitution of v and w and w for v', and Cockney pronunciations such as 'Toosday' and 'dooty' (Smart, 1836, pp.xl–xliii). This latter defect was also noted later in the century by Alford when he commented that 'there is a very offensive vulgarism, most common in the Midland counties, but found more or less everywhere: giving what should be the sound of the u in certain words as if it were oo: calling "*duty*", "dooty", "Tuesday", "Toosday"' (Alford, 1864, p.5). There were, however, even more appalling defects for Alford and worst of all was the dropping or adding of the aspirate 'h':

> First and foremost let me notice that worst of all faults, the leaving out of the aspirate where it ought to be, and putting it in where it ought not to be. This is a vulgarism not confined to this or that province of England, nor especially prevalent in one county or another, but common throughout England to persons of low breeding and inferior education, particularly to those among the inhabitants of towns.

As far as this defect goes, he argued, 'nothing so surely stamps a man as below the mark in intelligence, self-respect and energy, as this unfortunate habit' (*ibid.*, p.40). It was a feature that was stigmatised widely and Kington-Oliphant also railed against it. He wrote of 'the revolting habit, spread over too many English shires, of dropping or wrongly inserting the letter h'. The basis for such strong feeling is clearly social rather than geographic as new '(incorrect') modes of pronunciation signal the threat that the appearance of new shifts in the social order creates. Thus for Kington-Oliphant the self-made men of the mid-Victorian period (particularly the millocracy) were a major social and linguistic threat. He argued therefore that 'many a needy scholar might turn an honest penny by offering himself as an instructor of the vulgar rich in pronunciation of the fatal letter. Our public schools are often railed against as teaching but little; still it is something that they enforce the right use of the h '(Kington-Oliphant, 1873, pp.332–4). '*H*' then, the 'fatal letter', was a highly important social signifier and thus according to the same writer, 'few things will the English youth find in after-life more profitable than the right use of the aforementioned letter' (*ibid.*, p.333). The social importance of linguistic 'defects' or 'sub-standard' usage was enormous in Britain since they clearly marked out a person's social class. Moreover, given that this was the case, social rather than formal linguistic education was the most important factor in the eradication of 'defects'. As one writer made this point:

> Nor is grammar of much use in correcting vulgarisms, provincialisms and other linguistic defects, for these are more dependent on social influence at home and at school than on grammatical training.   (Sweet, 1891–8, p.5)

Which is to say that language was recognised to be a social phenomenon and one that could be taught most effectively by 'social influence' rather than formal pedagogy. However, for those children for whom the correct type of social influence at home and school did not exist, formal pedagogy did have a role since speech training in schools could help to eradicate those differences that were perceived as bearing such enormous social weight. In such cases, Sweet argued:

> When a firm control of pronunciation has thus been acquired, provincialisms and vulgarisms will at last be entirely eliminated and some of the most important barriers between the different classes of society will thus be abolished.   (Sweet, 1877, p.196)

The project to be undertaken was to eradicate distinctive non-standard forms and to raise the speech of all children to the 'standard' level, since as a later commentator put it, 'the elementary schoolchild began his education with his language in a state of disease, and it was the business of the teacher to purify and disinfect that language' (Sampson. 1924, p.28). The children of the poor then were the subjects around which a set of new organising principles and practices were to be set in motion as their writing and speech were to be standardised and 'purified' until freed of their defects.

In this period language became a crucial focal point of anxiety bound up with concern for social identity and the stability of such identity. Sweet identified linguistic anxiety that was related to stratification according to region, gender and class. He noted that:

The Cockney dialect seems very ugly to an educated Englishman or woman because he – and still more she – lives in a perpetual terror of being taken for a Cockney, and a perpetual struggle to preserve that *h* which has now been lost in most of the local dialects of England, both North and South.   (Sweet, 1890, pp.vi–vii)

However, this is not to argue that such linguistic discrimination was practised only by one class on the usage of all other classes. The practices and effects of such discrimination varied according to the other discourses and institutions with which such discrimination was involved. It is clear for example that the equation of 'good speech' and 'educated speech' would have a certain type of practice and effect in educational debates and the institutes within which such debates took place. Yet discrimination was not a unidirectional practice and Sweet for one noted that 'northern speakers often reproach Londoners with mincing affectation'. However, such a 're-proach' could easily be rebutted by the socio-linguist (an anachronism here) and discrimination could only be exercised if backed up with knowledge of the history of the language:

A century ago, when this reproach was first levelled against the Cockneys, there was really some foundation for it, for at that time the broad *a* in *father, ask,* was represented by the thinner vowel in *man* lengthened, the Northern *ask* and *man* being at that time pronounced with the short sound of the *a* in *father.*   (Sweet, 1890, p.vii)

Such 'internal' historical description could, moreover, be backed up by 'external' historical accounting of the type that was later to be described as 'socio-linguistics'. Sweet argued that the 'internal' pronunciation shift was brought about by external features such as the growth in importance of the mercantile class in Liverpool as a result of the expansion of the port's trade. The growth in the importance of this class led to specific linguistic alterations and thus, Sweet asserted, 'when the sugar-merchants of Liverpool began to "speak fine", they eagerly adopted the thin Cockney *a* in *ask,* which many of their descendants keep, I believe, to the present day long after this 'mincing' pronunciation has been discarded in the London dialect' (*ibid.*). The northern merchants' linguistic discrimination was evidently based on an inadequate understanding of the internal and external history of the language which could only be rectified by a proper study of the language.

In fact the social and historical development of Britain influenced the study of language in all sorts of ways at this period. Britain had become a largely urban nation in the latter half of the nineteenth century and by 1901 around 78 per cent of the population lived in towns (between 1871 and 1901 alone the number of towns with populations of more than 50,000 doubled). The pace of development differed of course from town to town and while some major industrial centres continued to expand prodigiously the lesser but still established pattern of 'urban spread' continued. One lexical effect of this expansion was the appearance of the term 'suburbia' in the 1890s but there were other linguistic effects since with the enormous expansion of the towns in the nineteenth century there appeared new forms of speech that arose out of the extensive and novel mixture of different groups. Yet the surprising thing is that most dialectologists did not see these new modes of speech as worthy of study and against the predominant direction of nineteenth-century geographic and demographic trends the dialectologists travelled from town to country rather than the reverse. The modern resurgence of dialect studies, with its concentration on large urban connurbations (Liverpool, Glasgow, Newcastle, Belfast, Leeds, London and Norwich in particular), would no doubt have stuck the nineteenth-century dialectologists as odd since when the modes of speech of the cities were noted it was usually in terms of reprobation. For example, Elworthy defended rural dialectal speech in contrast to urban dialects by arguing that 'the people are simple, and although there is a superabundance of rough, coarse, language, yet foul-mouthed obscenity is a growth of the cities, and I declare I have never heard it, and so it cannot be recorded by me' (Elworthy, 1875–6, p.xii). Although admitting that he had never heard such speech, Elworthy was nonetheless able to assert confidently what was a commonly held view. However, it was in fact not the emergence of large urban connurbations that accounted for this view, but the majority of the inhabitants of such towns, which is to say the first urban industrial proletariat. The threat posed by the working class was clearly perceived by various cultural commentators in the period covered by this text whether it be Kay-Shuttleworth on the Chartists, Matthew Arnold on the Hyde Park rioters or George Sampson on the General Strike. The responses to the threat were various but amongst linguists there was a clear shift *towards* (rather than away as most accounts have it) prescription and proscription. That is, a clear discrimination between various forms of language *and* the banishment of certain forms. In this development the unity of the language, and therefore its speaking and writing subjects in the nation, that had been posited earlier in the century was to be banished since the language (and thus its speakers) was to be divided into groups and sets and ranked into an hierarchical order. Certain forms were to be prescribed (the educated, cultured, good), others proscribed (the vulgar, rude, coarse), and the language was again to be divided in terms of social class.

The portrayal of working-class discourse as 'defective' or 'sub-standard' that was demonstrated earlier in this chapter is a part of this process and towards the end of the century the process hardens. A striking example is offered in George Gissing's *Demos, a Story of English Socialism* (1886). After the factory-owner Hubert Elden has sacked the workers of the New Wanley works he remarks to the vicar, Wyvern:

> We are all men, it is true; but for brotherhood – feel it who can! I am illiberal if you like, but in the presence of those fellows I feel that I am facing enemies. It seems to me that I have nothing in common with them but the animal functions.

Scarcely able to control such feelings Eldon continues:

> Absurd? Yes, of course, it is absurd; but I speak of how intercourse with them affects me. They are our enemies, yours as well as mine; they are the enemies of every man who speaks the pure English tongue and who does not earn a living with his hands. When they face me I understand what revolution means; some of them look at me as if they had muskets in their hands.   (Gissing, 1886, p.376)

No sign of unity here save that of common animality as the discourse of humanism is supplanted by that of war. There are a number of revealing shifts here as Eldon describes the sacked workers: they are enemies of the church (since Wyvern is the vicar), of the factory-owners, of everyone who does not earn a living with his hands, and of 'every man who speaks the pure English tongue'. The proletariat, the 'hands', pose a threat to every significant institution that Eldon can think of: church, capital and the English language. However, it is not the threat directly posed by the workers that most disturbs Eldon since the workers are not armed revolutionaries facing him and when he informs the workers of the sackings and evictions the text specifies that their response is almost muted: 'there was a murmur of discontent through the room, but no one took it upon himself to rise and become spokesman of the community' (*ibid.*, p.375). It is specifically not the threat that the workers pose but 'intercourse' with the workers that disturbs Eldon most. What disturbs the factory-owner is talking to them and having to listen to their 'defective' speech and murmurs which, in the words of a later commentator describing much the same phenomenon, 'never reach the level of ordered articulate utterance; never attain a language that the world beyond can hear' (Masterman, 1902, p.20).

In fact such examples give the lie to the belief that the introduction of universal elementary education would curb linguistic 'defects' through the imposition of a standard spoken language. And in fact the coercive nature of such linguistic training did not produce a uniformity of usage amongst all classes but a set of practices amongst 'sub-standard' speakers that was designed to counter stigmatisation and proscription. Cope noted that:

> Already I have found the children of parents who speak

among themselves the dialect of the country, ignorant of the meaning of words commonly used by their fathers. And even among the older people there is a growing disinclination, when speaking to educated persons, to use, what I may call, their vernacular dialect. So that when asked to repeat a word, they frequently – from a sort of false shame – substitute its English equivalent. (Cope, 1883, p.1)

These people who clearly do not speak 'English' adopt practices designed for self-protection and they 'correct' their speech when in the presence of the educated person or the linguist since the request to repeat a word is clearly taken as a signal of stigmatisation. And this might be an early recorded instance of what was later to become known in socio-linguistic methodology as the 'observer's paradox', in which the presence of the observer prevents an undistorted investigation of spoken language. However, an alternative to Cope's 'false-shame' thesis is the possibility that children simply learnt how to keep their schoolmistresses and masters happy as they gained the ability to switch 'codes'. Rather than acquiring the uniform standard speech that was to unite the social classes, they worked around the demands of their instructors by deploying specific usage in its 'correct' context and in that deployment their perceptions of class differences were clearly not eradicated but sharpened. As one dialectologist argued:

The school teaching sets the model for written language and home influence for everyday talk. The result is that at the present moment our people are learning two distinct tongues – distinct in pronunciation, in grammar and in syntax. (Elworthy, 1875–6, p.xliv)

Children learnt two codes: first, the 'written language' and its spoken standard version (the 'pronunciation' referred to in the quote argues for this); and second, the language of 'everyday talk'. The acquisition and practice of the 'standard language', however, evidently stopped at the school gates since as the same writer noted:

A child who in class or even at home can read correctly,

giving accent, aspirates (painfully), intonation and all the rest of it, according to rule, will at home, and amongst his fellows, go back to his vernacular and never even deviate into the right path he has been taught at school.   (*Ibid.*)

Thus the children became more adept linguistically and were able to switch codes in specific contexts, Tess of the D'Urbervilles being a case in point:

Mrs. D'Urbeyfield habitually spoke the dialect; her daughter, who had passed the sixth Standard in the National school under a London-trained mistress, spoke two languages; the dialect at home, more or less; ordinary English abroad and to persons of quality.   (Hardy, 1891, p.48)

In this text language is an important factor since, in one sense, the tragedy of Tess stems from her father's initial linguistic mistake when he notices the similarity between D'Urbeyfield and D'Urberville. In misreading a linguistic sound-law a process is initiated whereby moral, social and political laws or codes are also misread and broken. Moreover, Tess's ability to move between the form of language used in her home and that used by such as Alec D'Urberville also points to Hardy's own perception of the social and linguistic disruption produced by the new cultural processes. The rural situation was in some areas, such as the South-West, still relatively isolated and to some extent unaffected by many of the demands for mobility generated by industrial revolution; mobility, for example, was still largely restricted in districts such as Cardigan where, in 1901, nine out of every ten people in the rural area had been born in the county or just beyond its border. However, education, the branch expansion of the railway system, the delivery van and the national newspapers (to note but a few), were all developments that began to impose a novel and more national pattern of culture. It is these processes that Hardy works upon as the rural situation is infringed by new values and specifically values from the metropolis (Tess's teacher was 'London-trained'). In a sense this clash of values was the problem that was to face another of Hardy's characters, Jude the Obscure, and the author himself. Tess's dialectal forms were to become as deracinated as Hardy and the exigencies of the audiences both had to address forced them to premature conclusions. Hardy gave up novel-writing after the publication of *Jude the Obscure* and the consequent scandal; Tess's textual life was punctuated by an even more abrupt full stop.

More generally, however, the response to the imposition of particular patterns was not so defeatist (or defeated) and instead of Cope's concept of 'false shame' that accounts for code-shifting amongst 'sub-standard' speakers, it can be read alternatively as a process whereby such speakers refused the educated access to their discourse. Rather than viewing power as simply a coercive force in this context it is possible to see both power and resistance at work. Rather than 'shame', 'sub-standard' speakers could use their own forms as markers of difference and solidarity. As one commentator perceived, 'the working-classes speak quite differently among themselves, than when speaking to strangers or to educated people, and it is no easy matter for an outsider to induce them to speak pure dialect' (Wright, 1905, p.vii). Linguistic differences in this context are a part of that process whereby a class perceives itself as such since part of the construction of class solidarity lies in the process of the subjects of a class identifying themselves with each other and against others, part of which is this perception of 'insiders' and 'outsiders'. Furthermore, the argument that 'sub-standard' speakers reacted to the stigmatisation of their usage by passively accepting it and thus 'standardising' or 'correcting' their speech is not supported by much evidence. There is, on the contrary, evidence for a reverse process since those who did 'correct' or 'standardise' in any but the most necessary contexts were the recipients of the mockery and stigmatisation of their peers. Barnes, for example, noted that the dialect, 'will not, however, be everywhere immediately given up as the language of the land-folk's fire-side, though to outsiders they may speak pretty good English, since *fine-talking* (as it is called) on the lips of a home-born villager, is generally laughed at by his neighbours as a piece of affectation' (Barnes, 1869, p.v). He gives an example of this in his *Dorset Dialect Grammar*:

This will be understood by a case of which I was told in a

> parish in Dorset, where the lady of the house had taken a
> little boy into day-service, though he went home to sleep
> . . . the lady had begun to correct his bad English, as she
> thought his Dorset was; and, at last, he said to her, weeping,
> 'There now. If you do meäke me talk so fine as that, they'll
> laef at me at hwome zoo, that I can't bide there.   (Barnes,
> 1885, pp.34–5)

Clearly 'sub-standard' speakers did not share the zest for the
standard spoken language that gripped many linguists and
educated 'ladies' and 'gentlemen'. In Barnes's example it is
the standard spoken form and not the dialectal that is
stigmatised as it is the language of the educated that carries
with it the social handicap and not, at least in this context,
that of the uneducated.

Conclusion

It has been argued in the last two chapters that throughout
the nineteenth century specific forms of linguistic usage were
valorised and that this is a theme in continuity with the
linguistic practice of the eighteenth century. There appeared,
it was argued, from within the 'history of the language' and
the texts it enabled a concept of a standard literary language
and a standard spoken language. The standard literary language was traced as an historical phenomenon by the linguistic
historians as it emerged into its role as the national, uniform,
written language. The standard spoken language, however,
was not the same type of phenomenon. Although some linguists
did see it as a possible uniform mode of speech, others (the
majority) saw it as a form with a particular value deriving
from the social status of those who used it: the literate and
educated. This in turn created new ways of evaluating various
forms of spoken discourse as it gave certain values to specific
usage and devalued other usage. Within the ambiguous phrase
'standard English' the two concepts are often indistinguish-
able: sometimes it refers to the common language of writing
and sometimes to the valued spoken form. And its significance
in some senses stems precisely from this ambiguity since in

particular debates it could lend proscription (the banishment of certain forms of discourse) the more acceptable face of prescription (guidance in use) and thus be the more effective. The next chapter will contain a detailed examination of this term, and the hardening of the processes of pre- and pro- scription, in the work of two major early-twentieth-century British linguists. My aim will be to demonstrate how the politics of discourse can range across a number of apparently distinct fields, including the work of major 'linguistic scien- tists'.

5

Theorising the Standard: Jones and Wyld

Here, as elsewhere, the theories of the philologists have played a larger part in modern history than the historians have yet realised.

(*The Newbolt Report*, 1921, p.286)

Introduction

It has been argued over the last two chapters that the term 'standard English' was used to cover the literary language and a particular form of the spoken language that was defined in terms of its speakers. It was also argued that the ambiguity of such usage led to powerful possibilities in the use of this term in cultural, political and linguistic debates. In the present chapter it is proposed to consider the realisation of such possibilities in the work of two linguists in the early twentieth century by examining how they used the term in their theoretical and practical research and thus how the term itself was developed. This will be followed by a consideration of uses of the term in specific cultural and political debates in order to see what sort of role it played. Again this will involve a delineation of continuities and ruptures in the use of the term: continuities with the line of argument that has been developed and ruptures in the sense of new uses and possibilities. The two linguists whose work is to be considered are Daniel Jones and Henry Wyld, two of the most independent of the early-twentieth-century British linguists.

Theorising the spoken standard: Daniel Jones

A.J. Ellis had argued in his *Early English Pronunciation* that, 'at present there is no standard of pronunciation', and yet thirty years after the completion of that text the Wrights could distinguish between the past and present in this respect since:

> In the earlier New English period there was no such thing as a standard pronunciation in the precise sense that we now apply that term to the pronunciation of educated and careful speakers of the present day.   (Wright, 1924, p.3)

A clear shift had taken place and it is perhaps most easily traced in the texts of Daniel Jones, the Reader in Phonetics at London University. Despite his declared intentions, it will be argued that Jones undertook much of the work that was to facilitate the early-twentieth-century consolidation of the sense of the term 'standard English' as a standard to be met by all speakers.

There is no doubt that Jones's work was prescriptive in its intent, as is evinced in the preface to his *Phonetic Readings in English* (1912) which declared that the text, 'is designed primarily for foreigners desirous of acquiring the correct pronunciation of the English language. To be used with *Gramophone Records*' (Jones, 1912, p.iii). The text was intended as a pedagogical tool whereby non-native speakers of English could learn the 'correct pronunciation' that they were to imitate with the aid of 'gramophone records'. However, such pedagogical prescriptivism was not restricted to non-native speakers of the language since it was also to cover both the teachers of native speakers and certain classes of such speakers. In the preface to his text *The Pronunciation of English* (1909), Jones asserted that it was intended for:

> English students and teachers, and more especially for students in training-colleges and teachers whose aim is to correct cockneyisms or other undesirable pronunciations in their scholars. At the same time it is hoped that the book may be found of use to lecturers, barristers, clergy, etc., in short all who desire to read or speak in public. The dialectal

peculiarities, indistinctiveness and artificialities which are unfortunately so common in the pronunciation of public speakers may be avoided by the application of the elementary principles of phonetics.

As a further support to his phonetic work he cited 'the fact that the Board of Education has now introduced the subject into the regular course of training of teachers for service in public elementary schools [as] sufficient proof that its importance is now generally recognised' (Jones, 1909, p.vii). Jones specifies two principal points here: the intended readership and the intended use for the text. The readership was to consist of English students (in training colleges in particular) and teachers along with all those who 'desire to read or speak in public', and thus was clearly constituted by native speakers. The use for the text was to enable such speakers (particularly teachers) 'to correct cockneyisms or other undesirable pronunciations in their scholars' and to allow 'public speakers' to avoid offensive 'dialectal peculiarities, indistinctiveness and artificialities in their speech'. Such a text has become necessary and justified, he argued, since the subject with which it dealt had been newly introduced into teacher-training courses by the Board of Education. The intent then is evidently pre- and pro-scriptive. It is to guide by erecting a standard which can be followed and which can be used to banish the incorrect, undesirable, peculiar, indistinct, artificial and unfortunate pronunciations that now occur in speech. Thus if the 1912 text was designed for external legislation (ruling on non-native learning of the language), then this text was for internal legislation only. It drew up rules for the native speakers of the language and evaluated their usage.

The pedagogical purposes that Jones had in mind in the writing of these texts forced him, as he records, to adopt a particular form of the language and to take that as a 'standard'. Such an accomplished linguist could not, of course, be unaware of the 'hornets' nest' with which he was dealing in performing such a task since the vagaries of usage presented well-established and enormous difficulties. On this matter he noted, 'no two persons pronounce exactly alike. The difference may arise from a variety of causes, such as locality, early influences, social surroundings, individual peculiarities and the like' (*ibid.*, p.1). And these 'causes' were to be theorised for the first time only in this early-twentieth-century period. Yet in the face of such differences and 'for the purposes of the present book', Jones argued, 'it is necessary to set up a *standard*' (*ibid.*). Or, as he put the matter in his *Outline of English Phonetics* (1919), 'the existence of all these differences renders it necessary to set up a standard of pronunciation' (Jones, 1919, p.4). The necessity of setting up a 'standard of pronunciation' lay in the nature of the pedagogical task that Jones had set himself since if one were to write texts charting English speech sounds, transcribing phonetically English prose, describing English pronunciation, or giving outlines of English phonetics with phonetic readings in English, then one would need a good idea of what precisely were the 'English speech sounds' and 'English pronunciation' to start with. One would need to abstract from the total multifarious empirical uses of language a small number of 'typical', 'representative', 'average' (and so on) sounds that would count as 'English'. That is, one would need a 'standard'. As Jones pointed out when faced with such a task, 'the first question that confronts a person wishing to acquire a correct pronunciation of a foreign language is – which of the various forms of pronunciation ought he to learn?' It was a methodological problem that arose as a result of linguistic variation, as Jones argues in a repetition from an earlier text:

No two persons of the same nationality pronounce their language exactly alike. The differences may arise from a variety of causes, such as locality, social surroundings, early influences, or individual peculiarities.

For example he notes that, 'the pronunciation current among people educated in Manchester differs from those educated in Exeter, and both differ from those educated in Edinburgh or London'. Age and gender likewise cause problems: 'the differences between the pronunciation of old and young persons and between women and men of the same locality and social position are sometimes very marked' (*ibid.*, pp.3–4). Thus as was demonstrated in the previous chapter, at every stage at which one might expect to find stability the expectation is rebuffed since identity of nation, education, age, gender are simply no guarantee of identity of speech. Therefore for the person wishing to acquire this 'correct pronunciation' the methodological problem arises: which form ought to be chosen? Of course the problem is not restricted to the learner of a foreign language since precisely the same problem faces the native speaker too. Along with non-native speakers, which forms of the language are the English students and teachers, along with all those who 'desire to read or speak in public', to take as the 'correct' form?

Jones solved the problem for non-native speakers and native speakers seeking the 'correct pronunciation' by setting up a 'standard of pronunciation'. Given the multifarious usage he faced he settled upon one single form as the 'correct' or 'standard': the usage of a particular class from a particular region. It will be worth giving the various definitions that Jones gives for his 'standard' in the order in which they were produced:

> The pronunciation given is Standard English. It is based on my own pronunciation, a few modifications being introduced either for the sake of consistency, or where my pronunciation seems to be not in accord with the pronunciation of the majority of educated Southern English speakers.   (Jones, 1907, p.iv)

A year later;

> The pronunciation of the following words is intended to be that usually adopted by educated people in London and the neighbourhood.   (Jones, 1908, p.1)

In the 1909 text he declares that:

> The standard selected is that which forms the nearest approximation, according to the judgement of the writer, to the general usage of educated people in London and the neighbourhood. Where such usage varies, the style adopted by the majority will be preferred.   (Jones, 1909, p.1)

And in 1912 it is the 'pronunciation used by the educated classes in the South of England' (Jones, 1912, p.iii). Such definitions are of course much clearer (because much narrower) than a vague specification such as 'English pronunciation', but it may be useful to ask how much clearer? Who, for example, has consulted the 'majority' of educated southern English speakers? Or who has decided where the limits of 'Southern English' are? Evidently Jones considered this type of problem to be worthy of consideration since he continued to narrow the definition of 'Southern English speakers' to those of 'London and the neighbourhood', but then the limits here are not precise either. Then there is also the major problem of who is to say what counts as 'educated', which is the term that appears in all the definitions. Does educated mean basically literate, or with a secondary schooling, or a university education: what criteria are to be used here? Again Jones clearly held this to be an important point since he also defines 'educated' in more precise terms. In his *Outline of English Phonetics* (1919), he specifies that, 'the pronunciation represented is that of Southern Englishmen who have been educated at the great public boarding-schools.' Later in the same text it is asserted that:

> Many suitable standards of English pronunciation might be suggested, e.g. educated Northern English, educated Southern English, the pronunciation used on the stage, etc. It is convenient for present purposes to choose as the standard of English pronunciation the form which appears to be most generally used by Southern English persons who have been educated at the great English public boarding-schools.   (Jones, 1919, p.4)

And in his most detailed rendering, he attempts to clarify the definition precisely:

> The pronunciation used in this book is that most usually heard in everyday speech in the families of Southern English persons whose men-folk have been educated at the great public boarding-schools. This pronunciation is also used by a considerable proportion of those who do not come from

the South of England but who have been educated at these schools. The pronunciation may also be heard, to an extent which is considerable though difficult to specify, from persons of education in the South of England who have not been educated at these schools. It is probably accurate to say that a majority of those members of London society who have had a university education, use either this pronunciation or a pronunciation not differing very greatly from it.   (Jones, 1917, p.viii)

Unpicking the details of this definition reveals a clear geographic, gender-specific and class-specific basis, since although it is possible to find 'standard pronunciation' amongst the 'persons of education in Southern England', the surest speakers of the standard will be the men-folk educated at the 'great public boarding-schools' and their families. Even those who do not come from the South of England but who have been educated at these schools would speak this 'standard', and it could probably be said to be in use amongst the majority of the university-educated of London society (not least because this group would have largely been educated at such schools). Thus in shorthand terms the basis of 'Standard Pronunciation' is the pronunciation in use in the public schools, and it therefore followed that he would describe his 'standard' in the 1917 dictionary as 'Public School Pronunciation' (p.viii).[1]

This definition clearly narrows the possibilities down but there are still problems in ascertaining the 'standard'. Jones had specified macro-sociolinguistic causes of variation such as region, gender, education, social status and so on, and yet he gave recognition to other causes too. These would fall under the description of micro-sociolinguistic features and were concerned primarily with features of the context of speech and the 'style' or 'register' in which utterances were produced. Jones had offered a preliminary and untheoretical delimitation of such usage when he wrote of the pronunciation 'usually adopted' or of the 'general usage', and this was later to lead him to a further theorising of the 'standard'. He had argued in his 1907 text that there are at least three styles of speech used by the educated southern Englishman:

The first (Style A) is the pronunciation suitable for recitation or reading in public; the second (Style B) is the pronunciation used in careful conversation or reading aloud in private; and the third (Style C) is the pronunciation used in rapid conversation.   (Jones, 1907, p.iv)

One of these styles had to be selected in order to serve as that upon which the 'standard' could be based and in a later text he specified it in detail:

It must be noticed that even the best speakers commonly use more than one style. There is the rapid colloquial style and the formal orational style, and there are many shades between the two extremes. For our Standard Pronunciation we shall adopt . . . an intermediate style, which may be termed the *careful conversational style*.   (Jones, 1909, p.1)

It is possible to draw from these quotations a precise definition of Jones's version of the 'standard' that was to serve as the model for non-native and native speakers: it was essentially the careful conversational style of men educated at the English public schools in the South of England. That is, it was the formal, monitored style of the men of a particular class.

The editor of Jones's *English Pronouncing Dictionary* (1917) had no doubts about the form of speech taken as the 'standard' or its extended use. He wrote in the preface that he was 'disposed to ascribe the considerable extension of this form of speech during the last fifty years chiefly to the influence of women in the home, to the increased attention paid to speech in our educational system, and to quickened intercourse among members of the English-speaking world'. Rippmann, the editor, counted himself among the 'many', 'who think that for the purposes of social intercourse and of various kinds of public speaking (such as the pulpit and the stage), we require a "standard speech" and that, when a language is spread as widely over the world as ours is, a generally recognised form of speech is no less desirable than a common literary language' (Jones, 1917, p.v). There is again an argument towards two audiences here. The first is internal (those who will listen to the pulpit or stage) and the second external (those around the world listening to English). Moreover the 'standard' in both cases is proposed on the grounds of recognition: internally it is that form by which those whose home is elsewhere than southern England and whose 'dialect differs' from the 'standard', can make themselves 'more generally understood'. Externally it is the 'generally recognised form of speech'. Significantly, in both cases, the model for the 'standard of speech' is the 'common literary language' since the 'standard speech' is allegedly to function like the literary language in that it is to be nationally uniform, not belonging to any particular region or class. Its basis is alleged to be national intelligibility.

Dialects would be ruled out by this criterion since they are not nationally intelligible and not neutral in all areas:

> Every dialect has its interest and its appeal; but one who knows only his dialect finds himself at a disadvantage in social life, when once he passes beyond the limits within which that dialect is spoken, and it may well be doubted whether his aesthetic appreciation of our literature is not impaired.   (*Ibid.*, pp.v–vi)

Dialects are appealing and interesting but ultimately crippling since they put the speaker at a disadvantage socially and intellectually in that they prevent 'aesthetic appreciation' of the national literature. Failure to speak the national, common, 'standard speech' allegedly entails a failure to be able to 'read' the common, national literature and therefore dialects militate against the sharing of the 'common culture'. Rippmann continued:

> If in our schools we regard it as desirable to deal with the pupils' speech at all, we must have some idea of the kind of speech we wish them to acquire. . . . My own feeling is that our aim should be to secure a form of speech that shall be not merely intelligible but pleasing to the greatest number of educated speakers of English; and that implies not only unobjectionable pronunciation but good voice production. (*Ibid.*, p.vi)

There is a new element here since the 'standard' now must be 'not merely intelligible' but 'pleasing to the greatest number of educated speakers of English' and not only 'unobjectionable pronunciation' but 'good voice production'. There are again pertinent questions to be asked here: 'pleasing' on what grounds? Again who is to decide who are the 'educated'? What are possible objections to particular pronunciations? What is to count as 'good' voice production? The major contradiction in the argument is that the 'standard' in this case is clearly not the form uniformly intelligible but the form counted as 'pleasing', 'unobjectionable' and 'good'. In fact, however, another contradiction takes place earlier and is based on a false comparison between the 'common literary language' and the 'standard speech'. The 'common literary language' had a clearly delineated history as a uniform linguistic practice since, as was argued earlier, it had been and was still the form recognised by anyone who wanted to write in English. It was not the preserve of any particular region or class and there were no rivals to its use. With the spoken language, however, the situation was different since the 'standard speech' was not used by all who wanted to speak English, as it had not been and was not a uniform linguistic practice. It was, as its definition declared, *precisely* the preserve of those of a certain gender, class and region: the men educated at the private, fee-paying schools in the South of England. The exclusiveness of this definition could not have been clearer and given that it was a narrowly defined and privileged 'standard' that could be used to evaluate other forms, it could not become a uniform linguistic practice.

In fact many phoneticians had been very wary of setting up any particular form as the 'standard' to be met. Sweet, for example, argued in 1906 that, 'language only exists in the individual, and that such a phrase as "standard English pronunciation" expresses only an abstraction. Reflect that it is absurd to set up a standard of how English people *ought* to speak, before we know how they actually *do* speak' (Sweet, 1890, p.3). The curious and contradictory thing is that Jones agreed with this assertion. In the Introduction to the *Pronouncing Dictionary* (1917), he asserted that, 'the object of the present book is to record, with as much accuracy as is necessary for practical linguistic purposes, the pronunciation used by a considerable number of cultivated Southern English people in ordinary conversation'. He continued to argue that, 'the book is a record of *facts*, not of theories or personal preferences. No attempt is made to decide how people *ought* to pronounce' (Jones, 1917, p.vii). He describes himself as not 'a reformer of pronunciation or a judge who decides what pronunciations are "good" and what are "bad", but as an objective, scientific observer'. And continues to assert that he believes in neither the 'desirability or the feasibility' of constructing a 'standard', and that he does not consider the pronunciation of the public school speakers as 'intrinsically superior to any other'.

However, in spite of such self-justification, it is clear that Jones was instrumental in the theoretical and practical construction of a particular form of speech as the 'standard' to be met. In spite of any conscious intentions that he may have had, his work was placed within a context that could only have led it in one direction. In rendering the description of the 'facts' of public school pronunciation and in calling this the 'standard of pronunciation' Jones's texts fitted easily into a structure whereby the discourse of that class was counted as the 'standard' for evaluating the discourse of other classes. His intent may have been otherwise, but the effect of Jones's work was both prescriptive and proscriptive. It assigned a particular form of pronunciation as 'correct', 'educated', 'standard usage' and it banished other forms as 'cockneyisms', 'undesirable pronunciations', 'dialectal peculiarities', 'indistinct' and 'artificial'. The conscious intentions are not important for our purposes and we shall be more concerned with the texts and the effects they gave rise to in a larger context.

Henry Wyld

It has been argued that Jones produced increasingly precise definitions of the term 'standard English pronunciation' in the early twentieth century and we shall now consider the work of the other main theorist of the term in this period, the tutor of the study of language at the University of Liverpool, Henry Wyld. As with his contemporary, Wyld saw himself as a neutral, empirical scientist, an observer and tabulator of linguistic facts rather than their evaluator. Moreover, like many of his nineteenth-century predecessors he frequently used analogies with other sciences. For example, in commenting upon the variation within English he asserted that:

> The fact of the existence of these differences has a most important bearing, not only upon the question of the development of our language, but also upon the view which we shall take of the nature and habits of a living tongue. It should be noted that we have awarded, as a rule, neither censure nor praise to this or that variety of English. We have been content merely to attempt to show that variety exists, and to help the reader to know what he may observe for himself.

The 'attitude of the observer' should be that of the inquiring scientist and thus, 'our attitude to forms of English which differ from our own should, in the first instance, be merely one of curiosity. We collect varieties in speech as an entomologist brings together different kinds of moths. We do not love the one and despise the other: we simply observe and compare them' (Wyld, 1907, pp.68–9). By means of a close examination of Wyld's texts, however, it will be clear that his rhetorical claims for the 'neutral' basis of his study are false since rather than observation and comparison, processes of 'censure' and 'praise', 'love' and 'despite' will be demonstrated.

In his *Elementary Lessons in English Grammar* (1909) Wyld warns the reader against assuming that 'Standard English' is the only form of the language worth studying:

> You must not suppose that because only one variety or Dialect of English is here dealt with that the others are considered as lacking in interest, or unworthy of attention. This would be a very false view. As a matter of fact every form of English, every dialect whatever its origin, is

interesting, and important for those who make an exhaustive study of English in all its phases.   (Wyld, 1909, p.18)

Later in the same text he again warns the reader:

> Bear in mind that every peculiarity of sound, grammar, idiom or vocabulary which exists in a provincial dialect has its reasons and justification every bit as much as the peculiarities of Standard English. The careful study of English pronunciation must start with, and be based upon, the study of the native Dialect of English whatever that may be.   (*Ibid.*, p.209)

The study of English dialects seems to be given an enormous importance here since Wyld argues that a study of the native dialect must come before the study of all other forms and must form the basis for all other study. Dialects, it is argued, are not linguistically capricious or 'peculiar' but as law-governed as other forms of the language. Therefore, it follows, they are as worthy of our interest, and as important for our study, as all other forms.

In fact much of Wyld's work (particularly in the early texts) does evince such an interest in the dialects, as variation and its causes are described in lengthy detail. To take one example, he describes the existence of speech 'circles' (amongst friends, fellow workers, parents and children) in which, 'all the members of such a circle as we are supposing will pronounce the same words in the same way; they will make use of the same expressions, the same words, and none will have any glaring peculiarities in his way of speaking English, which will arouse surprise or laughter in others' (Wyld, 1907, p.42). These 'circles', or 'group of persons whose social intercourse is frequent and close' are the social bases of the dialects since:

> It is therefore a natural and inevitable circumstance that a community of more or less intimate friends should all speak in practically the same way. We say, in this case, that they speak the same *Dialect*. By *Dialect* is simply meant a *way of speaking*.   (*Ibid.*, pp.42–3)

Such 'circles' are socially circumscribed, which is to say that the definition of their boundaries is dependent upon social categorisation and thus the existence of differing 'circles' inevitably leads to different dialects. In this early work Wyld describes such social categories as: 'differences of interest and occupation' (p.43), 'differences of class' (p.44), 'difference of place of abode' (p.46), 'difference of age' (p.56), and differences of 'fashion . . . and even sex' (p.62). However, such an early account was still relatively untheorised and for a more sophisticated account we have to turn to a later work. In his *A Short History of English*[2] he outlined his theory of the 'differentiation of dialect' and used the important theoretical term the 'speech community'. He argued that, 'if we define *Speech Community* as a group of human beings between whom social intercourse is so intimate that their speech is practically homogeneous, then whenever we find appreciable speech differences we must assume as many communities, and it will follow that there will be as many Dialects as communities'. The completely 'homogeneous speech community' so beloved of one form of modern linguistics makes perhaps its first covert appearance here although it was in fact presupposed in Saussure's distinction between *langue* as a *fait social* and *parole* as individual, contextual usage.[3] Wyld's use of a basic version of the concept extends only as far as the dialect, although in itself this is open to question since he himself admits individual peculiarities (idiolectal characteristics) as further differentiating features. However he continues to argue that:

> Any factors that split up one community into 2 or more are also factors of differentiation of dialect. The main factors which divide one group of human beings from another are: (1) *Geographical and Physical* – seas, rivers, mountain ranges, distance, any features of the country which actually separate communities by interposing barriers between them; (2) *Occupational* – differences of employment, which lead in modern society to differences of class; (3) *Political*, or divisions which depend not on physical boundaries but on arbitrary lines of demarcation, drawn for purposes of government – e.g. county, or even parish boundaries, or frontiers between countries.   (Wyld, 1927, p.47)

Having described the causes of dialectal differentiation he

then describes the main features by which one can distinguish the dialects, and the single most important feature is the variation found in the sounds of speech since 'the most important test of dialect is pronunciation' (Wyld, 1907, p.47). This test is, however, accompanied by others since 'the diversity in the pronunciation of English, . . . is paralleled by an almost equally variable Vocabulary, Grammar, and set of Idiomatic expressions'. In fact he later argues against pronunciation as being the most important test of dialect when he makes grammar the basis which distinguishes between 'standard' and dialectal forms. In the same text he asserts that 'the Grammar of Standard English is practically fixed and uniform, so that among educated speakers, no matter how much they may differ in other respects, Pronunciation, Vocabulary and Idiom, they will generally agree in using the same grammatical forms'. Therefore it follows that, 'divergences of Grammar of any great extent are usually assignable to Regional Dialects' (*ibid.*, p.58). It is clear from this that Wyld holds there to be a central form which is recognisable, fixed and from which deviations can be measured. Which is to say that there is a 'standard' that can be used to evaluate other forms, what is not 'standard' being designated as dialectal. However, it is not the case that Wyld is arguing at this point for the dialects as sub-standard (rather than non-standard) varieties since that shift was largely made later. He argues here for the recognition of the propriety of particular forms of speech within their specified limits:

> Many grammatical usages that speakers of Standard English would consider terrible vulgarisms occur in these dialects, and are there perfectly '*right*' in the sense in which it is permissible to use this word when speaking of language – namely, in that they are the regular and habitual forms of the dialects. (*Ibid.*, pp.59–60)

However, if such uses of grammar, vocabulary or pronunciation occur outside the limits of dialectal use (say in 'Standard English' contexts), then they immediately become 'provincialisms' and 'vulgarisms'. The two categories are distinguished in terms of the gravity of the linguistic offence and although 'a *provincialism* is a pronunciation or expression which definitely belongs to a provincial or regional dialect', a vulgarism is of a different order. A vulgarism:

> is a peculiarity which intrudes itself into Standard English, and is of such a nature as to be associated with the speech of vulgar or uneducated speakers. The origin of pure *vulgarisms* is usually that they are importations, not from a regional but from a class dialect – in this case from a dialect which is not that of a province, but of a low or uneducated social class.

He continues to specify the status of vulgarisms:

> Thus, a *vulgarism* is usually a variety of Standard English, but a bad variety. An example of what is meant is the pronunciation of *tape* so that it is indistinguishable from the word *type*. Again the so-called 'dropping of an *h*', as when people say *'orse* for *horse*, is distinctly a *vulgarism*. (*Ibid.*, p.55)

The provincialism is regional, the vulgarism class-bound, and it is always possible for a provincialism to become a vulgarism. This occurs under certain circumstances: 'a *provincialism* be-comes a *vulgarism* by being familiar to, and familiarly associated with, vulgar speakers'. However, there are reservations to be borne in mind here since:

> It is very important . . . to bear in mind that pure provincial dialects in themselves are not vulgar. It is a profound error to imagine that dialect speech is an attempt to imitate Standard English; it is nothing of the kind, but is a separate and independent form of English. It is only when a speaker *is* attempting to speak Standard English, and lapses into provincial forms, that these are liable to sound vulgar. (*Ibid.*, p.56)

Wyld's claims to neutral observation seem already to be on slippery ground here since there is a quite evident tone of censure in these comments. Simple observation and comparison would lead the linguist to note that there are forms that are used in differing contexts, say regional and class dialectal forms that are occasionally used by speakers of the dialect referred to as 'Standard English', or 'Standard English' forms used by the speakers of regional or class-dialects. However, Wyld goes further than this in categorising such uses as 'provincial' (not central) and 'vulgar' (with tones at least implicitly of distaste) and proscribing their use. Therefore, although the dialects are all of equal interest they are not all of equal potential since some specifically cannot be used in certain contexts without infringing linguistic and therefore social propriety. As he argued in a later text:

> The first thing is to realise that in itself a Provincial or Regional Dialect is just as respectable, and historically quite as interesting, as Standard English. The next thing is to realise that if you want to speak good Standard English, pronunciations which belong typically to a Provincial Dialect are out of place. It is probably wise and useful to get rid of these Provincialisms since they attract attention, and often ridicule, in polite circles. The best thing to do, if you have a native Provincial Dialect, is to stick to it, and speak it in its proper place, but to learn also Standard English.   (Wyld, 1909, p.208)

There are a number of interesting steps in this argument which reveal a clear tendentiousness. The first is to reassure the dialect speakers that their mode of speech is, *de jure*, as respectable and as historically interesting as 'Standard English'. The second is to argue that the dialects are, *de facto*, not as respectable as 'Standard English' since he warns quite explicitly that provincial forms will excite 'attention' and 'often ridicule' in 'polite circles'. Evidently if such forms excite such censure then they cannot be as 'respectable' as 'Standard English' and in the proper context of 'polite circles' only one form of speech is respected and that is 'Standard English'; all others are to be banished. Thus for the native dialect speaker there are two things to do: first, to learn how to speak 'Standard English', and second, to learn when to speak it. Or to put it in another form, to learn that the 'proper place' for the dialect is not in 'polite circles' since to act in any other way is to invite the censure of the educated and polite.

It is clear that social changes and pressures were exerting their influence in various ways through the newly formed patterns of British society and one effect of such influence was the continuing belief amongst linguists that the dialects (class and regional) were in the process of eradication. As we have noted already, this belief was widely articulated in the nineteenth century and was to continue in interesting ways in the twentieth century. Wyld commented that 'Regional and Class Dialects are giving way before the encroaching Standard English' and then gave the reasons as he saw them:

> The main factor in obliterating Regional Dialects is our system of Primary Education, which places, in schools all over the country, teachers trained according to a uniform scheme, whose own pronunciation and general way of speech has been carefully supervised in Pupil Teachers' Colleges or Training Colleges. Another important class of speech missionaries are the Clergy of the Church of England; and last but by no means least in importance as an agent in smoothing out the most marked peculiarities of dialect, is the wonderful increase in facilities of locomotion, which enables the population to move about freely.   (Wyld, 1907, pp.124–4)

Through the newly formed institutions and cultural patterns, the 'censure' and 'praise' given to certain forms of speech were taking effect in that schools would insist on 'Standard English', the clergy would deliver God's word in 'Standard English', and trains would bring people into contact for the first time with this non-indigenous form used in 'polite circles'.

Otto Jespersen, another major early-twentieth-century linguist, also argued that increasing standardisation was taking effect. Declaring that 'Standard languages are *socially* determined', he continued to assert that, 'it is also worth while to insist strongly on the fact that the various forces which contributed in earlier times to produce and preserve linguistic unity were never since the world began so strong as they were in the last half of the nineteenth century and as they are now in the twentieth'. He too outlined the main causes as:

> greater mutual intercourse owing to the vast development of the means of communication – railways, tramways, motors, steamships, telephones, wireless, etc., cheap books and newspapers in the interest of literary communism – finally the enormous growth of many great cities which attract a population from outside. (Jespersen, 1925, pp.43–4)

All these factors led to an increasing eradication, or so it was thought, of the dialects in favour of 'Standard English'. Wyld argued much the same point when he concluded that 'the increase in the facilities of travel has also been responsible for making many persons familiar with the sound at least of Standard English, who in earlier days would normally have spoken and heard nothing but the dialect of their own village all their lives' (Wyld, 1909, p.207). And of course such people would not simply have become familiar with 'the sound' of the 'Standard English' but with its social significance too. In hearing the sounds of 'Standard English' they recognised it as the form spoken by the polite, as the form institutionalised in particular contexts and as the form used when speaking to persons of a particular social class. They recognised it, in other words, as the form of speech not belonging to them and saw it as an alien, difficult form to which they were outsiders.

Given that Wyld had argued that the dialects were as respectable and as historically interesting (in their place) as 'Standard English', then it follows as a corollary that, linguistically, 'Standard English', was as respectable and as historically interesting as the dialects but not more so. Wyld himself argued that this is the case:

> When we speak of Good English, or Standard English, or Pure English, as distinct from what is known as Provincial English, or Vulgar English, we must remember that there is nothing in the original nature of these other dialects which is in itself inferior, or reprehensible, or contemptible. In a word, the other dialects are in reality, and apart from fashion and custom, quite as good as Standard English considered simply as forms of language.

Linguistically then the dialects and 'Standard English' are equal since 'no form of language is, *in itself*, better than any other form'. However, the all-important rejoinder in Wyld's statement is 'apart from fashion and custom', since it precisely is in this powerful sense that 'Standard English is Better than Other Forms'. Moreover, along with 'fashion and custom' Wyld cites other factors:

> It is natural that the language of the Court should come to be regarded as the most elegant and refined type of English, and that those who do not speak that dialect naturally, should be at the pains of acquiring it. This is what has happened, and is still happening to the dialect which we call Standard English. Of course, since this form of English is used in the conversation of the refined, the brilliant, and the learned, it has become a better instrument for the expression of ideas than any other dialect now spoken. This is the result of the good fortune which this particular dialect had to reach its position of pre-eminence over the others.   (Wyld, 1907, p.49)

There are contradictions in these last two assertions since Wyld argues in the latter that 'Standard English' and the dialects are precisely *not* equal (though they may have been once). He asserts that as a result of being used by a specific class of speakers, 'Standard English' 'has become a better instrument for the expression of ideas than any other dialect now spoken'. If this were true 'Standard English' could be qualitatively distinguished from other dialects on the grounds of its better potential for 'the expression of ideas', and this would mean that more than 'fashion and custom', the power of the language itself would give grounds for preferring it. What is significant also is the elision of the process whereby such a development takes place since Wyld simply declares that such a process is 'natural' and a result of 'good fortune' rather than explicable by reference to any historical or social activities. In other words, the reasons that other forms of language 'have not the same place in general estimation . . . have not been so highly cultivated, and . . . have not the same wide currency' are either natural (and thus unchangeable) or a result of chance (and thus not open to influence). In any case, for whatever reason, 'Standard English' is taken here as the language of 'the refined, the brilliant, and the learned' and the other forms of the language are not.

If we look at the definition of 'Standard English' in grammatical terms again we find a certain peculiarity:

> The Grammar of Standard English is practically fixed and uniform, so that among educated speakers, no matter how much they may differ in others respects, Pronunciation, Vocabulary and Idiom, they will generally agree in using the same grammatical forms. (*Ibid.*, p. 58)

The peculiarity is that there appears to be little or no stability to the features that one might expect to find within a linguistically unified entity, and this might lead one to question what it is precisely that 'Standard English' consists in. Evidently it is not a stability in regard to 'Pronunciation, Vocabulary and Idiom'. But then if read carefully it is not a stability of grammatical forms either since the grammar is not fixed, it is '*practically* fixed and uniform'. There is no fixed agreement in grammatical forms since the speakers only 'generally agree'. Clearly exceptions are permissible; but then how does one prevent an exception from being classified as a 'provincialism' or a 'vulgarism'? Wyld was aware of the problem:

> There are, however, a few points of this order in which speakers of Standard English may disagree, in very colloquial speech, without it being necessary to attribute such difference of habit to separate Regional or Class Dialects. The differences we speak of are in reality due to the adherence on the part of some speakers to a more old-fashioned mode of speech. (*Ibid.*)

Evidently there are problems here that cannot simply be resolved by Wyld's solution and the explanation of the 'old fashioned mode of speech' will not do. Is this 'old fashioned mode of speech' a new category that can take its place in the line of 'Standard English', regional and class dialects, 'vulgarisms' and 'provincialisms' (and finally the 'old fashioned mode of speech')? If so, why isn't the 'old fashioned mode of speech' a 'vulgarism' or 'provincialism' since the former, like the latter two forms, intrudes upon the smooth discourse of the learned and refined? Or to pose another question, are not the sayings of 'the old fashioned mode of speech' also to be categorised in terms of regional and class dialects since at least certain of the 'old fashioned' terms must be regional or class-dialectal? Wyld's introduction of this new category is intended to smooth over the problem of the variation within the forms of 'Standard English' but instead it highlights the problem. Perhaps there can be no purely linguistic definition of 'Standard English'. Perhaps, as the nineteenth-century linguists discovered, the only definition of 'Standard English' to be made has to be couched in extra-linguistic terms.

This was certainly a possible move for Wyld in the face of his problems and it is a move that he undertook. He defined 'Standard English' in one of his early works as a *'class dialect*, which is practically the same, at the present day, in all parts of the country'. Again, however, differences are acknowledged as existing since 'Standard English' is 'practically the same' all over the country but not quite, and therefore a more stable factor has to be introduced into the definition. Therefore, he continued:

We have referred to the fact that all over England there exists a form of language, which is common to the more educated classes in all districts.

This is a kind of English which is tinged neither with the Northern, nor Midland, nor Southern peculiarities of speech, which gives no indication, in fact, of where the speaker comes from – the form of English which is generally known simply as *good English*. It is the ambition of all educated persons in this country to acquire this manner of speaking, and this is the form of our language which foreigners wish to learn. If we can truthfully say of a man that he has a Scotch accent, or a Liverpool accent, or a Welsh accent, or a London accent, or a Gloucestershire accent, then he does not speak 'good English' with perfect purity.   (*Ibid.*, p.48)

'Standard English' according to Wyld's definition, 'is not now confined to any one province but is spoken by people of corresponding education and cultivation all over the country'. In this definition a kind of stability appears that had previously not been present in that Wyld has specified that grammatical, lexical or phonetic uniformity is not present but the stability of the group who speak this form of the language guarantees the stability of the form itself. That is, the one stable factor in all definitions of the 'Standard Language' is once again the group who speak it: the educated. Or at least some of the educated since the specification is of 'the more educated' and there are, he notes, educated persons who clearly do not speak the 'Standard Language' but whose ambition it is 'to acquire this manner of speaking'. We shall return to this further specification later and compare it to Jones's definition of standard speakers. The other point to note at this stage is that the 'purity' of 'good English' depends upon a concept of accentual neutrality, in that speakers of 'Standard English' cannot be pinned down as to their regional origin. However, such neutrality can only refer to geographic origins since in social terms it would be perfectly clear 'where the speaker comes from'. The 'neutral accent' is neutral only in specific contexts and only for particular users and receivers since in other contexts its neutrality would be brought into question. For anyone who doubts this it might well be worth the while of any native English speakers who do not consider themselves to have an accent, or consider their 'standard English' and 'received pronunciation' to be neutral, to imagine contexts in which it would not be classified as such. Speakers with such a 'neutral' accent might find for example that in a bar in the Falls Road, Belfast, their 'accent neutrality' might sound anything but 'neutral'. And the consequences of such linguistic naïvety might also be anything but neutral. However, this type of view was not shared by Wyld since he perceived such usage as free from the type of social significance that tends to distinguish other 'non-standard' forms. In the Preface to his text on *The Teaching of Reading in Training Colleges* he asserts,

'I do say that the pronunciation recorded in the text is free from blatant Provincial or Class peculiarities – is in fact, that of an educated person who has listened all his life to 'good' speakers' (Wyld, 1908, p.vii). In fact the 'neutrality' of this form of English and this alleged liberty from class-related and provincial peculiarities again led to another significant conflation. In his *Elementary Lessons in English Grammar* (1909) he argued that:

Our business is only with one main form of English, that form that is generally called 'Educated English', that is a sort of general average English which has a wide circulation among educated people, and is what is generally referred to by the rather vague name 'correct English', or better, *Standard English*. Unless it is otherwise stated, therefore, 'English' in this book means only this particular dialect of English.

Wyld has allowed his terminology to slip and has to warn the reader against precisely the conflation that he has consistently made, since 'English', he warned earlier, is not to be confused with 'Standard English' alone since the language is more an aggregate of all the dialects together. Yet his concern with his terminology at this point reveals that to all intents and purposes the term 'Standard English' does in fact stand as shorthand for 'the language' itself.

There is another interesting and familiar conflation in the early work that returns later and this is the conflation centred upon the concepts of the standard spoken language and the standard literary language. Wyld writes of the east Midland dialect in the Middle English period that it was 'destined to have a wonderful history, for it becomes, first, the form in which all English literature in future is written, and, secondly, the main spoken form throughout the country' (Wyld, 1907, p.120). Later in the same text he argues that 'the same form of English which became the vehicle of literature came also to be regarded as the best and most 'correct' form of *Spoken* English' (*ibid.*, p.123). And in a later text:

We shall have a good deal to say later concerning both

literary and standard Spoken English. It is enough here to say that they are very closely related; that the origin of both is the same; that the starting point was in the language of London as spoken by the Court and the Upper ranks of Society and in the transaction of business from the fifteenth century.   (Wyld, 1927, p.16)

Here it is variously stated that the standard spoken and standard literary languages are the 'same' because of their origin in the east Midland dialect; or, as the later version has it, that they are at least very closely related. This is a conflation that was consistently made by the theorists at the time: speech was conflated with writing, or rather a certain type of speech was conflated with a certain form of writing. This conflation was to have the sort of complex effects that will be demonstrated below.

Further theoretical developments

We have concentrated so far upon Wyld's earlier work and outlined the main theoretical developments that he made. At this point it will be necessary to outline the further theoretical developments made in his later work. Wyld's description of the language in the early work had been based upon a tripartite division of his object into the standard language, the regional or provincial dialects, and the class dialects. However, his appreciation of the difficulties involved in the study of language led him to a rejection of such a simplistic categorisation and we find in his later work a more sophisticated account of variation and difference. For example, in his *History of Modern Colloquial English* (1920), Wyld develops the concept of 'Standard English' by making new distinctions and the first of these is 'Received Standard English' which is 'the type which most well-bred people think of when they speak of "English"'. He asserted of this form of the language that:

As regards its name, it may be called good English, Wellbred English, Upper-class English, and it is sometimes, too vaguely, referred to as Standard English. For reasons which will soon appear, it is proposed here to call it *Received Standard English*.

Clearly this new concept was in need of definition and he provided it immediately:

> This form of speech differs from the various Regional Dialects in many ways, but most remarkably in this, that it is not confined to any locality, nor associated in any one's mind with any area; it is in its origin, as we shall see, the product of social conditions, and is essentially a *Class Dialect*. *Received Standard* is spoken, within certain social boundaries, with an extraordinary degree of uniformity, all over the country ... *Received Standard* is spoken among the same kind of people, and it is spoken everywhere, allowing for individual idiosyncrasies, to all intents and purposes, in precisely the same way.   (Wyld, 1920, pp.3–4)

'Received Standard English' (RSE) is a socially bounded form of the language, a 'product of social conditions' and more ostensibly than any other form a 'Class Dialect'. Evidently the history of such a form would need to be traced and the task became part of Wyld's project since 'if Received Standard is now a Class Dialect, and the starting point of other Class Dialects, it must once have been a Regional Dialect'. Wyld traces this form to the thirteenth century and its use in 'a large number of writings ... which were produced in London, and apparently in the dialect of the capital', including the works of Chaucer. He concluded that:

> London speech then, or one type of it, as it existed in the fourteenth century, is the ancestor of Literary English, and it is also the ancestor of our present day Received Standard. Written Standard may be said to have existed from the end of the fourteenth century, although it was not used to the complete exclusion of other forms for another hundred years or so. It is more difficult to date the beginning of the existence of a spoken standard.

The 'spoken standard' is more difficult, of course, since it involves evaluations and judgements, social pressures and attitudes and these problems were recognised by Wyld in his argument that:

> The question is, How soon did men begin to feel that such and such forms were 'right' in the spoken language, and that others should be avoided? For it is the existence of this feeling that constitutes the emergence of a favoured or standard dialect.   (*Ibid.*, p.5)

Again the 'standard language' is not constituted by purely linguistic features alone but by 'feelings' that particular forms were 'right' and others to be avoided, which is to say that the existence of the standard is constituted by social and not linguistic forces. On this basis Wyld concludes from 'the remarks of grammarians and others in the sixteenth century' that 'the first recognition of the superiority of one type over the others must be placed as early as the fifteenth century, and perhaps earlier still'.

In fact Wyld's increasing interest in the social stratification of forms of the language leads him to a closer examination of the history of RSE and leads him to ask when 'the ancestor of our present Received Standard became a Class Dialect'. Or to put the question another way, 'how early do appreciable and recognisable divergences appear between the speech of the upper and lower classes in London'. Having posed the question he proceeded to answer it:

> There are general reasons for believing that social dialects would arise quite early in a large community; it may be possible, though not easy, to establish from documentary evidence a probability that they actually did exist in the fifteenth century; it is quite certain that in the sixteenth century a difference was recognised between upper-class English and the language of the humbler order of people. (*Ibid.*)

By reading back into historical documents such as Puttenham's *Arte of English Poesie* (1589), Wyld and other contemporary linguists perceived social processes at work in the language at that time that they also perceived in the language of their own time. Spoken language was taken to have been as socially stratified in the fifteenth and sixteenth centuries as it was in the early twentieth century and what was, and is, to be counted as 'correct', 'proper' and 'standard' became increasingly clearly the result of social and historical forces rather than nature or chance.

Wyld's increasing sensitivity to the social stratification of language led him to reject the simple tripartite model of Standard, Regional and Class Dialects. Yet although he adapted the concept he still retained the notion of a 'standard' in the form of a 'Received Standard'. Moreoover, given that the 'Standard English' had previously been defined as the language of the 'educated', the question to be asked is, who are the speakers of RSE? The answer to the question shows Wyld's increasing precision in his theoretical definitions. He had argued earlier that 'Standard English' was 'common to the more educated classes in all districts', and that 'it is the ambition of all educated persons in this country to acquire this manner of speaking'. There is a clear differentiation here between different groups: there are the 'more educated' who speak the 'standard' and there are the 'educated' whose 'ambition' it is to acquire the 'standard'. And this leads to Wyld's later theoretical developments. He still maintains that the 'standard' is spoken by 'all educated persons' but within both the social group (the educated) and the form of language itself (the 'standard') he makes clear distinctions.

The first distinction is that RSE is the domain of the 'more educated' as he had named them, which is to say that Wyld joined Jones in defining a particularly prestigious form of the language as deriving from the English Public Schools. As Wyld put it, 'if we were to say that Received English at the present day is *Public School English*, we should not be far wrong' (Wyld, 1920, p.3). Or as the presupposition is more clearly laid out in the 'Rules for Pronunciation' according to his *Universal English Dictionary* (1932):

The sounds which the writer of this dictionary had in mind are those in use among the majority of persons who speak *Southern Standard*, or better, *Received Standard English*. If this description is considered too vague, it must suffice here to say that *Received Standard* is spoken by those who have been educated at one of the older Public Schools. (Wyld, 1932, p.vi)

The order of stratification places RSE and its public school speakers in the most prestigious position since RSE and its speakers are privileged in being imitated by the educated, in being considered as the model upon which others should form themselves. Non-RSE speakers, of course, were also to be distinguished since not all non-RSE speakers were to be counted as speaking the same form. This in turn led to a further categorisation of the language and even to a further division of the 'standard language'. In this division, after the 'more educated' RSE speakers came the educated 'Modified Standard' speakers; that is, those who were not RSE speakers but not either purely regional or class dialectal speakers. Wyld asserts that:

The fact is that those types of English, which are not Provincial or Regional Dialects, and which are also not Received Standard, are in reality offshoots or variants from the latter, which have sprung up through the factors of social isolation among classes of the community who formerly spoke, in most cases, some form of Regional Dialect. It is proposed to call these variants *Modified Standard*, in order to distinguish them from the genuine article. This additional term is a great gain to clear thinking, and it enables us to state briefly the fact that there are a large number of Social or Class Dialects, sprung from what is now Received Standard, and variously *modified* through the influence of Regional Standard on the one hand, on the other, by tendencies which have arisen within certain social groups. (Wyld, 1920, p.3)

Wyld makes it quite clear that 'it is a grave error to assume that what are known as "educated" people, meaning thereby highly trained, instructed and learned persons, invariably speak Received Standard'. 'Education' is no guarantee of speaking this form since it can in fact lead to hyper-correction, or 'over-careful pronunciation'. Examples given by Wyld include the pronunciation of *t* in 'often', 'or when initial *h* is scrupulously uttered (whenever written) before all personal pronouns' and so on. 'Education' then, in general, was no guarantee and it was clearly more a case of birth, class and a 'proper education' at one of the public schools. Wyld comments on such 'modifications' of the standard by declaring that 'all these things, and countless others of like nature, are in no wise determined by "education" in the sense of a knowledge of books, but by quite other factors. The manner of a man's speech from the point of view we are considering is not a matter of intellectual training, but of social opportunity and experience' (*ibid.*, p.4). By the time a person might worry about the way in which they spoke it would be too late since they either had RSE or they did not, and if they did not, there was little point in trying to learn it.

By the later 1920s Wyld had abandoned his earlier more simplistic model in favour of a more highly stratified account. This consisted of 'the old provincial or local dialects, which it is convenient to call *Regional Dialects*, [which] owe their long-standing differences to the factors of geographical isolation'. Along with 'the other kind of dialects which owe their variations from each other primarily to social causes, [which] we may for convenience call *Class Dialects*'. Then there is 'the vulgar English of the Towns, and the English of the villager who has abandoned his native Regional Dialect' which is 'Modified Standard':

> That is . . . Standard English, modified, altered, differenti-
> ated, by various influences, regional and social. Modified
> Standard varies from class to class and locality to locality;
> it has no uniformity, and no single form of it is heard outside
> a particular class or a particular area.

Finally there is *Received Standard* which is:

> that form which all would probably agree in considering
> the best, that form which has the widest currency and is
> heard with practically no variation among speakers of the
> better class all over the country. This type might be called
> Public School English.   (Wyld, 1927, pp.148–9)

The best English: the superiority of Received Standard English

It was argued earlier that the early modern British linguists and their nineteenth-century counterparts saw themselves as scientists, neutral observers of facts or phenomena which they neither praised nor censured. In earlier chapters it was also shown that the nineteenth-century linguists' self-image was a fiction and that in fact such linguists had been deeply involved with social and rhetorical concerns in their study of language. Their work was not neutral but prescriptive and proscriptive in selecting particular forms and assigning them value and banishing other forms as inferior. It will now be shown that Wyld, the most advanced theorist of the concept of 'Standard English' of this period, was likewise pre- and proscriptive.

This will begin with an examination of an essay published by the *Society for Pure English* by R.W. Chapman, entitled 'Oxford English'. The essay is interesting not least for its rejection of the term 'Oxford English' in favour of the term 'Standard English'. In it Chapman describes 'Standard English' as 'in essentials the best of the English dialects, and therefore – though foreign languages may excel it in this or that quality – one of the most subtle and most beautiful of all expressions of the human spirit' (Chapman, 1932, p.562). A definite assertion then of the superior excellence of 'Standard English' on the grounds that this form of the language is the best of all the English dialects and therefore among the finest of the languages of the world. Though it may be rivalled or even excelled in particular characteristics it is, overall, an excellent example of the 'human spirit' expressed in language. Chapman specifies his perception of its strength more clearly in his argument that 'the strength of standard English lies in its prestige, which is still very great, and – as I hope we can believe — in its intrinsic value' (*ibid.*, p.563). Its strength falls into two categories: first there is its prestige, which means that its strength at least in part derives from the fact that people consider it to be strong. And second, there is its 'intrinsic value', that is, its value which exists apart from any judgements of praise or censure, prestige or ridicule, that may be passed upon it. This second point is a new factor since previously the overwhelming agreement was that 'Standard English' was superior in that it was the language of the educated but now there again appears the possibility that 'Standard English' is the language of the educated because of its intrinsic value. As with Wyld's shift in the basis of his definition, Chapman also argues in such a way that its former extrinsic value has become internalised, and this is a point we shall return to later.

Chapman did, however, also subscribe to the theory that 'Standard English' was the 'best' partly because of its speakers, and illustrates this in talking of the broadcasting of 'Standard English' to the nation through the medium of radio. He argues that 'the fine flower of Standard English is the product of qualities and opportunities which cannot be broadcast. It is the speech not of a region, but of a class within that region: of a class which, though not arrogantly exclusive, is necessarily limited in numbers. Its traditions are maintained, not primarily, by the universities, but by the public schools' (*ibid.*, p.561). However, although it cannot be nationally inculcated through the radio it might prove possible to do this in the schools and therefore, if speech-training is to take place, 'by precept or example, the speech taught in this island must, in the main, approximate to standard English'. Unlike many other cultural commentators of the period Chapman was doubtful as to the possibilities of achieving this task even through the schools. And even if it were achieved, for Chapman at least the effect would be harmful since, he argued, 'I am so undemocratic as to believe that the best, in speech as in other things, can never be widely and rapidly disseminated without damage to itself' (*ibid.*, p.560). Even without the attempt to disseminate it to the masses, mass-consumer society appeared to threaten the purity of the language. It was the modern world itself that appeared to threaten its existence:

> Whether standard English will long be able to maintain its position and its integrity seems open to doubt. It is exposed, as we have seen, to dangers from within. . . . As the speech of a very small minority of English speakers it is obviously exposed to gradual absorption by the surrounding mass, and perhaps also to deliberate attack. It is well-known that

English vocabulary and idiom are undergoing penetration
from America and elsewhere. . . . Even our grammar is
threatened. (*Ibid.*, p.562)

The superior language then, the form 'intrinsically' better
than all other forms, is under attack and the danger lies both
within the language itself (from forces of decay and corruption)
and without it (from the unconscious and conscious attacks
made upon it). The 'surrounding mass' with their popular
newspapers, fiction, slang, dialects and Americanisms evidently threaten the purity of the vocabulary, idiom, and even
grammar.

There have, of course, consistently been purists and those
who profess concern for the 'decaying state of the language',
from Socrates to Mencken. And in this sense Chapman's essay
could be noted as the pleading of a purist who sees his superior
form disappearing (as 'superior' forms tend always apparently
to do). However, his essay is important in that it fits in with
a general trend of thinking about language at this period that
was common to both linguists and non-linguists, despite the
denials of the former. To demonstrate this point Wyld's 1934
essay will be examined in order to show its similarities to
Chapman's arguments; the essay was also published as a tract
of the Society for Pure English in 1934 entitled *The Best English:
The Superiority of Received Standard English.*

Wyld had argued in his earlier work that he had no interest
in awarding 'censure nor praise to this or that variety of
English' and that as a linguist he did not 'love the one and
despise the other: we simply observe and compare them'. He
had specifically asserted the equality of all forms of the
language as forms of language since 'in a word, the other
dialects are in reality, and apart from fashion and custom,
quite as good as Standard English considered simply as forms
of language' (Wyld, 1907, p.49). Or in other words, no form
or variety of the language was intrinsically better than any
other. On the evidence of the early work, then, Wyld appears
to be wholly opposed to Chapman; and yet it will now be
demonstrated that Wyld, like Jones, moved to a position in
his later work which contradicts the basic tenets of the
earlier research. He became interested in social and rhetorical

concerns that influenced his linguistic research and led it in a particular direction.

In his 1934 article Wyld begins by citing two earlier SPE tracts on the subject of phonetics and it is from one of these (Aikin's 'English Vowel Sounds') that Wyld takes the 'text for this paper'.[4] Aikin had argued that, 'it is best, from a phonological point of view, to combine the condition of maximum resonation or sonority, with the clearest possible differentiation of sounds' (Aikin, 1927, p.184). Wyld takes this as the basis for his own paper and thus the aim of his paper becomes a question of identification:

> The questions for English speakers then are – which among the various Regional or Provincial dialects on the one hand, or which of the innumerable Class dialects on the other, best exhibits the desired conditions; and further, whether intrinsic superiority can really be claimed for one type of English above all others in respect of these questions of sonority and distinctness.   (Wyld, 1934, p.604)

There are a number of developments here. First Wyld agrees with Aikin that phonologically (and presumably in terms of intelligibility) it is best for a form of language to combine maximum 'sonority' with 'the clearest possible differentiation of sounds'. Second, Wyld then proceeds to argue that the form of English which best matches these conditions will be 'intrinsically' superior; that is, it might not simply be regarded as the best but will be the best. And a few lines after posing this question Wyld declares that he has already discovered this 'best' form of the English language in his assertion that: 'I believe that the form of English which best satisfies Dr. Aikin's conditions, and also several others of hardly less weight, is that which I take leave to call *Received Standard*' (*ibid.*). Wyld defends his position in terms precisely similar to those that Chapman had proposed earlier, that is, in terms of both its prestige (stemming from the social status of its speakers), and its intrinsic value. He argued that:

> I suggest that this is the best kind of English, not only because it is spoken by those often very properly called 'the

best people', but because it has two great advantages that make it intrinsically superior to every other type of English speech – the extent to which it is current throughout the country, and the marked distinctiveness and clarity in its sounds. (*Ibid.*, p.605)

There are three factors used in the argument for RSE as the 'best' form of English, one extrinsic and two intrinsic: the fact that it is spoken by the 'best' people, along with its currency throughout the country and the distinct and clear sounds it utilises. The first argument will not, however, stand up to scrutiny since to argue that because the 'best speakers' speak a certain form of a language then that form must be the best is either tautological or, at the very least, highly contentious. If there were general agreement about who are the best speakers, or even general agreement upon the means by which this could be decided, then the 'best speakers' could be ascertained and one could then simply say that the speech of the best speakers is by definition the best speech. However, there is in fact no such agreement since estimations of who are to be counted as the 'best speakers' vary enormously and moreover to appoint as the best speakers that small group to which the speaker making the judgement belongs is to lay oneself open to deep scepticism. The second argument, that the currency of 'Standard English' throughout the country is an argument for its intrinsic superiority, will likewise not bear examination. There are two reasons for this; first, 'Received Standard' is not, by Wyld's own arguments, current through-out the country. Wyld had consistently argued that 'Received Standard' was current amongst only a tiny minority, consti-tuted by the public-school-educated men of the South. It was not even the form current amongst the 'educated' since 'education' was no guarantee of speaking RSE, though it could well have counted as a necessary and sufficient requirement for speaking 'Modified Standard'. However, and this is the second reason that Wyld's second argument fails, even if it were the case that 'Standard English' were 'current throughout the country', that would still not be an argument for counting 'Standard English' as *intrinsically* superior to other forms. The fact that a particular form is widely used is to say nothing about the intrinsic nature of the form but is rather to state a fact which is *extrinsic* to the form. To argue otherwise would be akin to arguing that because a particular practice is carried out throughout a community at regular intervals, then this practice is intrinsically good, whereas the fact that it is widely and regularly practised is an extrinsic fact that argues for nothing save the fact that it is a practice widely and regularly used. Arguments as to the nature of the practice are of a different order; whether it is good or bad, useful or not, pleasurable or not, harmful or not, destructive or not, are distinct from arguments covering its currency. These are questions that demand debate, judgement and evaluation, and moreover it is crucial that they should be recognised as such. Once such recognition is made, it then becomes impossible to think of the practice as intrinsically superior, inferior, or anything else. In the case of 'Standard English', its currency is extrinsic and its 'superiority', if it depends on its currency, is likewise so: a result of evaluation and judgement.

We come then to the third argument, and the second for the 'intrinsic superiority' of RSE; that is, the argument that RSE 'is superior, from the character of its vowel sounds, to any other form of English, in beauty and clarity' (Wyld, 1934, p.606). Wyld's argument here is largely non-existent: for example, he argues that 'sonority is an element of beauty in language', which already begs the question of who, at what point, and according to which criteria, has made this evaluation. However, even given this he then goes on to define a 'sonorous language' as 'one which possesses a considerable number of sonorous vowel sounds'. He then states that RSE 'has a fair share of such sounds, more, I fancy, than any single provincial dialect'. These are, of course, weak arguments since they produce no evidence and Wyld realises this and moves to concrete examples. However, the first of these demonstrates the tenuous nature of such evidence as he argues of the 'sonorous vowel sounds' that the 'chief of these is the sound popularly expressed by *ah* [a], as heard in *path, chaff, task, hard*, etc. It is surprising how rare this sound is in provincial speech. In some dialects the vowel is short, and even if nearly the same in actual quality, this short vowel lacks the solidity and dignity of the RS Sound' (*ibid.*, p.607). The quality of the evidence here is thin: firstly it is asserted that the chief 'sonorous vowel sound' is 'ah [a]'. Yet there is no definition of why this sound is 'sonorous', it is simply asserted to be so. Second, there is the problem that this sound is said to be 'popularly expressed'; but then he quickly argues that this sound is 'rare' in provincial speech. Is it the case then that the bulk of provincial speech is minor as compared to the major bulk of 'standard speech'? Clearly not since RSE is the preserve of a small elite. Where then is this sound *popularly* expressed in language? Third, there is the argument that the RSE sound has 'solidity and dignity'; but these too are evaluations and surely cannot be taken as evidence for RSE as being objectively a more 'sonorous' language than the dialects. If they were to be taken in this manner then the evidence would be just as convincing as if RSE were hailed as a 'weak and undignified language' on the grounds of its sonority. These are assertions open to debate, not linguistic facts open to simple verification as they are presented; which is to say that an assertion such as, 'this sound [ae] is neither as sonorous nor as beautiful as [a]' is not a statement of a linguistic fact, but an opinion or judgement.

However, after reviewing and evaluating a number of different vowel sounds, Wyld concludes that:

> If it were possible to compare systematically every vowel sound in RS, with the corresponding sound in a number of provincial and other dialects, assuming that the comparison could be made, as is only fair, between speakers who possessed equal qualities of voice, and the knowledge how to use it, I believe no unbiased listener would hesitate in preferring RS as the most pleasing and sonorous form, and the best suited to be the medium of poetry and oratory.

What is precisely at stake is the assumption that there is a basis upon which the comparison could be made as well as the position and status of the unbiased listener. If, for example, someone were to challenge the conclusion and insist on the inferiority of RS on the grounds of 'sonority', would that then indicate a degree of bias? Or if, for example, there were a speaker who preferred *The Prelude* read in an accent associated with the Cumbrian area, or Burns read with a particular Scottish accent, would that speaker then be biased? The answer must be yes, as biased as the speaker who prefers the RS version: not less but then certainly not more. Wyld then moves on to the argument concerning clarity as he claims that 'the merit of clearness is possessed by RS to a degree not approached by any of the provincial and vulgar forms of English. The reason is that all those vowels in the former, which are not diphthongs, are definite, individual and perfect types of their several kinds' (*ibid.*, p.608). Again there are problems with this. First, there is the problem that a great deal of phonetic overlapping takes place in the production of sound sequences and thus in speech there would be no such thing as a 'definite, individual and perfect type' of vowel since the vocal organs themselves move so rapidly as not to allow for such articulatory 'perfection'. The second, and more important point for our purposes, is that any such perception of clarity is as likely to depend upon the context of any dialogic exchange as it is on the linguistic nature of the speech sounds involved. 'Clarity' in this sense would be more than simply a linguistic concept and would depend upon the perceptions of the audience since there is at least the possibility that RSE would be unclear in particular contexts due to the expectations and even biases of the audience. Though, of course, the audience that hears RSE as perfectly clear also has its own expectations and biases too.

These objections notwithstanding, Wyld argues that RSE is extrinsically and intrinsically the superior form of the language. It follows therefore that those non-RSE forms must be 'inferior' and 'unpleasing' and he continues to assert the problems for non-RSE speakers consequent upon such facts. He argues that an orator using Modified Standard 'will of necessity speak a dialect which is in many respects unfamiliar to most of his speakers' unless the speaker is addressing an audience within his or her own locality and class. If the speaker is not in such a position, however, she/he will inevitably alienate most of his or her audience since, it is claimed:

Most people find it distressing to listen to a discourse

uttered with a pronunciation unfamiliar to them. The effect is a continuous series of surprises which startle and distract the attention from the subject under consideration, and at last excite amusement or disgust.

He then gives an example:

Some time ago I listened in to a speaker, a noble lord I regret to say, broadcasting his belief that there was still a 'stight of dinejer' in the political atmosphere of Europe – or else that there was not – I am not sure which, for my attention was diverted from following his argument by the interest excited by his cockney accent.   (*Ibid.*, p.606)

The interesting point to note here is that Wyld confines this argument to 'modified standard' speech and yet from his own arguments to the effect that RSE is the speech of public-school-educated men it must follow that an RSE speaker will almost always and everywhere speak in a way 'in many respects unfamiliar to most of his hearers' since the public-school-educated men are a tiny minority. If it is true that 'most people find it distressing to listen to a discourse uttered with a pronunciation unfamiliar to them' then RSE speakers must labour under this difficulty constantly and they must consistently be met with the problem of hearers who do not listen to the substance of what they say but react with 'a continuous series of surprises which startle and distract' their attention. The RSE speakers must suffer from the difficulty of being able to communicate at ease with none other than that tiny number of their fellow alumni.

Having established 'objectively' that RSE is the 'best' form of the language from a purely linguistic point of view Wyld then goes on to describe other forms of the language and again he does so in terms of censure and dispraise. He asserts that:

It is urged, however, that to introduce provincial sounds into what is intended to be Standard English, addressed to educated people, is distressing and distracting. For the various forms of Modified Standard of towns which reflect class influence, and are of the nature of plain vulgarisms, there is little to be said except in dispraise. (*Ibid.*, pp.613–14)

Again 'provincialisms' and 'vulgarisms' are stigmatised as liable to distract one's audience or even to distress it. Even worse, however, than 'plain and downright vulgarism or provincialism' is another form of Modified Standard, the 'over-refined and affected'. This is the language of the new middle classes and for this, Wyld argues, 'a few words in dispraise may not be out of place':

First of all it should be noted that the kind of speech referred to is a tissue of affectations. Nothing is natural, everything – vowels, the cadence of the sentence, every tone of the voice – bears evidence of care, and the desire to be 'refined'. The result is always ludicrous, and sometimes vulgar. The whole utterance is pervaded by an atmosphere of unreality, and the hearer not infrequently gets the impression that the speaker is endeavouring with the utmost care, by means of a mincing, finicky, pronunciation, to avoid, or cover up, some terrible natural defect. We feel in listening to such speakers, that they are uneasy, unsure of themselves, that they have no traditional social or linguistic background, but have concocted their English upon some theory of what is 'correct' and 'refined' instead of absorbing it, and reproducing it unconsciously, from the converse of well-bred and urbane persons.   (*Ibid.*, pp.614–15)

The new members of the middle class betray themselves in their speech by their affectations and unnatural endeavours, and it will be shown later how such fears about self-betrayal were deeply felt. What is of interest here is Wyld's use of the terms 'natural', 'tradition', 'well-bred' and 'urbane'. What Wyld does in this passage is to hail the discourse of one class as superior because its speakers sound 'natural' and have behind them a long-standing social and linguistic tradition of being 'well-bred and superior'. Moreoever, theirs is not a form of language that can be consciously learnt since it is a form that one is born with or that one can unconsciously absorb. Wyld goes on to describe this unworried, superior form of language and its speakers:

It is characteristic of RS that it is easy, unstudied, and natural. The 'best' speakers do not need to take thought for their utterance; they have no theories as to how their native tongue should be pronounced, nor do they reflect upon the sounds they utter. They have perfect confidence in themselves, in their speech, in their manners. For both bearing and utterance spring from a firm and gracious tradition. 'Their fathers told them' – that suffices. Nowhere does the best in English culture find a fairer expression than in RS speech.   (*Ibid.*, p.614)

RS speakers are not 'careful' speakers since they do not need to be as they have all the confidence of knowing that their speech, manners and their very selves are superior to all around them. The reason for this is, of course, the patriarchal tradition in which they find themselves graciously but firmly situated: their fathers told them they were superior and they were right. They are, according to this theory, not merely superior but the 'best' that English culture has to offer in the form of language. Formerly Wyld had defined RS speakers as the men educated at the English public schools but now he sees the necessity of narrowing the definition further. He asserts:

If I were asked among what class the 'best' English is most consistently heard at its best, I think, on the whole, I should say among officers of the British Regular Army. The utterance of these men is at once clear-cut and precise, yet free from affectation; at once downright and manly, yet in the highest degree refined and urbane.   (*Ibid.*)

Amongst the officer class of the British Army then one is sure of finding the best English since their speech is unaffected, refined, urbane and (necessarily of course since he is referring to the male officers' mess) manly.

Conclusion

In Chapters 3 and 4 an attempt was made to show the

development of different concepts of the 'Standard Language'. The first of these, as argued in Chapter 3, was the concept of the 'Standard Language' as the central literary form of the language, the form which became used nationally as the form in which writing was to take place. The second concept of the 'Standard Language', argued in Chapter 4, was that which took the 'Standard Language' as the standard spoken language and then derived that standard from the discourse of the literate or the educated. In this chapter we have largely been dealing with the second of these conceptions. It has been shown that the early-twentieth-century linguists Jones and Wyld, just like the earlier nineteenth-century linguists, saw themselves as neutral scientists, observers without discrimination. It has also been shown that in so far as this particular concept was concerned their self-images were false, since when they developed their theories concerning the 'Standard Language' they constructed them along the lines of the preferences and prejudices that had been present in the nineteenth century and earlier. They argued that the 'Standard Language' was the 'best' language and that it was the language of the 'best' class, the language of public-school-educated men or of the male officer class. Other forms of language were all well and good in their place but when they obtruded in the domain of public discourse they became 'vulgar' and 'provincial', exciting censure, dispraise and ridicule.

It is clear from the development of the concept of 'Standard English' in the work of eminent linguists such as Jones and Wyld that the study of language was still a field dominated by social and rhetorical concerns. That is not to argue that such linguists did not carry out other work that was pioneering and highly interesting since they clearly did. It is rather to point out the constitutive effect that particular social and political values had on certain branches of the field. The research into language carried out at this time was not 'purely scientific' since it was influenced to a large extent by certain cultural presuppositions and thus became part of a larger formation whose task was to set out the politics of discourse. In the next chapter of this book this study will be extended further by moving away from the direct work/of linguists and on to the many others in early-twentieth-century Britain who viewed language and discourse as socially and politically crucial. We have concentrated so far on linguists, or students of language, who were directly or indirectly influenced by particular social and political concerns; we turn next to political theorists, politicians, historians, educationalists and cultural commentators of various sorts, who took a direct or indirect interest in the politics of discourse in early-twentieth-century Britain.

6

Language
Against
Modernity

The language in which we are speaking is his before it is
mine. How different are the words *home, Christ, ale, master*,
on his lips and on mine! I cannot speak or write these
words without unrest of spirit. His language, so familiar
and so foreign, will always be for me an acquired speech.
I have not made or accepted its words.
(Joyce, *A Portrait of the Artist as a Young Man*, 1916)

Language and class

The fifty years spanning 1875–1925 are generally taken by
cultural historians as the period in which the familiar patterns
of British working-class and middle-class living were first
produced. Hobsbawm, for example, argues that, 'in a word,
between 1870 and 1900 the pattern of British working-class
life which the writers, dramatists and T.V. producers of the
1950s thought of as "traditional" came into being'
(Hobsbawm, 1969, p.164). In the same vein Stedman-Jones
recently proposed that a distinct working-class culture though
formed earlier, first gained recognition at the beginning of
the twentieth century (Stedman-Jones, 1983, p.183). Such
historians perceive a fundamental shift in the British social
formation as new patterns and new perceptions (new ways of
experiencing and new ways of seeing experience) emerged in
the structures of British culture. Significantly, these historians
see new and important roles for the language, concepts and
experiences of class in British society. Stevenson, for example,
gives a clear account of the growing importance of class

differences (Stevenson, 1984, pp.31–49), though the direction of his argument is countered by Waites's contention that 'there was a simple shift in emphasis in the language of class away from descriptions of an elaborately ranked society towards accounts of a more simply structured society' (Waites, 1976, p.49). Nonetheless, though different in their direction both agree that perceptions of class were themselves felt as social phenomena of ever-increasing importance. However, even if Waites is correct that the use of class as an indicator of status in society begins to change at this period, and is gradually replaced by class as a more simple mode of describing social structures, then it is also true that the language, concepts and experience of class at the time became much more bitter and antagonistic. On this point Bullock argues that 'nothing is more striking in reading through the speeches and newspaper comments of the early 1920s than the frank recognitions by both sides that industrial relations had become a running class war and the concessions or rejections of wage-demands, symbols of victory or defeat for one side or the other' (Bullock, 1960, vol. 1, p.150). In any case the language of class, it is generally agreed, played an important role in British culture since it was a mode of perceiving economic relations and a way of perceiving behaviour, fashions, lifestyles and most significantly for our present purposes, language itself. Therefore, this section will attempt to demonstrate how contemporary cultural observers thought of class in their accounts of British society and what role language played in those perceptions.

In 1901 the early sociologist C.F.G. Masterman wrote of the 1880s:

Beyond the actual political arena there was everywhere a great stirring and an agitation. The great mass of the people, so long silent, seemed to be slowly breaking into articulate speech. Trades Unionism was penetrating into the depths of hitherto unorganised, unskilled labour with apparently astounding success. . . . Popular discontent, especially in London, appeared gathering to a focus; riots, strikes and noisy demonstrations seemed to give a foretaste of the coming struggle between capital and labour. . . . The future that almost all competent observers foretold was the active realisation of that 'class war' which haunts the mind of so many German Economists: a struggle growing ever more bitter between the holders of property on one hand and workers on the other.   (Masterman, 1901, p.2)

And yet in 1901 Masterman concluded that such radicalism had largely spluttered out and noted that not only had the 'class war' not been realised, there was as yet no likelihood of its realisation either (though the perception of the threat remained). For Masterman the reasons were clear: imperialism was the first since 'the lust of domination, the stir of battle, the pride in the magnitude of the empire' (*ibid.*, p.4) had largely served to de-radicalise the working class in his view. The second was the reformism of the working-class organisations that had sought change since in the Independent Labour Party, he argued, 'socialism has been largely abandoned' and 'the condition of the people problem . . . appears local, parochial, a problem of gas, water and drains' (*ibid.*). However, although its representatives had largely (in Masterman's eyes) betrayed it, the urban proletariat in particular still posed a threat to the fragile social fabric with their novel and unfamiliar appearance:

Our streets have become congested with a weird and uncanny people. They have poured in as dense black masses from the eastern Railways; they have streamed across the bridges from the marshes and desolate places beyond the river; they have been hurried up in incredible number through tubes sunk in the bowels of the earth, emerging like rats from a drain, blinking in the sunshine. They have surged through our streets, turbulent cheerful indifferent to our assumed proprietorship.   (*Ibid.*, p.2)

These are the 'new city race', 'the people of the abyss' that caused a 'cloud on men's minds' and Masterman characterised them as, 'a mammoth of gigantic and unknown possibility. Hitherto it has failed to realise its power. . . . How long before, in a fit of ill-temper, it suddenly realises its tremendous unconquerable might?' (*ibid.*, p.4). It was the question of the period. Moreover, it was a question that was to be posed more often and more urgently as the century wore on. Sir Henry Newbolt, for example, later described the 'new bitterness' of the political scene after the First World War:

> Then came the propaganda of the new Russian political system, under the influence of which there was to be heard up and down the country so much talk of confiscation and the class war that it was thought by some worth while to try the experiment in earnest. Even that, even the memory of our nine days' civil war is rapidly fading into the twilight of history; but it remains true for the present that we are no longer in any sense a nation at peace within itself.   (Newbolt, 1927, p.8)

A society at war with itself seems a fair summation of the common perception at the time since early-twentieth-century Britain was perceived by contemporary observers as a society divided by mutually antagonistic classes in bitter struggle.

Classes are constructed by economic differences in the production and distribution of wealth and they are also the bearers of other types of differences that we recognise as cultural. Thus the society that was divided in terms of the production and distribution of wealth was also divided in cultural terms. In language in particular this was the case and in fact this medium even came for some to be more significant as an indicator of class than any other economic or cultural feature. Galsworthy, President of the English Association in 1924, asserted for example that 'there is perhaps no greater divide of society than the differences in viva-voce expression' (Galsworthy, 1924, p.8) And in his portrait of Victorian England Young had also described this intense awareness of the social importance of linguistic (along with other) differences:

> The world is very evil. An unguarded look, a word, a gesture, a picture or a novel, might plant a seed of corruption in the most innocent heart and the same word or gesture might betray a lingering affinity with the class below.   (Young, 1936, p.2)

A single word could assign you to an inferior class and reveal a hidden history in a moment. Such perceptions, values and traditions evidently were being formed around cultural and class boundaries since as Reynolds, another early British sociologist, asserted:

> Between the man of one tradition and another, of one education and another, of one domestic habit and another, of one class feeling and of another class feeling – that is where the line of cleavage runs through town and country alike.

He continued to argue that 'class antagonism is a very powerful force, growing rather than diminishing, acting in all sorts of unexpected ways, cropping up in all sorts of unexpected places' (Reynolds and Woolley, 1911, pp.xviii–xix). In 'all sorts of unexpected ways' new perceptions of class and of its importance for social identity were becoming clear. Through education, to take one new mode, the children of a specific class would experience a shift in their view of their relation to their parents that would have been unlikely for their parents in relation to their own mothers and fathers. Reynolds gives a good example of this from Seacombe, a small fishing village in which he lodged with the Widger family, when he declares that 'the growth of the class spirit, as opposed to the old village spirit, can be seen plainly when Bernie returns from school saying: "Peuh! Dad's only a fisherman. Why can't 'er catch more fish an' get a little shop an' be a gen'leman"' (Reynolds, 1909, p.199). The term 'gen'leman' is an excellent example of a lexical indicator of class since it could be applied only to a specific class of person, and certainly not to a fisherman. The social gap between a 'man' and a 'gen'leman' was clearly perceived and Reynolds reports an exemplary dialogue:

> 'Who gie'd thee thic ha'penny?' Mrs Widger asked Jimmy.
> 'A man to beach.'
> 'G'out!' said Mabel, 'T'was a gen'leman.'
> 'Well . . .'
> 'Well, that ain't a *man*!' (*Ibid.*, p.17)

Later in the same text, in a section entitled 'The Language of Class', Reynolds gives an analysis of this and other distinctions:

In Under Town, I notice, a gentleman is always *gen'leman*, a workman or tramp is *man*, but the fringers, the inhabitants of the neutral zone, are called *persons*. For example: 'That *man* what used to work for the council is driving about the *gen'leman* as stays with Mrs Smith – the *person* what used to keep the greengrocery shop afore she took the lodging house on East Cliff Street.

He gives other examples of class-determined vocabulary:

Jimmy and Tommy have a name of their own for the little rock cakes their mother cooks. They call them *gentry-cakes* because such morsels are fitted for the – as Jimmy and Tommy imagine – smaller mouths of ladies and gentlemen. The other day Isobel told me that a boat she had found belonged not to a boy but to a *gentry-boy*.   (*Ibid.*, p.18)

The use of terms such as 'gentleman' and its corresponding term 'lady' was also discussed by linguists such as Wyld under the rubric of 'differences due to class'; it was described as 'felt by many to be contrary to the best usage' (Wyld, 1907, p.64).

Not the least interesting aspect of Reynolds's account is the fact that it is amongst the earliest well-documented evidence of the sort of linguistic issues that have dominated the modern study of sociolinguistics. One such issue has been the process of code-switching by certain speakers in particular contexts. In his account Reynolds describes how the oldest daughter of the family with which he lived would return home on holidays from domestic service with her friends and fall between two 'codes' in manners and speech:

In imitating the one code,   nsuccessfully, they lose their hold on the other. Their very peech – a mixture of dialect and standard English with false intonations – betrays them. They are like a man living abroad who has lost grip on his native customs, and has acquired ill the customs of his adopted country.   (Reynolds, 1909, p.217)

What is at stake here is a form of linguistic alienation in which the entry into domestic service entails both a geographic and social removal. As Jenny enters the service of a different class she has to learn the manners and speech appropriate to it and yet she cannot acquire such features 'correctly', of course, since as Wyld had argued it is more a question of birth (and, in part, unconscious education) than of conscious acquisition. The result is that Jenny is unable to function easily in the new patterns but in the attempt to do so finds herself also removed from the older patterns and thus is alienated from both as both become strange and uneasy. Reynolds, on the other hand, drawn from a different social class, describes himself as having 'managed to preserve the ability to speak dialect in spite of all the efforts of my pastors and masters to make me talk the stereotyped, comparatively inexpressive compromise which goes by the name of King's English'. He then continues with a comparison of the dialect and 'Standard English' by arguing that 'the flexibility and expressiveness of dialect lies largely in its ability to change its verbal form and pronunciation from a speech very broad indeed to something approaching Standard English'. He then specifies examples:

> 'You'm a fool', is playful; 'You'm a fule', less so.
> 'You're a fool', asserts the fact without blame; while 'Thee't a fule', or 'Thee a't a fule!' would be spoken in temper, and the second is the more emphatic. The real difference between 'I an't got nothing', 'I an't got ort', and 'I an't got nort' – 'Oo't?' 'Casn'?' 'Will 'ee?' and 'Will you?' – 'You'm not', 'You ain't', 'You bain't' and 'Thee a'tn't' – are hardly to be appreciated by those who speak only standard English. *Thee* and *thou* are used between inmates, as in French. *Thee* is usual from a mother to her children, but is disrespectful from children to their mother.   (*Ibid.*, pp.82–3)

It is clear from these accounts that language was a crucial social marker and bearer of social and cultural difference. Therefore, whether the evidence be lexical, phonetic or grammatical, it points to the fact that language was always out of the control of the speaker in the sense that language always betrayed social status. The nature of the society determined how the speaker would be heard rather than any determining consciousness since the reception of idiom, accent and grammar was socially constructed rather than 'purely' linguistic. The reception of the speaker's words was at least in part determined by the evaluations, biases and preoccupations of the hearer, and these were constructed in accord with the politics of discourse.

The articulate and the barbarians

The division of society could be made in various ways and one of the most interesting in early-twentieth-century Britain was that which divided British society in linguistic terms into the articulate and the barbarians. One educationalist argued, in his work on 'the school teaching of English', that his pupils could be assigned to three classes: those 'who have a natural inherited taste for good prose and poetry' (by which, he specifies, he means those pupils from a middle-class background with access to books); those 'who, under wise and sympathetic treatment can be made to enjoy and profit by the literature lesson'; and finally 'those stolid young barbarians who appear to have absolutely no interest in literary expression' (Wilson, 1905, pp.80–3).[1] Social classes were evidently thought of in relation to access to literature and language and what is more this 'fundamental cleavage' was perceived as one across which it was almost impossible to pass. The articulate and the barbarians could not even address each other since there was no apparent language for the purpose, no 'shared knowledge' to facilitate communication. On this point Reynolds argued that, 'the articulate classes, moreover, are actually so little acquainted with the inner life of the poor that there is no groundwork of general knowledge upon which to base conclusions (Reynolds, 1909, p.166). In this case he attacks 'the articulate classes' for pre-judging the poor since they could not know what their life was like and this was a difficulty also noted by another social observer, Margaret Loane, who commented that 'it was difficult for members of the educated classes to keep up any conversation with the poor' (Loane, 1905, p.93). The articulate and the barbarians could not communicate because there was no shared system of language or knowledge and no equality of access to the media in which particular discourses took place. Education, for example, was clearly one such discourse and by definition the 'educated' had had access to it and, also by definition, the barbarians had not. However, when the problem was raised it was not inequality that was challenged but its results since as Reynolds observed:

> It was but natural that the fully articulate class, among whom discussion is fast and fairly free, should concentrate their attention chiefly upon the very apparent diseases of the less articulate classes, which can only speak for themselves, at best, through the comparatively clumsy machinery of elections and trade unions. Social reform came very largely to mean reform of those inarticulate classes. (Reynolds and Wooley, 1911, p.168)

The 'less articulate classes' had a limited access to discourse (democratic though it was) and their 'very apparent diseases' were to be remedied by a large-scale reform of the 'inarticulate'. The remedy proposed was that the barbarians were to be given a share in the common, 'standard language'.

Images of the barbarians were usually lurid and menacing and Masterman reported that many social observers saw the new city race as:

> charged with a menace to the future. They dread the fermenting, in the populous cities, of some new, all-powerful explosive, destined one day to shatter into ruin all their desirable social order. In these massed millions of an obscure life, but dimly understood and ever increasing in magnitude, they behold a danger to security and all pleasant things. Therefore the cry goes up as foretold by Mazzini: 'The Barbarians are at our gates'. (Masterman, 1904a, pp.61–2)

These 'massed millions' were a 'menace' and 'a danger to security and all pleasant things' and the principal reason for this is that they stood outside the city, excluded from its environs and banging on the gates. The barbarians were always alien and foreign, a forceful mass only 'dimly understood' and thus threatening ruin. Reynolds had given an example of one such barbarian in the figure of Jenny. Taken into domestic service she is in such a role a foreigner, one with peculiar 'manners and speech' that need reforming in order to allow her to carry out her function properly. He gives another example in his text *The Holy Mountain*, in which the protagonist is accompanied by Jim, a fisherman, upon a trip to London and then France:

> Upon our third-class weekend tickets was stamped, 'Issued subject to the Aliens Immigration Act'. I had visions of being herded with exceptionally venomous aliens into a big wooden room; of trying to convince an East-country inspector of human cargoes, that Jim's broad Devonian tongue, with its modified *u*, was not foreign English; of having to worry our way back to our own England. 'I bain't no alien!' said Jim. But had it not been remarked that he singularly resembles a Breton fisherman in build and, as if to confirm it, had not a London 'busman shouted out to him in the Strand in Cockney French?   (Reynolds, 1910, p.271)

Again the economy of exclusion is marked: the aliens that British law attempts to exclude have to be 'exceptionally venomous' and yet the evident danger is that Jim can be taken as such. Jim's 'broad Devonian tongue with its modified *u*' clearly marks him out as an alien, a barbarian, a 'foreign English' speaker; and thus it is clear that it would not be Jim who would argue with the inspector, but the articulate protagonist. Every time Jim spoke he unintentionally signalled his exclusion: 'I bain't no alien!' simply serves to confirm his alien status. Arguing against the stigmatising of a particular form of discourse *in* that form was an impossible task since every time you opened your mouth you ensured your own condemnation. Other features are significant too but it is the language that counts as the most important in this economy of inclusion and exclusion.

The barbarians then were internal exiles whose very appearance caused shock and whose carnivalesque behaviour disrupted the order of the city:

> We gazed at them in startled amazement. Whence did they all come, these creatures with strange antics and manners, these denizens of another universe of being? . . . They drifted through the streets hoarsely cheering, breaking into fatuous irritating laughter, singing quaint militant melodies. . . . As the darkness drew on they relapsed more and more into bizarre and barbaric revelry – where they whispered now they shouted, where they had pushed apologetically, now they shoved and collisioned and charged. They blew trumpets, hit each other with bladders; they tickled passers-by with feathers; they embraced ladies in the streets, laughing generally and boisterously. Later the drink got into them, and they reeled and struck, and swore, walking and leaping and blaspheming God.
> (Masterman, 1902, p.3)

These are the barbarians, 'strange', 'bizarre' 'denizens of another universe of beings' whose 'strange antics and manners' disrupt order and regularity. These are the unpredictable creatures who were transformed by the fall of night and drink, and commit acts of 'barbaric revelry', swearing and blaspheming God. 'Barbarian', however, did not simply mean strange, or even hostile since its etymological origins demonstrated its force as a marker of language-related exclusion. In Greek there are a number of terms and concepts that reveal this linguistic alienation: βαϱβαϱίξω, to behave or speak like a barbarian, to speak broken Greek, to speak gibberish; βαϱβαϱοφωνέω, to violate the laws of speech, to commit barbarisms; βαϱβαϱοστομία, a barbarous way of speaking; βαϱβαισμός, the use of a foreign tongue, or the use of one's own tongue amiss; βάϱβαϱοι, all the non-Greek speaking peoples, that is not ῞Σλληνες. Language is the central component of these criticisms since it is upon this basis that the judgements of exclusion are made: barbarian, according to at least one etymology, referred to the speakers whose mouths could utter nothing but the rough sounds 'Bar-Bar'. This pattern of linguistic difference as a threat, a marker of cultural difference, and an aberration from a central form of the language, is a factor in patterns of cultural exclusion ranging from the Greeks to the biblical mispronunciation of 'shibboleth' (Judges, 12.6) to the examples given here. And the nineteenth-century and early-twentieth-century barbarians like their ancient counterparts were geographically and culturally on the wrong side of the barriers, beyond the pale but on its margins demanding entrance. When they did gain entry, as Masterman pointed out, their appearance was perceived as noisy and raucous: 'they reeled and struck and swore, walking and leaping and blaspheming God'.

The concept of the standard spoken language can be seen as functionally equivalent to the Hellenic language, the central, 'correct' and 'pure' language spoken by the best speakers (ἕλληνες). The barbarians of course did not speak it since they spoke dialects, vulgar or provincial forms of speech, non-standard forms full or errors and corruptions. On this point, as well as the opinions of linguists such as Jones and Wyld, useful evidence is provided by that whole host of early sociological observers of the urban poor of the opinion of the 'articulate' classes towards the 'barbarians'. Loane, a district nurse attending to the urban poor, noted that 'compulsory education has had a great effect on the vocabulary of the poor, and has swept away many differences of pronunciation, but errors in grammar are perhaps as frequent as ever' (Loane, 1905, p.65). It was a view shared by Wilson, who argued that 'it is a fair subject for discussion whether, in some districts, the effect of our speech drill in schools will ever be strong enough to prevail against outside influences, many of which tend not merely to the provincial, but to the vulgar'. He continues to wonder 'if it is possible to eradicate provincialisms, some of which, at least, are probably due to climactic causes' (Wilson, 1905, p.38). Such defects would be beyond redemption since they are naturally occurring results of the climate in which the poor live.

There was, then, a very clear perception of the differences between the sub-standard language of the barbarians and the standard language of the articulate and Loane gives an extended appraisal of the matter:

At the present day the language of the poor differs from that of the upper and middle classes only in the following points:
(i) *Intonation*, which cannot possibly be reproduced or even indicated.
(ii) *Pronunciation and accentuation*: the differences, although unmistakeable, are often too slight to be represented by any arrangement of the alphabet, however distracting and uncouth.
(iii) *Vocabulary*. This is more limited but the difference in that respect rapidly decreases; the poor are beginning to use freely the language that they see in print, while the rich carefully avoid any bookish tinge. . . . There are, of course, different words in use among the poor for some things. . . .
(iv) *Superabundance of negatives*, e.g. 'I shouldn't think none couldn't guess that, not nohow'.
(v) *Other grammatical errors*. These are nearly all on the lines of simplification; for example, hisself and theirselves, comed, goed, seed, bringed; the verb not agreeing with the subject (I go to school still and are still in the sixth standard). Use of thee.
(vi) The constant use of 'as' for 'that'. . . .
These carried out in detail exhaust the differences which mark the speech of the poor as I know them.

Given this, it is no surprise that Loane prefaces her list with the comment that she had 'often listened to the poor day after day until the sound of a cultured voice strikes on my ear like the rarest and most exquisite music' (Loane, 1905, pp.112–15). There can be no doubt that the language of the barbarians was viewed as a cacophany, a discordant clash of sound that provokes abhorrence, fear and exclusion. For some it was pestilence to the ear because it was corrupt and infected since, as the educationalist Sampson put it, the children of the poor begin education with their 'language in a state of disease' (Sampson, 1925, p.28).

Such stigmatisation led to an effect that many of the early sociological observers believed they saw, which was the silencing of the barbarians, or at least the refusal of audience or readership to the discourse that they produced. Reynolds

reported one working-class informant as arguing that the role
of education should be to teach the children how to compete
in discourse. He asks what sort of education working-class
children should have and is told that 'they ought to learn 'em
to read and write and reckon *well*, which they don't do, and
to speak for themselves, so that them as can chatter shan't
browbeat 'em down' (Reynolds, 1909, p.310). Masterman, on
the other hand, perceived what appears to be an actual
silencing taking place as he describes a queue of working-class
women and men outside a pub on a Sunday lunchtime waiting
for the opening as a 'strange, silent crowd'. He noted that
'there is no speech nor language, no manifest human discourse,
no human aim or visible object' (Masterman, 1902, p.86).
One way of accounting for this silence would be to put it
down to eager anticipation since Masterman later describes
the pub as humming with noise. A more interesting way of
reading it, however, would be to account for it theoretically
since in linguistic and discourse theory there is a distinction
between speech and discourse on the one hand and noise or
mere sound on the other. A noise or sound cannot be counted
as a speech sound until it has a place within the linguistic
system and users who use it. At this point it rises from the
status of a noise to that of a speech sound with structured
possibilities, or to put the point in the terminology of post-
Saussurean linguistics, it changes from being a phonetic unit
to a phonemic unit.[2] If we extend this theoretical distinction
to Masterman's claim it follows that the working-class
speakers make noise but are not counted as engaging in
discourse because the noises they make are not part of the
'standard language' system. They may well be able to converse
amongst themselves, but in the public sphere that demands
the use of a specific form of discourse their speech sounds are
relegated to the status of mere noise. It is in effect a form of
noisy silence.

In a section of *From the Abyss* entitled 'Of the Silence of Us'
Masterman comments on the 'silence':

> If the first thing to note is our quantity, the second is our
> silence – a silence that becomes the more weird and uncanny
> with the increasing immensity of our number. That one or

a few should pass through life dumb is nothing noteworthy; when the same mysterious stillness falls upon hundreds of thousands the imagination is perplexed and baffled. In some forms of disturbed dream a crowded panorama occupies the scene; each figure acts his part in the dumb show; there is apparent activity and motion, but no sound discernible. And the terror of the situation is somehow interwoven with this silence; it weighs down as with a sense of physical oppression; could one only once cry aloud, it appears, the fantastic vision would vanish away. A similar feeling is experienced in the contemplation of the moving crowds of the abyss; could they but in a moment of illumination be stimulated to a united utterance, one feels that strange events would follow. (Masterman, 1902, pp.18–19)

Each line of this remarkable description of the situation of the barbarians is interesting: the silence is 'weird and uncanny', a 'terror' with 'a sense of physical oppression'. This is the fear that one might witness in encountering the 'dumb', or those who can make noises but cannot speak, those whose noise is not elevated to the level of 'sound', those who are forced to communicate in other, more gestural, semiotic codes. This is the 'mysterious stillness' that leaves the observer 'perplexed and baffled' since it is like a 'disturbed dream', a nightmare or a 'fantastic vision' in which thousands take part but in which the actors, or 'figures', are silent, acting parts in a 'dumb show'. They act, or at least there is 'apparent activity', but they do so with 'no sound discernible'. Therefore, to rid oneself of this silent nightmare one has to imagine its antithesis; to overturn the mysteriously still dumb show of physically oppressed figures one had to imagine instead a 'moment of illumination' that could bring about a 'united utterance' from which 'strange events would follow'. At the moment, however, the 'united utterance' is distant and possibly only in the imagination. The actual situation is silent:

always noisy, we rarely speak; always resonant with the din of many-voiced existence, we never reach that level of ordered articulate utterance; never attain a language that the world beyond can hear. We boast no leaders, no interpreters, no recognised channels of expression. (*Ibid.*, p.20)

Again we see the very careful distinction that Masterman draws here between 'noise' and 'ordered articulate utterance' since there is noise here but it is the noise of many voices that amount to no more than a din. There is noise but not 'ordered articulate utterance', noise then but no language. This is the situation of the barbarians again, since if classically they were those who did not speak Hellenic Greek now they are those who do not speak the standard language, the language of the 'educated', 'articulate', 'best speakers'. They are the speakers who make a din from which educated speakers such as Loane have to flee in order to return to the 'rarest and most exquisite music' of a 'cultured voice'. These barbarians are reduced to silence because they have no language, or at least no language that counts as language since they lack 'a language that the world beyond can hear'. Thus:

We are very silent, so silent that no one to this hour knows what we think on any subject, or why we think it. . . . We take up the burden of silent work through long years of silent endurance. We rear up others to compete against us in a similar life. At length, at the closing of the day, we pass to a silent grave; of the meaning of this dim, silent life existence we have no power to ascertain. (*Ibid.*, pp.24–5)

Language, nation and citizenship

Masterman clearly thought the 'moment of illumination' to be distant and felt that the barbarians had no power to alter their 'silent life existence'. Yet he had also commented earlier upon the disruptive (though marginal) appearance of the barbarians as they upset the normal patterns of existence by their carnivalesque creation of disorder. What is more, the barbarians were 'charged with a menace to the future' (inarticulate as it was) and even more disturbing, they were at the gates of the citadel. If in 1902 the 'moment of illumination' appeared distant, there were times over the next twenty years when it appeared close at hand and the 'dumb show' became dramatic history. In Yeats's words from 'Easter 1916', many resigned their part in 'the casual comedy' of 'meaningless words' to take on different roles.

In the first quarter of the twentieth century the British state was shaken to its core by a pattern of events that appeared to indicate that a moment of menacing 'united utterance' had arrived. Working-class militancy in the periods 1911–13, 1919–20 and, of course, during the General Strike, brought about fears and anxieties that are clearly indicated in the debates and practices that took place across a number of different fields from the extensions of the Defence of the Realm Act to the educational reforms passed by the Education Minister Fisher. There were other barbarians who also found their voices at this time too as the militancy and persistence of the Suffragette movement radically altered at least the official status of women in British society. And of course the 'wyld Irysh' renounced the 'casual comedy' of Gaelic brotherhood and declared the war upon Britain that was to lead to the secession of the 26 countries. These were indeed alarming times as new voices demanded the right to be heard and it reminded some observers of events scarcely a century before when the Chartists had articulated radical demands that also produced powerful effects. In fact the Newbolt Report *On The Teaching of English* (1921) explicitly cited the parallel and commented that just as the Newbolt Committee was set up to confront the dangerous menace now threatening, in the same way an earlier committee had been founded to confront another dangerous 'threat'. The Report noted that:

> Fear of the danger to the State that an illiterate population might constitute became a powerful motive after the Reform Bill of 1832, and in 1833 the House of Commons made its first grant towards the cost of education. In 1839 the Committee of the Privy Council on Education was created, Sir James Kay-Shuttleworth becoming its first Secretary. (Newbolt, 1921, p.41)

In the early part of the nineteenth century the danger was

posed by the Chartist movement; in the early part of the twentieth century the danger was posed by the 'inarticulate' barbarians at the gates of the city.

The response to the threat posed by the barbarians at the city gates in the twentieth century was to be the same as that proposed in the nineteenth: to 'civilise' the barbarians. Etymologically, at least, this was a proposal to bring the barbarians into the citadel and thus to make them citizens. Placed outside the city, at the gates, the barbarians are dangerous since they are beyond the pale of 'civilised law and order' and it is possible that they could break open the gates and cause 'startled amazement'. By bringing them in the threat would at least be lessened since they would then be open to the force of law and order and in this process would become 'better people'. And if one could not physically bring them into the city then an alternative was to extend the city boundaries in order to include them, thereby extending the force of the law and order of civilisation in order that it gained new subjects for its domain. It was in such an extension that a specific view of language was to have a significant role.

In an interesting debate 'On the Terms Briton, British, Britisher', the linguist Henry Bradley and the poet Robert Bridges debated the historical (and therefore contemporary) meanings of these terms in a pamphlet of ᵗhe Society for Pure English. Evidently such terms were important since the whole period was rent with anxiety about international and intra-national identity and they noted that:

> In both Europe and Asia legislators are at this time anxiously in search of the factors that determine nationality, and among the determinants it would seem that language, which prescribes our categories and forms of thought, shapes our ideals, preserves our trade, and carries all our social relations and intercourse, had the most solid claims.
> (Bradley, 1928, p.11)

Such anxiety had largely been caused by the after-effects of the most important of all the early-twentieth-century crises (though linked to them all and therefore not isolable as an event in itself), the First World War. Internationally such

problems were clear in the treaties and conferences instituted
to settle national territories and identities, and within Britain
too the effects of the catastrophe were pronounced. This was
the first war in which the whole population was directly or
indirectly involved (with large numbers of young men and
women leaving their districts, to say nothing of their country,
for the first time), and it was the first in which the population at
home received widely disseminated (though often inaccurate)
information about the casualties of the conflict. It was a war
that revealed that when the British people were medically
examined *en masse* for the first time in 1917 (for the purposes
of conscription), 10 per cent of its young men were totally
unfit for service, 41.5 per cent of them had 'marked disabilities'
and 22 per cent had 'partial disabilities'. It was also a war
that increased all of those percentages by its end. The effects
of the war are now difficult to perceive (in the sense of being
difficult to disentangle from those of the general crisis of the
period), but at the time it appeared as though the whole basis
of nationality and citizenship would need to be renegotiated.
As the influential political theorist Ernest Barker wrote during
the war:

> This, after all, is perhaps the real thing which those who
> return – whether they return in flesh or whether they come
> back to us in the spirit – will wish to say. . . . It will be
> much when we make peace with the enemy. It will be more
> when we make a real concord one with another, and when,
> instead of fighting each as for his own hand, we solemnly
> covenant ourselves into one Commonwealth, one country,
> one college, and one factory. We shall only have won the
> war by consenting to be one body, and each one of us a
> member thereof, doing his appointed function for
> it.   (Barker, 1917, pp.21–2)

This is again a Burkean appeal for 'the solemn partnership of
the living and the dead' or, as Barker called it in a piece
entitled 'The City of God', 'the communism of the quick and
the dead in a common citizenship'.

    In fact the problem of what constituted a common national-
ity or citizenship was theoretically addressed by Barker in a

number of texts in this period. He argued first that 'our citizenship is an historical formation; and we shall best understand its nature and its obligations if we study its growth and examine its history'. And second that 'a nation is a material basis with a spiritual superstructure' (Barker, 1927, pp.v & 2). For Barker, what made a nation a nation is 'essentially the unity which it is in virtue of that "spiritual superstructure" which it has built by its own hands for its own dwelling' (*ibid.*, p.7). Race, territory, and occupation are only relatively important since 'it is one, and has a character of its own, by virtue of the unity of its tradition' and thus, 'a Nation is not the physical fact of one blood, but the mental fact of one tradition' (*ibid.*, p.12). What Barker calls the 'material' basis is important but not as important as the cultural superstructure since he argues that 'what divides a nation internally may be even more differences in culture than economic differences' (*ibid.*, p.222). Cultural unity therefore was crucially important to the unity of the nation and an important factor in such unity was the 'superstructural' feature of language. Barker concluded on this point that:

> Just because a nation is a tradition of thought and sentiment, and thought and sentiment have deep congruities with speech, there is the closest of affinities between nation and language. Language is not mere words. Each word is charged with associations that touch feelings and evoke thoughts. You cannot share these feelings and thoughts unless you can unlock their associations by having the key of language. You cannot enter the heart and know the mind of a nation unless you know its speech. Conversely, once you have learned that speech, you find that with it and by it you imbibe a deep and pervasive spiritual force.   (*Ibid.*, p.13)

Language is the key as it is 'a deep and pervasive spiritual force' for unity and a community with a single language is a nation. He can therefore explain the 'historical formation' of 'our citizenship':

> The State does not create the national language, but it can

make a local dialect into a national possession, as it did in England, in France, and in Germany; and when a national speech is formed, and a national literature is developed, the bonds of a common written tradition and a common culture of the mind are added.   (*Ibid.*, p.12)

Barker fails here to draw the distinction between the concepts of a 'national speech' and a 'national literature' since as was argued earlier, the 'common written tradition' may be traceable, but the 'common culture' of speech offers a much more difficult conceptual and empirical problem. However, even if the argument were correct (since we are not for the moment interested in contesting that), Barker's conclusions would still be wrong. Even if it were true that a nation is a group with a common 'material basis' and common 'superstructure of language and culture' it would still not follow that England, in these terms, was a nation. Indeed, England in these terms would specifically *not* be a nation since economic and cultural differences divided it in many ways, not least in the realm of language. However, what is of interest is not whether Barker was wrong about the 'common culture' (since what it would mean to be right about this question is not yet altogether clear), but the vehemence and force with which he makes the argument. As with the nineteenth-century repetition of the link between language and nation it is explicable only in the light of the historical reality that he faced: a divided and heavily stratified culture that anatomised and categorised the supposedly common spoken language according to the class status of its speakers.

The historical reality of early-twentieth-century Britain was outlined by the Minister of Education in the War Cabinet, H.A.L. Fisher, in his speeches in favour of passing the 1918 Education Act. In his speech upon the introduction of the Bill into the Commons Fisher argued that 'the Bill is urgently demanded and connected with the circumstances of the war' since it is 'a time when national unity is a grave and dominant consideration' (Fisher, 1917a, p.1). However, the introduction of such a Bill during war-time was extraordinary and clearly in need of the sort of explanation given in a speech to the Liverpool Education Committee. In it Fisher explained that 'there does exist throughout the community a vague and undefined expectation that the end of the war must see radical changes in our social and educational structure' (Fisher, 1917b, p.1). The war had in fact produced a demand for change and a demand that was not the 'vague and undefined expectation' claimed by Fisher. The demand was much clearer than that suggested by Fisher since as he noted in the same speech, 'there is hardly a meeting of trade-unions that does not pass some resolution in favour of popular education'. Moreover, the war ostensibly produced a different way of viewing the urban proletariat since if previously they were viewed as a threat to the state, now they were viewed as possible aides-in-war. Fisher asserted that:

> These ordinary children from a Liverpool slum are not merely to be considered as hands in a factory. They have within them the potentialities of great service to the State, they have something in them which, when the call of civic duty comes, will prompt them to give their all to their country.   (*Ibid.*, p.9)

In fact the war altered many perceptions of the barbarians since the threat they posed at the city gates was postponed by the war and, as Fisher argued, there were new expectations appearing, new demands being voiced, and new perceptions required. Fisher described this as a 'movement of opinion' that had taken place during the war years and he states the changed perceptions in his speech to the House of Commons (1917). He noted:

> The increased feeling of social solidarity which has been created by the War. When you get conscription, when you get a state of affairs under which the poor are asked to pour out their blood and be mulched in the high cost of living for large international policies, then every just mind begins to realise that the bonds of citizenship are not determined by wealth, and that the same logic that leads up to desire an extension of the franchise, points also to an extension of education.

The barbarians have been brought into the citadel as the force of the law and order of civilisation (conscription) has made them its subjects and they can now be made full citizens (after having 'proved' themselves in war) by the bestowal of the right to vote and to be educated. The 'logic' of awarding voting rights to the barbarians also demands that they be given the means by which they could become 'articulate' since if the vote was a right to make your writing count, education (as will be argued later) was to have the aim of making your speech count as an articulate citizen by 'enabling' you to use the 'correct' form of discourse.

Fisher writes as though the desire for the extension of the franchise was current amongst parliamentarians and the middle classes generally, though of course it was not (*The Times*, for example, did not accept the principle of democracy until 1914). The desire and campaign for the franchise came primarily from those who did not have it and they were working-class men and all women. Yet towards the workers in particular attitudes were changing and Fisher noted that:

> There is a growing sense, not only in England but throughout Europe, and I may say especially in France, that the industrial workers of the country are entitled to be considered primarily as citizens and as fit subjects for any form of education from which they are capable of profiting. I notice also that a new way of thinking about education has sprung up among many of the more reflecting members of our industrial army. They do not want education in order that they may become better technical workmen and earn higher wages. They do not want it in order that they may rise out of their class, always a vulgar ambition; they want it because they know that, in the treasures of the mind, they can find an aid to good citizenship, a source of pure enjoyment from the necessary hardships of a life spent in the midst of changing machinery in our hideous cities of toil.   (Fisher, 1917a, p.4)[3]

There is a clear linkage here between being considered as a citizen and as a fit subject for education on the basis that education was a requisite component for being civilised. Moreover, Fisher claims to perceive a shift in the attitude of the new citizens towards their new right since he argues that the workers no longer see education as the way to become better workers in order to earn better pay, though there is little, if any, evidence to show that this was ever an important factor in the demand for education. He also argues that workers do not want education in order that they can rise out of their class as individuals though in fact, given that the two most popular subjects demanded by workers were Political Economy and English, one might conclude that many workers saw education as a possible means of rising with their class rather than out of it. And he concludes by asserting that the new citizens know the real reason for educational provision: access to 'the treasures of the mind' which will act as a pleasurable palliative to the 'necessary hardships' of the worker's life, since this, of course, tends towards the creation of 'good citizenship'.

To be strictly chronological, the civilising process of education was bestowed upon the new citizens before they gained the right to vote as citizens since Fisher's Act, tabled in 1917 and passed in 1918, slightly pre-dates the two Acts extending the franchise (1918 and 1928). Yet the two developments are so closely linked that the discourses used of them were often mixed. Morley, for example, as President of The English Association, argued that 'this wholescale admission then, of the principle of Universal franchise, male and female, into the world of letters is one mark of our time' (Morley, 1913, p.3). The widening of educational provision became a frequently cited argument in favour of the extension of the franchise since once the barbarians had been civilised through initiation into 'the world of letters' and 'the treasures of the mind' they could then be trusted with the vote. Indeed for some commentators citizenship and being a member of the world of letters were similar on other grounds too., H.C. O'Neill, for example, argues that 'one may enjoy the privilege of living under the protection of a country without possessing that full use and right which comes from citizenship. Similarly, one may learn the craft of letters without achieving the firmness and lucidity of grasp which come from an insight into the reason of things' (O'Neill, 1915, p.v). He addresses what are clearly viewed as faults and half-acquisitions of citizenship and 'the craft of letters': just as one may be under the protection of a community without being a member of it, without understanding it fully, likewise one may be able to read 'literature' without understanding, without having insight into the reason of things. Or to combine the two faults: one may be able to inscribe an 'X' on a ballot paper without understanding the duties and obligations of citizenship that this allegedly entails. In fact the aim of O'Neill's text, *A Guide to the English Language, its History, Development and Use*, was to correct these faults and to produce the educated, literate citizen. That is to say, the citizen who realises the duties and rights of the social contract, or in other words, the citizen who is both educated and civilised (according to a specific set of criteria). It is, as Trench had said some sixty years before, an initiation into both the language and the nation. The aim, as for Trench, was to induce an insight into the reason of the language in order to produce a desire for full citizenship of the nation. For other writers too, education was not merely inculcation into English citizenship but citizenship of a more universal type. R.B. McKerrow noted that 'among the minor results of the Great War has been a revival in the interest taken by educationalists and by the general public in the historical study of English literature and of the English language'. After describing such a result as 'minor', however, he then goes on to elevate it to universal status. The question is, he asks, 'to what extent will the study of English increase the student's own enjoyment of life and make him a better citizen of the world. For, after all, this is surely the main purpose of education' (McKerrow, 1921, p.3). The study of English language and literature is to fulfil the humanist purpose of producing better world citizens: civilised and educated citizens of both the English nation and humanity itself.

What sort of nation, one might ask, was it that the new citizens were to enter? One reading of history might inform us that it was a divided nation in which both cultural and economic differences were the foci of deep unrest and anxiety leading to bitter struggle. Contemporary accounts, however, describe the nation differently and Barker asserts that 'there is nothing that comes so near to being the very authentic voice of England as the bells of her village churches, falling and swelling, pealing and dying, from the north to the south and the east to the west' (Barker, 1917, p.9). Here there is a different citizenship on offer, a citizenship of a nation which is both geographically united (from north to south to east to west) and socially united (around the church). The 'authentic voice of England' for this writer is the voice of the rural scene and the falling and swelling of the bells strike a tune with the ups and downs of history, they are not opposed to it. Or to put it in different terms, the 'hideous cities of toil' are inauthentic England since authentic England was the organic rural community gathered around its church.

Romantic Ireland may have been dead and gone, but the myth of Romantic England was alive and flourishing and was, in fact, an important part of the political rhetoric of a politician far more astute and influential than Barker, Stanley Baldwin. Baldwin, Tory Prime Minister in the crucial years 1923 and 1924–9, was properly concerned with the type of nation that the new citizens were to inhabit. He describes what he imagines 'when I ask myself what I mean by England' by answering:

The sounds of England, the tinkle of the hammer on the anvil in the country smithy, the corncrake on a dewy morning, the sound of the scythe against the whetstone, and the sight of a plough team coming over the brow of a hill, the sight that has been seen in England since England was a land, and may be seen in England long after the Empire has perished and every works in England has ceased to function, for centuries the one eternal sight of England. The wild anemones in the woods in April, the last load at night of hay being drawn down a lane as the twilight comes on, when you can scarcely distinguish the figures of the horses as they take it home to the farm, and above all, most subtle, most penetrating, and most moving, the smell of wood smoke coming up in an autumn evening, or the smell of the scutch fires: that wood smoke that our ancestors, tens of thousands of years ago, must have caught on the air when they were coming home with the results of the day's forage, when they were still nomads, and when they were still roaming the forests and the plains of the continent of

Europe. These things strike down into the very depths of our nature, and touch chords that go back to the very beginning of time and the human race, but they are chords that with every year of our life sound a deeper note in our innermost being.   (Barker, 1927, p.7)

The 'sounds' of England, or its 'authentic voice' as Barker described it, were essentially rural: the England of blacksmiths, ploughmen, haymakers and woodsmoke that will last beyond empire and factory. These are the sounds of the organic community at work renewing itself, replenishing itself eternally from the beginning of time to the other end of English history (if there is to be an end). 'The sounds of England', however, were being drowned out by other noises and Baldwin himself asserted that 'these are the things that make England, and I grieve for it that they are not the childish inheritance of the majority of the people to-day in our country' (*ibid.*). Evidently 'the sounds of England' were not the possession of the majority of the people who were citizens of the English nation and though the barbarians were being incorporated as citizens, that process in itself (along with others) meant that they became citizens of a greatly altered nation. Instead of the rural, organic community echoing to the sounds of self-renewal, the new citizens of England were faced with a 'many-voiced existence' in which the voices belonged to different discourses competing for different ends. It was a situation recognised by Baldwin and one which he felt needed opposing:

There is only one thing which I feel is worth giving one's whole strength to, and that is the binding together of all classes of our people in an effort to make life in this country better in every sense of the word. That is the main end and object of my life in politics.   (*Ibid.*, p.16)

For others too such unity was politically critical and in this crisis language and education were to play a significant role.

Language and education

It was commonly held that education was in a state of crisis in early-twentieth-century Britain and this was a view shared alike by the Education Minister and the practitioners of the profession. MacCarthy, President of the Headmasters' Association, argued in 1915 that:

> The victory we hopefully look forward to and the great pacification which is to follow, will teach us the same lesson [of the need for educational reform], for fierce light will have beat upon our dimly-seen deficiences, and fresh impetus will be given to reforms and reconstructions, social and educational. People will be less tolerant than they have been of established machinery or methods, however venerable. . . . My plea for the extension of educational opportunities in the ways I have indicated for the industrial population of poor, backward, 'unenthusiastic' England is based on the irrefutable facts I have given.   (MacCarthy, 1915, pp.3)

Educational reform in particular was viewed as crucial since the war had revealed the inferiority of the English education system in comparison to that of the German nation. Lloyd George, speaking in 1918, asserted that 'the most formidable institution we had to fight in Germany was not the arsenals of the Krupps, or the yards in which they turned out submarines, but the schools of Germany. They were our most formidable competitors in business and our most terrible opponents in war' (quoted in Baldick, 1983, p.83). And Lloyd George, like MacCarthy, issued an explicit warning that education would have to be reformed if 'dire consequences' were to be avoided. The 'dire consequences' were not simply the possibility of losing a future external struggle with a better-educated nation but also the possibility of an internal conflict. 'People', particularly 'the industrial population of poor, back-ward, "unenthusiastic" England' were becoming less tolerant of the established methods as Fisher had noted in his comments on trade union demands. Education then would have to be reformed, but not necessarily in any politically radical manner since curricular changes could be introduced for explicitly conservative purposes. English literature and language could be used again to inculcate a love of England and a respect for social unity. After all, its major author had allegedly directly recommended as much and was often cited in such a way: the literary critic De Selincourt for example held that Shakespeare was 'no subtle political theorist' but even so, 'the first lesson that he read in past history was the imperative need for national unity. The house divided against itself cannot stand'. As for Shakespeare's theory of the State, he evidently believed that 'the state is a complicated human machine in which each separate part contributes its quota to the general efficiency, and it may at any time be thrown out of gear by the failure of one part to perform as its allotted function' (De Selincourt, 1915, pp.20–1). De Selincourt's comment on this is that this 'has just as much value for us as they had for the Elizabethan audience'. Subtle political theorists are not required in order to understand the political direction of an education based on such literary readings as these. However, it is not the intention here to consider the 'social mission of English criticism' in this period since that has been undertaken by Baldick's *The Social Mission of English Criticism 1848–1932* and our principal concern is with the study of language at this time.

Arguments for the centrality of the study of the English language in education were to become increasingly frequent and as early as 1906 Wyld had argued that:

> Not until the English language is placed upon a sound and secure footing as a necessary part of the course in the Secondary Schools of this country, beyond the reach of controversy, can it be said that it occupies the position of dignity and importance in National Education which is its right by every educational and patriotic importance. (Wyld, 1906, p.34)

Wyld himself recommended that the English language, particularly 'the history of the language', should be taught in schools and colleges and therefore produced texts geared to ensuring that such a curriculum could be possible. However, the loudest, most confident and most effective arguments for such study were not presented until the critical 1920s and they were arguments that ranged over the whole scope of the issues that this text addresses: prescription and proscription, the 'standard language', language and citizenship, and language and history. The principal texts were the *Newbolt Report* of 1921 and George Sampson's *English for the English* (1921 and 1925 editions).[4]

Perceptions of the divisions in British society were clear in the 1920s and language in particular was viewed as a powerful dividing factor. Sampson argued that 'in this country classes are sundered by difference in language – difference of speech is a symbol of class antagonism' (Sampson, 1925, p.44). Such a 'superstructural' feature (to use Barker's terms) was often cited as a far more powerful agent of division than more 'material' features and the Newbolt Report itself argued that 'many of the differences between the lot of one class and another are of little importance' but class-related linguistic difference bore enormous significance. The Report asserted that:

> Two causes, both accidental and conventional rather than national, at present distinguish and divide one class from another in England. The first of these is a marked difference in their modes of speech. If the teaching of the language were properly provided for, the difference between educated and uneducated speech, which at present causes so much prejudice and difficulty of intercourse on both sides, would gradually disappear.   (Newbolt, 1921, pp.22–3)

British society was divided to its very core in all cultural fields and yet both the Commissioners and Sampson in his independent study agreed that 'culture', and specifically the study of the English language and literature, could bring about unity and heal divisions. The idea was not an original one since Arnold (along with Burke the most frequently cited cultural commentator in the Report) had argued a similar case fifty years earlier. In fact the Commissioners misquote Arnold in their presentation of his argument but the case they make is substantively similar to his. They argue that the propagation of 'culture' through a rational education would unite classes since:

> If there were any common fundamental idea of education, any great common divisions of the curriculum, which would stand out in such a way as to obliterate, or even to soften, the lines of separation between the young of different classes, we might hope to find more easily the way to bridge the social chasms which divide us. (*Ibid.*, p.6)

The 'social chasms' were evident to even the casual observer and thus any 'instrument' for the eradication of cultural division took on enormous significance and, by corollary, any 'instrument' that fostered division was to be opposed with equal enthusiasm.

It followed from this that the training of children in schools appeared to be of particular significance and thus Sampson declared that 'as long as the elementary school is the chief means of humanising the masses, it is the most important school in the country' (Sampson, 1925, p.16). This demonstrates that education had taken on a new and significant status since it was again to become the focus of calls for national and social unity, as the site at which the last stand against the destructive forces of mass civilisation would take place. Yet the Commissioners noted anxiously that there was no 'common fundamental idea of education [or] great common divisions of the curriculum' and argued that 'in this country we have no general or national scheme of education' (p.5). It was evident therefore that their task was to establish such an idea and such a curriculum.

The public schools had, in the eyes of the Newbolt Commissioners, acted as a harmful influence with their favouring of the classics since they had thereby detracted from the possibility of attaining a national culture. Which is to say that they had prevented the teaching of the one subject of which it was possible even to conceive of teaching in all schools to all classes: English. The effect of this curricular ordering was clear to the Commissioners:

> Greek would enable a clergyman to read the New Testament in the original, Latin would qualify a barrister to study Roman law, or a doctor to write his prescriptions; Mathematics was essential to the soldier, sailor, or engineer. But for English there seemed no call. (Newbolt, 1921, p.98)

By 1920, however, the call for English seemed deafening and the study of English language and literature was now viewed as a necessary force for social unity and the inculcation of citizenship. The Newbolt Report argued that a 'liberal education' built upon English:

> Is the greatest benefit which could be conferred upon any citizen of a great state, and that the common right to it, the common discipline and enjoyment of it, the common possession of the tastes and associations connected with it, would form a new element of national unity, linking together the mental life of all classes by experiences which have hitherto been the privilege of a limited section. (*Ibid.*, p.15)

That is to say, the Commissioners were arguing for the construction of a 'common culture' through careful study of 'English for the English'.

The Report notes the direct effect that the war had had on education as students turned mainly to 'historical or social' subjects. Yet the whole thrust of the Report was that the study of English was social, historical and much more besides, and was therefore to be the cornerstone of English education. The franchise, education and the teaching of English were often linked in these critical debates as in the literary critic Dover Wilson's observation that 'it is no accident that 1832 and 1867, the dates of the two great Acts of political enfranchisement, coincide with dates equally important in the history of education' (Dover Wilson, 1928, pp.22–3). He also noted 'the fashion in which the development of our educational system keeps step with development of our constitution as a whole'. Thus the extension of the franchise to ever larger sections of the population meant that education would need to be extended too and English was the only subject that could bear the weight of such an increase. Sampson put the argument succinctly:

> There is no class in the country that does not need a full education in English. Possibly a common basis of education might do much to mitigate the class antagonism that is

dangerously keen at the moment and shows no sign of losing
its edge. . . . If we want that class antagonism to be
mitigated, we must abandon our system of class education
and find some form of education common to the schools
of all classes. A common school is, at present, quite
impracticable. We are not nearly ready yet to assimilate
such a revolutionary change. But though a common school
is impracticable, a common basis of education is not. The
one common basis of the common culture is the common
tongue.   (Sampson, 1925, p.39)

English was to be the cornerstone because through it alone
could the masses be reached and the barbarians civilised since
'through English, humane culture first becomes a possession
and then a delight' (Newbolt, 1921, p.201). Moreover, in such
a process class antagonism would at least be 'mitigated' or,
at best, eradicated with the disappearance of classes, as both
Arnold and the Commissioners intended. However, if this
process was to take place then the study of the native language
would have to have a central role since only then would the
results be unifying:

The English people might learn as a whole to regard their
own language, first with respect and then with a genuine
feeling of pride and affection. More than any mere symbol
it is actually a part of England: to maltreat it or deliberately
to debase it would be seen to be an outrage; to be sensible
of its significance and splendour would be to step upon a
higher level. In France, we are told, this pride in the
national language is strong and universal; the French artisan
will often use his right to object that an expression 'is not
French'. Such a feeling for our own native language would
be a bond of union between classes, and would beget the
right kind of national pride.   (Newbolt, 1921, p.22)

The language could be used to stimulate pride and affection
and to encourage sentiments of outrage and splendour, and
thus through a process of strong and universal policing of
language bonds of class and national unity could be forged.
Work on the ideology that lay behind the construction of a

'national language' and its deployment in French education has become an area of interest to French scholars recently, but it is interesting that precisely the same interest was demonstrated by the Newbolt Commissioners.[5] They added an Appendix, 'On the Teaching of the Mother Tongue in France', to the Report and analysed the advantages of the French system thus:

> The great interest of the system lies in the fact that we have here a conscious effort to give every child a liberal education through the only medium which can reach the vast majority of the people – the mother tongue; to lead the child through the appreciation of the language and literature of his race to the development of social consciousness and love of country. (*Ibid.*, pp.370–1)

And such was clearly the intention of the educational reforms which placed English at the centre of the liberal English education just as it had been the stimulus for Trench's first appeals earlier.

The classics were to be ousted from their position at the centre of the liberal and humane education since the Commissioners held it to be 'an incontrovertible primary fact' that 'for English children no form of knowledge can take precedence of a knowledge of English, no form of literature can take precedence of English literature: and the two are so inextricably connected as to form the only basis possible for a national education' (*ibid.*, p.14). Indeed they saw the English language as 'the only foundation upon which in this country all else can be built' (p.342) since it was not simply that 'the teaching of English as the instrument of thought and the means of communication will necessarily affect the teaching of every other subject' (p.23), but that English was a subject without bounds, merging across the curriculum. They argued that 'it is impossible to teach any subject without teaching English; it is almost equally impossible to teach English without teaching something else' (*ibid.*, p.63). All subjects involve the English language and it merges with all subjects and, therefore, its educational hegemony was complete.

What was the point of the educational reforms sought by

the Newbolt Commission and Sampson as they saw it? On this the report and Sampson's text are very clear: it was to give language to the 'barbarians'. It aimed to use the educational process to 'civilise' the bad speakers and to provide them with a form of language that would enable them to function as the articulate citizens (newly enfranchised) that they were expected to be. The elementary school had a very clear task:

> Plainly, then, the first and chief duty of the Elementary School is to give its pupils speech – to make them articulate and civilised beings, able to communicate themselves in speech and writing, and able to receive the communication of others. It must be remembered that children, until they can readily receive such communication, are entirely cut off from the life and thought and experience of the race embodied in human words. Indeed, until they have been given civilised speech it is useless to talk of continuing their education, for in a real sense, their education has not begun. (*Ibid.*, p.60)

Such speech as they had was not counted as a form of communication and therefore their education had to begin with the acquisition of 'civilised speech', the only form of discourse that was to count as language. As Sampson put it, 'as our aim is to make the children articulate intelligible human beings, we must equip them with language' (Sampson, 1925, p.xi).

Attitudes towards the language of working-class children were particularly harsh and in the infant department or infants' school (in which children were entered at 4–5 years of age), the Newbolt Report argues that some children were almost etymologically justified in being there since they were without speech (*in fans*). It commented that 'many children, when they first come to school, can scarcely talk at all. Sometimes, a witness told us, they cannot even name their eyes, ears, toes, and so forth' (Newbolt, 1921, p.68). After four or five years of silence in their working-class homes the children are to be given speech since as Sampson says, 'what they lack most of all is language' (Sampson, 1925, p.23). It is difficult to see whether what is meant here is phonetic silence or phonological silence; that is, whether the children cannot speak or whether they cannot speak in such a way as to have their discourse counted. It is akin to Masterman's distinction between noise and 'ordered articulate utterance' and it is a point that Sampson takes up:

> Come into a London elementary school and see what it is that the children need most. You will notice, first of all, that in a human sense, our boys and girls are almost inarticulate. They can make noises, but they cannot speak. Linger in the playground and listen to the talk and shouts of the boys; listen to the girls screaming at their play – listen especially to them as they 'play at schools'; you can barely recognise your native language.   (*Ibid.*, p.21)

Sampson continues on the same page to quote a letter from a schoolboy as an example of illiteracy. Yet it is important to distinguish the charges here. It is clearly correct that basic literacy should be demanded of the schools but it is not literacy that concerns Sampson in the main since it is not access to the standard literary language but to the standard spoken language that concerns him. These elementary schoolchildren cannot speak standard English and therefore 'in a human sense', 'can make noises, but they cannot speak'. Their discourse, no matter how noisy, is reduced to a form of political and cultural 'silence' since they are barbarians outside the bounds of the 'human'. Barbarians make noises but not, by definition, the sounds of 'civilised', 'educated', 'articulate' discourse. However although it was one thing to be *in fans* it was quite another to use barbarian noises and these were the subject of harsh dealing by the Commissioners. They asserted that 'among the vast mass of the population, it is certain that if a child is not learning good English he is learning bad English, and probably bad habits of thought; and some of the mischief may never afterwards be undone' (Newbolt, 1921, p.10). As with Trench's linguistic work, the discourse of morality begins to creep in here as 'good' and 'bad', along with 'mischief', become terms to be used of the language. The fixed binary opposition is clear since it is either 'good English' or 'bad English' and the effects, if bad, may be permanent. Morality was also invoked directly by Sampson when he argued that 'it is specially upon Speech that our work must be bottomed if it is to hold firm. Boys from bad homes come to school with their speech in a state of disease, and we must be unwearied in the task of purification . . . good speech is the firmest foundation of success in all departments of school life' (Sampson, 1925, p.xii). 'Bad' homes produce 'diseased' speech and the poor intelligent child 'has a clear right to have his language cleansed and purified, and we must accept the burden of effort' (*ibid.*, p.24). Just as 'bad homes' produce 'bad English', then by corollary 'good homes' produce 'good English':

> The great difficulty of teachers in Elementary Schools in many districts is that they have to fight against the powerful influences of evil habits of speech contracted in home and street. The teachers' struggle is thus not with ignorance but with a perverted power. That makes their work the harder, but it also makes their zeal the fiercer. A child with home advantages hears English used well, and grows up to use it well himself. He speaks grammatically, he acquires a wide vocabulary, he collects ideas.   (Newbolt, 1921, p.59)

Again moral terms are prominent as 'evil habits of speech' and perversion are pitted against fierce 'zeal' and speaking 'well'. What is again also clear is the marked binary division as bad homes and bad streets produce disease, perversion, evil, and good homes produce good grammatical English, wide vocabulary and intellectual curiosity. In his own work Sampson uses identical terms as 'good English' opposes the 'bad English' of street and home, 'insuperable hostile forces' are ranged against the teacher who is involved in a struggle with 'evil knowledge' and 'degraded English', 'the more powerful forces of evil', and 'a heap of rubbish' (Sampson, 1925, p.24). The speech of the mass of the population is stigmatised as inferior and is clearly not non-standard so much as sub-standard. Moreover such judgements were not confined to the teaching profession since the Newbolt Commission also consulted those who would employ the 'mass of the population' and cites their evaluations as useful evidence:

thus, Messrs. Vickers Ltd., 'find great difficulty in obtaining junior clerks who can speak and write English clearly and correctly, especially those aged from 15 to 16 years'. Messrs. Lever Brothers Ltd., say 'it is a great surprise and disappointment to us to find that our young employees are so hopelessly deficient in their command of English'. Boots' Pure Drug Co say: 'Teaching of English in the present day schools produces a very limited command of the English language'.   (Newbolt, 1921, p.72)

Evidently some remedy was required for this state of affairs and the barbarians against whom teacher and employer struggled would have to be taught a new language of 'civilisation'. Thus in the eyes of the Commissioners the 'earlier stages of education' for all children must consist of:

> First, systematic training in the sounded speech of standard English, to secure correct pronunciation and clear articulation: second, systematic training in the use of standard English, to secure clearness and correctness both in oral expression and in writing: third, training in reading. Under this last head will be included reading aloud with feeling and expression, the use of books as sources of information and means of study, and finally, the use of literature as we have already described it, that is, as a possession and a source of delight, a personal intimacy and the gaining of personal experience, and an end in itself and, at the same time, an equipment for the understanding of life.   (*Ibid.*, p.19)

There are in fact more than three steps here: first, 'systematic training' in the sounds of 'Standard spoken English' with the aim of imposing a uniform mode of pronunciation and articulation. Second, lexical training to secure clarity and correctness in speech and writing. Third, training in 'public speaking' involving problems of intonation. Fourth, an introduction to the 'use of books' involving technical details such as how to use an index, or a catalogue. Finally the use of 'literature' or how to 'read' which involves more than basic literacy and is a training in how to 'read' for certain purposes:

as a source of 'delight', 'experience', and 'the equipment for the understanding of life'. Everything from basic skills to sophisticated techniques for reading; everything from the ability to read to knowing how to read well.

Our primary interest at the moment lies with the first three points and the means by which they could be taught and on this the Report is clear in its summary:

> The means relied on for teaching correct speech should be the correction of mistakes as they arise, the great power of imitation and (at a later stage) the teaching of the general rules to which our standard speech conforms.   (*Ibid.*, p.358)

The mistakes of 'uncouth speech [which] has been assumed to be the natural heritage of the children for whom elementary schools were originally instituted' (p.64) were to be stamped out by constant correction, imitation and learning of a new set of rules. And the process was to be ambitious since the report held that:

> It is emphatically the business of the Elementary School to teach all its pupils who either speak a definite dialect or whose speech is disfigured by vulgarisms, to speak standard English, and to speak it clearly, and with expression. . . . It is not sufficient merely to correct the various errors of pronunciation as they occur, or to insist on children 'speaking out'. They should learn to recognise every sound in standard English, should observe for themselves how sounds are produced and modified by the position of the speech organs, and should practise producing them properly. (*Ibid.*, p.65)

'Standard English' speech then, in a theoretical return to the formulations of Jones and Wyld that indicates the power of such linguistic research, was speech that was not dialectal or provincial and its sounds would have to be described and learnt by the methods of the phoneticians. Sampson was likewise committed to 'systematic training in standard English speech' on the grounds that:

> This country is torn with dialects, some of which are, in

the main, degradations. Enthusiastic 'localists' cling to their dialects – and cling, sometimes, to the merely ignorant mispronunciations, blunders and lapses which they fondly imagine to be part of dialect. . . . The language of all English schools should be standard English speech. It is not the job of teachers either to cherish or destroy a local dialect; they have simply to equip their pupils with normal national speech – as a sort of second language if the grip of the patois is very strong.   (Sampson, 1925, pp.40–1)

As to the question of what 'standard English speech' might be, Sampson is quite clear:

There is no need to define standard English speech. We know what it is, and there's an end on't. We know standard English when we hear it just as we know a dog when we see it, without the aid of definition. Or, to put it another way, we know what is *not* standard English, and that is a sufficiently practical guide. If any one wants a definite example of standard English we can tell him that it is the kind of English spoken by a simple unaffected young Englishman like the Prince of Wales.   (*Ibid.*)

'Standard spoken English' can be defined for this writer in two ways: first in terms of difference, which is to say that we know what 'Standard English' is because we know what it is not (it is not vulgar, provincial, uneducated, inarticulate, uncivilised, bad, evil or perverted English). Second, we know what it is because we recognise who speaks it, such as, for example, 'a simple unaffected young Englishman like the Prince of Wales'. Or to put it another way, 'Standard English' is spoken by those who are not vulgar, provincial, uneducated, inarticulate, uncivilised barbarians.

The Newbolt Report appears to be more circumspect in its definition of 'Standard spoken English' and argues that in the teaching of it, 'the problem is not really one of the use of phonetic symbols, but of what standard English pronunciation is. This is a much debated question, but for our present purpose it should suffice to say that it is a pronunciation free from provincialisms and vulgarisms' (Newbolt, 1921, p.66).

Essentially this is the definition given by Jones and Wyld, and like these two linguists the Newbolt Report ostensibly denies that 'Standard spoken English' is 'socially superior than the other forms'. The Commissioners assert that they did not:

> advocate the teaching of Standard English on any grounds of social 'superiority', but because it is manifestly desirable that all English people should be capable of speaking so as to be fully intelligible to each other and because inability to speak standard English is in practice a serious handicap in many ways.   (*Ibid.*, p.67)

English children, they continue, have the entitlement to be taught 'the accepted speech of their own country' (p.63). There are two arguments for the teaching of 'Standard English speech' presented here: first, that it enables communication since it is the nationally 'accepted speech of their own country'. Second, because the inability to speak 'Standard spoken English' is in practice a handicap, though not on the grounds that 'Standard English' is considered socially superior to other forms. Both of these arguments can be demonstrated to be problematic. First, it is clear from much of the evidence that 'Standard spoken English' was not accepted nationally but merely amongst a small group and moreover, given that it was so clearly the prerogative of an exclusive group, it tended to make communication more difficult not less so. Rather than being a neutral tool for the purposes of communication between classes it functioned as a clear marker of class difference. Therefore the imposition of 'Standard spoken English' was not experienced by its recipients as a mode of enfranchisement but as a form of denial of their own practice since rather than enabling discourse it often prevented it, as linguists often commented. Once the non-standard speaker heard the 'standard accent' silence fell. Second, the inability to speak 'Standard spoken English' was in practice a handicap primarily because the 'standard' form *was* taken as 'socially superior'. And in fact the Newbolt Report did advocate its tuition on the grounds of 'social superiority' since there seems to be no other way of reading epithets such as 'good', 'articulate', 'civilised' rather than 'bad', 'uneducated', 'evil' speech. These are precisely social values since they are values ascribed to the language and to its speakers and they articulate a very clear hierarchy of discourse.

There are many examples given in the text of the Commissioners' sensitivity to the social stratification of forms of language. Pupils in the private preparatory schools 'have, as a rule, much better home opportunities for learning English than elementary school pupils have' the Report declares, and it continues to argue that 'in the Preparatory Schools the dialect difficulty seldom requires to be dealt with' (p.96). Thus, in childhood access to certain forms of language was determined by social class. Such access, however, was also determined by gender since the teaching of 'phonetics' and 'speech training' in schools was strongly recommended by the Report. Most schools, of course, did not teach such subjects but some did:

> Time should be found for phonetics in the many schools that do not yet attempt this subject, though in the girls' schools, speech training generally based on a study of phonetics is not now uncommon.   (*Ibid.*, p.108)

Other than this the report does not comment on this acceptance of the new subject in the girls' schools yet it is clear that this acceptance is part of a more generalised pressure upon women, particularly those of a specific social class, to conform to the 'accepted' patterns of speech. Although this is an interesting example, it is generally in terms of class that linguistic stratification is most clearly dealt with in the report and in such terms that the attitude to the 'standard spoken language' can best be analysed. The report takes up Wyld's insistence on the difficulty of speaking 'Standard spoken English' since, as Wyld had specified, if you are not born to it then the only possible method is to practise imitation of the 'best speakers'. Quoting approvingly from a *Memorandum on Commercial Instruction in Evening Schools* from the Board of Education (1919), the Report declares that:

> There is only one method by which power over the mother-tongue can be acquired: by practice. Those have the best

command of English, who from birth have lived in an environment where accurate language, a copious vocabulary, a pure pronunciation, and the habit of reading are characteristic. All that can be done in a school, therefore, is to reproduce these conditions, so far as is possible. The pupils should be enabled to read good English, to hear good English, and should be practised with a view to their speaking and writing good English.   (*Ibid.*, p.137)

Those who have the 'best command of English' are those who come from a specific type of environment, which amounts finally, in the words of the Report, to those who 'can procure books, and can sit in comparative peace in a warm and well-lit room' (*ibid.*, p.59). The barbarians were not, by definition, from that civilised class and yet it was evidently felt important to 'elevate' them, to 'raise' their status in order that they too could become 'articulate' and 'civilised' speakers of (at least modified) standard English. At particular points of crisis such pressure became direct since it was hoped that giving the barbarians language would not only enable them to function as voting, educated, employable citizens, but would also guarantee their civic responsibility. This was the case since:

Lucidity and command of language . . . will be of service not merely in commercial life, but also in those political and social activities, such as trade union meetings and the like, which are becoming the preoccupation of an ever-increasing number of working people, and where sincerity and clear-headedness are matters of national concern. (*Ibid.*, p.146)

Or as Sampson put it in more stark and negative terms:

Deny to working-class children any common share in the immaterial, and presently they will grow into the men who demand with menaces a communism of the material. (Sampson, 1925, p.x)

By the immaterial here Sampson means the standard spoken language (among other things) and the argument is that the acquisition of this form of speech by the barbarians will lead to their being civilised and articulate citizens, able to communicate 'in a human sense' with their fellow citizens without any class feelings. However, even if there were such a possibility of imposing a 'neutral' form of the language, unaffected by social stratification, it cannot of course follow that 'class-antagonism' would thereby be mitigated. The more important point, however, is that such a possibility is not open: 'Standard spoken English' was not a 'neutral' form of the language but a form recognised by its speakers, by those who did not speak it, and by linguists who specified it in their texts, as the discourse specific to a particular class. Indeed, *that* is the most important basis of its definition.

Conclusion: language against modernity

The *Newbolt Report* and Sampson's *English for the English* both argued for language as an important unifying force socially and nationally and yet both did so in a way which reflected rather than circumvented division. However, to choose language as an important factor of unity and value against forces of decay and corruption was not an untypical gesture in early-twentieth-century Britain. The study of language and of the English language in particular, was invested with enormous social significance across a number of different discourses ranging from literary criticism, to linguistics, to broadcasting, to prime ministerial speeches. The Newbolt Report used a familiar Baconian image in order to argue that:

> The expert in language can perform a real service not only to students but to the community at large by keeping it continually alive to this transvaluation in the meaning of words, and thus helping to free it from the dominion of the idols of the market place.   (Newbolt, 1921, p.220)

Words, as they altered their meanings to keep pace with the changes of the modern world, were to be subjected to the wary critique of the 'expert in language', that careful guardian of the linguistic tradition. And in the early twentieth century groups of such guardians gathered to form societies for these purposes. Logan Pearsall Smith, commenting on the origins of the *Society for Pure English* in 1913, for example, argued that it stemmed from a sense of 'concern about the state of the English language and the danger which seemed to be threatening it under modern conditions' (Pearsall Smith, 1931, p.481). On the one hand language seemed to be threatened by the disintegrative forces of modern mass civilisation, but on the other the growth of the study of language offered the possibility that increased knowledge could prevent the victory of such forces. With this in view, Bridges commented upon Bradley's work on the *OED* in this way:

> He recognised the national importance of that work. He understood thoroughly the actual conditions of our time, and the power of the disruptive forces that threaten to break with our literary tradition. He also knew that these conditions differ from any that we have ever encountered before in as much as we are now possessed by the scientific knowledge and social organisation which can to some extent control the adverse forces, and enable us to guide, if not determine, the development of our speech.   (Bradley, 1928, p.50)

Historical work on the past development of the English language such as that undertaken by the *OED* workers could offer some answers to the linguistic problems of the future, and of course such problems were not viewed as purely linguistic but as having enormous social significance. Against the modern forces of forceful shattering the English language was to be offered once again as an example of unity and gradual evolution. In a reference strikingly similar to nineteenth-century claims the Newbolt Report referred unproblematically to 'the direct linguistic descent of modern English from Anglo-Saxon' (p.224). The modern English nation and language may be threatened by forces of disruption and decay but its strong historical tradition will act as a prophylactic and thus contemporary division can be healed by reference to the unity of the past.

The forces of linguistic destruction were often specified by the linguists and educationalists of this period and they indicated the increased use of slang and jargon as the main threats. Bradley's article on 'slang' in the *Encyclopaedia Britannica*, for example, argued that, 'as the prevailing tendency of words is toward degeneration of meaning, one of the most frequently recurring needs of language is that of words of dignified and serious import to take the place of those which have become cheapened through ignoble use' (Bradley, 1928, p.155–6). He continues to define slang thus:

> Slang, in what is now the usual sense, [is] a general name for the class of words and senses of words, more or less artificial or affected in origin or use, which are not recognised as belonging to the standard vocabulary of the language into which they have been introduced, but have an extensive currency in some sections of society either as a means of concealing secrets or as intentionally undignified substitutes for those modes of expression that are employed by persons who value themselves on propriety of speech. (*Ibid.*, p.145)

The most dangerous thing about 'slang' is that it is 'a conscious offence against some conventional standard of propriety', which is to say that 'slang' is a deliberate ('conscious' and 'intentional') attempt to offend against 'good English' and a deliberate use of non-standard forms in order to disrupt established values. The person who uses slang, according to the literary critic Raleigh, is not using language for its proper end of the communication of thoughts and ideas since the slang-user prevents this type of communication by setting off other questions in the hearer. He argues that 'the strong vivid slang word cannot be counted on to do its work. It sets the hearer thinking, not on the subject of my speech, but on such irrelevant questions as the nature of my past education and the company I keep' (Raleigh, 1926, pp.20–1). Slang contributes to the decay of established values, communication, and also to the destruction of literature:

> The growing tendency of our indulgence in slang, in useless and inelegant colloquialisms, in vulgarisms both clumsy and gross, and in a slackness as opposed to a virility of

speech, threatens a degeneracy of speech which will end by corrupting our literature to a more or less extent. (O'Neill, 1915, p.114)

Evidently all sorts of social values are considered to be at stake in the use of slang, and yet the opprobrium for the use of jargon, though more personalised, is not less keen. Sir Arthur Quiller-Couch, for example, adapting Ben Jonson's assertion in his *Timber, or Discoveries* that 'Language most shows a man: speak that I may see thee', argues on his own part that 'language . . . is your reason, your λόγος. If your language be Jargon, your intellect, if not your whole character will almost certainly correspond' (Quiller-Couch, 1918, p.105). Corruption in language then brings about social, literary and personal decay.

What is of interest in such statements is not simply the anxiety that they demonstrate about language in early-twentieth-century Britain but the fact that such views are missing from most accounts of the history of the study of language in this period. Such views fit more accurately, according to such histories, in earlier periods of the study of language since the views expressed above would not be out of place alongside those Augustan tracts condemning corruption and change in language (say Swift's *Proposal*). Such prescriptive and proscriptive views do not, however, fit the self-images of the nineteenth century and early twentieth century as ages of linguistic objectivity and 'scientificity'. Social and rhetorical issues, however, *were* constantly involved in thinking about language and in the early twentieth century many linguists and educational theorists saw the English language in the early modern period as the last bastion of 'sweetness and light' (to use Arnold's phrase) for cultured values. This led many of them to what was primarily a moral investment in the language. Sampson asked rhetorically:

How is the enemy's growing tyranny to be most effectively fought today? . . . It is because I know that the power of the evil is so strong, and the power of the good as yet so small, that I beg the place of honour in the fight for our own great native force – 'the illustrious, cardinal, courtly and curial vernacular' of England. (Sampson, 1925, p.109)

Moreover, for some slightly more overtly political figures language was a useful site of arguments for morality and politics. Baldwin, for example, constantly argued for 'propriety' in language in his political addresses. Citing Locke's *Essay Concerning Human Understanding* (Bk III, Chapter XI, Para. 4) to the effect that we should 'well consider the errors and obscurity, the mistakes and confusions, that are spread in the world by an ill-use of words'; and Bentham's assertion in his *On Evidence* (Bk III, Chapter 1) that 'error is never so difficult to be destroyed as when it has its roots in language', Baldwin then continues to draw the moral and political conclusions for the English people in his own *On England*. He argues, in an essay called 'Truth and Politics', that, 'no small part of education lies in learning the right use of words, in tracing their birth and behaviour, in fitting them closely to facts and ideas' (Baldwin, 1926, p.80). Furthermore:

> False words, said the dying Socrates, are not only evil in themselves, but they infect the soul with evil. Although the use of words may be abused and the fight for their honour may at times seem hopeless, we must never give up the struggle to use them solely in the service of truth. Let us aim at meaning what we say and saying what we mean. (*Ibid.*, p.91)

Language was to be the site of the struggle for truth, for the intentional coincidence between words, meaning and the world itself. Yet Baldwin did not merely engage in the rhetoric of political philosophy since he also found more concrete examples of the force and potential of the English language. The English language, for Baldwin, particularly through its most accomplished media (The English Prayer Book and The Authorised Version of The Bible) had an unconscious moral effect on the English people:

> Fifty years ago all children went to church, and they often went reluctantly, but I am convinced, looking back, that the hearing – sometimes almost unconsciously – of the superb rhythm of the English Prayer Book Sunday after Sunday, and the language of the English Bible leaves its

mark on you for life. Though you may be unable to speak
with these tongues, yet they do make you immune from
rubbish in a way that nothing else does, and they enable
you naturally and automatically to sort out the best from
the second best and the third best.   (Baldwin, 1928, p.295)

Even unconscious exposure to hearing the 'best English' had
a moral and political effect since it enabled the listeners to go
and sift the language they heard in search of 'rubbish' and
'false words'. Evidently Baldwin had good cause to worry
about the power of rhetoric (including his own) and the use
of 'false words' in the 1920s since it was a period of fierce
challenge to established values and the discourses in which
they were fixed. However, though anxious, Baldwin clearly
thought that he had language on his side as he revealed in an
important Commons speech on national unity entitled 'The
Gospel of Hate' in 1923:

But I am quite certain that whether they [the Labour
Party] succeed or fail, there will never be a Communist
Government, and for this reason, that no gospel founded
on hate will ever seize the hearts of our people – the people
of Great Britain. It is no good trying to cure the world by
spreading out oceans of bloodshed. It is no good trying to
cure the world by repeating the pentasyllabic French
derivative 'Proletariat'. The English language is the richest
in the world in thought. The English language is the richest
in the world in monosyllables. Four words, of one syllable
each, are words which contain salvation for this country
and for the whole world, and they are 'Faith', 'Hope',
'Love', and 'Work'.   (Baldwin, 1926, pp.59–60)

Physical bloodshed is compared to the damage wreaked upon
the language by the use of an imported French pentasyllabic
word in order to suggest that those propagating the 'Gospel
of Hate' would bring about cultural and bodily damage. The
English language itself, however, is on Baldwin's side as,
stocked with monosyllables rather than those devious French
pentasyllabics, it is the more 'virile', 'plain' and straightfor-
ward language of the common English man. Even 'Charity',

a trisyllabic Latin derivative, has to make way for the Anglo-Saxon monosyllabic 'work'. English in Baldwin's rhetorical scheme is not the language of rhetoric since it is the direct, plain, unadorned language of truth. But then what better example of a rhetorical claim could there be?

Language then became the focus of new pressures and new values as cultural patterns changed and one of the founders of a crucial cultural shift at this period, involving a massive revaluation of the national past, also saw language as an important upholder of values. F.R. Leavis argued that:

> At the centre of our culture is language, and while we have our language tradition is, in some essential sense, still alive. And language is not merely a matter of words – or words are more than they seem to be.   (Leavis and Thompson, 1948, p.81)

'But words are words', says one Shakespearean character in a horrible underestimation of the potency of language, since words have an indeterminate multiplicity of uses and potential uses, of causes and effects, of values and functions. In the early modern period one such function became dominant for linguists, literary critics, educational theorists and politicians, and it is best described by the critic I.A. Richards:

> From the beginning civilization has been dependent upon speech, for words are our chief link with the past and with one another and the channel of our spiritual inheritance. As the other vehicles of tradition, the family and the community, for example, are dissolved, we are forced more and more to rely upon language.   (Richards, 1929, pp.320–1)

Language had not been, in Müller's phrase, 'brought back to itself' but was deeply engaged with 'social and rhetorical' concerns again. Across a whole network of different areas of social life the views and evaluations of distinct forms of language that had been evolved in various forms of linguistic research in the nineteenth and early twentieth century were making themselves felt. In debates about education, the formal study of language, the political rhetoric of parliamentarians and the measures such rhetoric enabled them to enact, to name but a few such areas, the politics of discourse exercised its regulative influence.

7

Conclusion: Past and Present

A band of efficient schoolmasters is kept up at much less expense than a body of police or soldiery.
(Nineteenth-century MP, quoted in Leith, 1983, p.167)

Introduction

The 1980s in Britain have been years of crisis. The post-war consensus which had largely been adhered to by the major political parties and public opinion has been under severe attack. Institutions and practices that not long ago seemed safe from challenge are now subject to ruthless ideological and political assault. The provisions of the welfare state, the free health service and the state education system have all been faced with fundamental alteration by perhaps the most radical and confident Tory government of the century. Across many fields the onslaught has taken place and it has been accompanied by a marked shift in political discourse. The ground has shifted so fast that at times it appears bewildering: competition, efficiency, profit and individualism have become buzz-words in the revision and reversal of values, opinions and practices which has taken place in the ideology of the new Toryism. Given that this has been the recent historical context in Britain, the aim in this conclusion will be to see whether the general drift of our argument can fit this period of cultural and political crisis. The argument has been, in short, that language becomes a crucial focus of tension and debate at critical historical moments, serving as the site upon which political positions are contested. This conclusion then will attempt to demonstrate that the argument in this book does fit the recent historical period in Britain as the English language has again been placed on the agenda for right-wing ideologists.

One of the notable features of the new form of Toryism is its apparent willingness to blame the 1960s for all that is wrong in contemporary Britain. The 'permissive society', if we are to believe the ideologists of the new right, is responsible for everything from the rising crime rates under Thatcherism to slack morals in public life, declining standards of politeness among the young, bolshie union bosses and much more besides. Not least in the litany of offences that the evil decade has visited upon us is the alleged decline of standards in education, with the level of literacy a favoured topic. Despite the fact that more people are educated, and to a higher level, than ever before, there is still a widespread populist belief (which is given ideological force by the views of certain educationalists and politicians) that the British population is in grave danger of becoming illiterate. There appears to be a terrible threat that the English language and its users are menaced by teachers and educationalists who no longer believe in standards and deliberately undermine 'good English'. Therefore this conclusion will attempt to examine the views of the new right educationalists in order to demonstrate the continuity of their thinking with the sort of pre- and proscriptive attitudes that have been outlined in this text. The aim will be to show how the language has again become the vehicle for a crusade for specific types of contemporary values and to examine the political implications of those values in the sphere of linguistic education.

Mellifluous rhetoric: the language trap

A good example of new right educationalists' thinking about language is given in John Honey's pamphlet *The Language Trap: Race, Class and the 'Standard Language' Issue in British Schools*, published by the right-wing pressure group the National Council for Educational Standards as one of a series of 'Kay-Shuttleworth Papers on Education'. Examples of Kay-Shuttleworth's educational thinking and aims can be found in Chapter 1. Honey's pamphlet opens with a paragraph on 'Threatened Standards in English' which begins: 'In the past two decades there has been increasing concern on both sides of the Atlantic, over the standards of written and spoken English by the products of our school system' (Honey, 1983, p.1). He then cites complaints from employers along with mistakes on insurance forms and advertising cards in shop windows as evidence of such a decline in linguistic standards. They are, he asserts, 'a sad commentary' on the level of achievement of our educational provision. This argument is interesting from a rhetorical point of view in that it deploys a familiar tactic of contemporary reactionary thought by dehistoricising the problem that it seeks to address. The claim is that linguistic standards have become a concern over the past two decades and thus the implication, formulated explicitly elsewhere in the pamphlet by Honey, is that the problem causing such concern has likewise arisen only in the past twenty years. However, the evidence presented in this text shows Honey's claim to be what it is, a piece of clever rhetoric, as it demonstrates that such concern has been voiced widely over the past century and a half at least. Even a small amount of research would discover the previous politicians, educationalists and employers who voiced their concern in almost precisely the same terms as those used by the contemporary critics. This 'new' concern for 'standards' has to be put in the historical context of a long and continuing debate about the level of educational provision, about what is to be taught in our schools and how it is to be taught. To present the concerns that are being voiced today as if they are specific only to the past two decades is both tendentious and misleading.

A central claim made by Honey is that such concerns have arisen as a direct result of a recent form of linguistic theorising. Described by the new right as the 'new orthodoxy' amongst linguists, it is characterised here as 'a pseudo-scientific theory' which has been 'handed down by incautious academics first to school teachers and their like, ultimately to become the stock-in-trade of lightly educated politicians' (*ibid.*, p.3). The 'new orthodoxy' must clearly be a dangerous form of thought and so it will be worth while quoting its central tenets in the words of its upholders as given in Honey's text. He cites Professor John Lyons, for example, as holding to the menacing belief that 'every language has a sufficiently rich vocabulary for the expression of all the distinctions in the society using it'. Dr V.K. Edwards holds to the threatening view that 'it is an established fact that no language or dialect is superior to another'. And Professor Michael Stubbs holds to the 'pseudo-scientific theory' which maintains that 'it is accepted by linguists that no language or dialect is inherently superior or inferior to any other, and that all languages and dialects are *suited to* the communities they serve'. Essentially then the radically destructive 'new orthodoxy' appears to be the belief that any one language or dialect is linguistically, and in terms of the needs of its users, equal to any other language or dialect.

Honey's view of the 'new orthodoxy' is that it is dangerous, misleading, and responsible for the 'annual crop of total illiterates' who leave our educational system each year. He maintains that the upholders of the 'new orthodoxy' 'under-mine attempts by teachers to meet the demands of parents and employers that pupils should be able to speak and write "good English"' (*ibid.*, p.3). No doubt those teachers and educationalists under attack here might argue that what is precisely at stake in such debates is the question of what is to count as 'good English'. As we shall see, however, begging the question is not the most serious of the flaws in Honey's argument. The aim of this pamphlet is to stop the 'ritual incantation' of the 'new orthodoxy' and to 'examine the implications of what these theorists and their acolytes are doing'. However, as the accusations and claims already cited show, his text is replete with rhetorical flourishes designed to discredit the claims of his academic opponents in what he insists is a 'spirited exchange of ideas'. Many of his contentions are in fact intemperate in tone but he does present two arguments which are of interest and worth examination. Therefore these should be countered before we move to a demonstration of the sort of political values that inform his text. The first of his arguments worth considering is his attack on what he calls 'relativism', by which he apparently seems to mean the belief that 'every language or dialect has a sufficiently rich vocabulary; always keeps pace with its speakers' social development; is entirely adequate for their needs, and as a communicative system; and is as good and efficient as any other' (*ibid.*, p.5). The way in which Honey deals with such claims is illustrative of his manner of debate. What he does with this argument is to misread its central claim by shifting the ground of the argument from a view of language *per se*, to a philosophical claim about the 'needs' of particular human communities. Taking Peter Trudgill's claim that 'all varieties of a language are structured, complex, rule-governed systems which are entirely adequate for the needs of their speakers', Honey responds by arguing:

> Thus, if a speech-community is found whose language does not already possess the extensive vocabulary which would enable its members to handle any given aspect of modern technology (say), or modern medicine, or modern communications, then we are presumably to infer that the members of that community do not *need* any of those commodities. (*Ibid.*, p.5.)

There are two points to note here. First, Honey shifts Trudgill's claim from one concerning varieties of a language to a claim about a language in itself. The second and more important point is that he distorts Trudgill's argument by making it into a qualitative judgement on the cultural, economic and political state of the speech-community rather than a claim about the language of that community. Trudgill does *not* claim that a speech-community which is not in possession of the language or facilities of modern medicine has no *need* of them since his argument is simply that for the state in which that speech-community exists, its language fulfils the requirements of the speech community. Trudgill does not concern himself with what the needs of the speakers are or could be, whether that is decided by themselves or by exterior agencies, but with a logical claim about the functioning of language. Honey's false inference turns Trudgill's linguistic point into a claim about relative stages of cultural development and enables him to accuse Trudgill, in essence, of proposing to deny underdeveloped groups the means to advance. There is no such proposal in Trudgill's work since he confines himself to the linguistic point in dispute. To present the case otherwise is to misread seriously.

It is claimed in *The Language Trap* that 'even a first year student of the Philosophy of Education' knows that there are many philosophical implications of the word 'needs' and if that is true then it is clearly meritorious and those who teach the subject are to be congratulated. It must be said, however, that John Honey has a very particular and idiosyncratic view of the needs of particular speech-communities. He argues for example that:

> speakers of different languages have different potentialities open to them: that if you belong to a 'primitive' tribe whose language has a total vocabulary of a few thousand words or less, there are things which you simply cannot say, compared with speakers from modernised societies whose dictionaries list hundreds of thousands of words.   (*Ibid.*, p.5)

This is presented as being a contentious view though it is not in fact opposed by any of the linguists cited by Honey. And no doubt such linguists might wish to point out that by corollary there are things which you simply cannot say in the languages of modernised societies that can be said in those of '"primitive" tribes'. Nonetheless Honey proceeds from this claim to ask, rhetorically, how speakers from the "primitive" tribe' can cope '*in their own language*, with the concepts of higher mathematics, or Wittgensteinian philosophy, not to speak of biochemistry or nuclear physics?' The answer to the question, which we already know since it is a rhetorical question, is of course that they cannot and do not cope with such tasks in their own languages. This, we are assured, is attested by 'anyone who has actually tried to translate a scholarly paper in physics, psychology, or semantics from a major world language into the speech of a preliterate jungle tribe'. Now it is important to be clear on the distinctions and claims being made here. It is evidently the case that the concepts of higher mathmatics will not be available to the speakers of a 'preliterate jungle tribe' in their own language. Though perhaps it is important to say that such concepts are not yet available to such speakers at all for political and economic reasons. But the main point to be recalled here is that it is not the case that they could *never* be available in such a language since if the social nature of the speech-community changed so that such concepts became important to it, or to put it alternatively, became part of the needs of that community, then it would also happen that their whole pattern of linguistic living would likewise change. The processes of semantic expansion, word-borrowing, neologisms and so on would be developed in that language just as they have in the history of the English language in order to meet the requirements of its speakers. The requirements of the speakers, as they are worked out and realised in the social life of the community, would be embodied in the language that they use since the language and forms of life of that community would be as closely interwoven as they are in our own. Though of course communities are never in themselves homogeneous and there will often be clashes of interest or need within them. However, Honey's claim against the main point amounts to arguing that such languages could never adapt to such functions and that therefore such underprivileged speakers should adopt the languages of the 'modernised' societies. Such an argument fails to appreciate one of the lessons of language and history: the language and forms of life of the past are not adequate to the present, and the language and forms of life of the present will not be found adequate to the future. That is why change takes place.

As regards the case of the translator of the scholarly paper in semantics from a major world language into the speech of a 'preliterate jungle tribe', one can only say that if such projects are being undertaken they must be conducted by: (i) people who have a lot of time and money to waste; (ii) people who have an odd sense of humour; or (iii) people who are seriously misled. No doubt John Honey will be at the forefront of the fight to achieve a fairer distribution of the world's resources in order that 'preliterate jungle tribes' will be able to partake of the benefits of modern medicine, technology and communications, though if he thinks that such preliterate speakers need such a redistribution in order to fulfil their 'need' (in his sense of the term) for scholarly papers in semantics then he has his priorities wrong. One would imagine that such speakers would prefer a few more basic things first.

It should be clear, however, that John Honey's argument

is not part of a Utopian vision that seeks to ensure an egalitarian distribution of resources and the power that goes with them. His 'anti-relativist' argument is designed instead to serve the function of allowing him to gain the high ground of moral and political certainty in order to evaluate and put into a non-relative hierarchy particular languages and forms of language. This will serve his purpose later when he extends the argument concerning the relationship of 'preliterate jungle tribes' to the languages of 'modernised' societies, to the relationship of dialect speakers to 'standard English'. Of course there is no reason to suppose that even if Honey's claims about the preliterate speakers were true, that the argument could then be transposed to the speakers of non-standard English, but we will allow the analogy to stand for the moment since before discussing Honey's claims in this distinct area we shall have to examine Honey's second substantive argument against the 'new orthodoxy'. The second argument is directed against the American socio-linguist and practical founder of the 'new orthodoxy', William Labov. Labov's work in this area, largely conducted in the 1960s and early 1970s, sought to investigate whether the 'verbal deprivation' assigned to black American ghetto schoolchildren had any basis in fact. To do this Labov examined the use of Black English Vernacular as used by such speakers in order to ascertain whether it was inferior to 'standard English' as a vehicle of logical discourse. The results of his work, as published in the article 'The Logic of Nonstandard English' (Labov, 1972, Ch. 5), demonstrated that from an analysis of a specific interview between a Black English Vernacular speaker and a 'standard English' speaker, it was the Black English Vernacular speaker who showed verbal fluency and 'quick, ingenious and decisive' skills in argument. The 'standard English' speaker on the other hand is described by Labov as tending to produce verbiage and to be 'overparticular and vague' in discussion. Now the results of Labov's work are open to interpretation in various ways – Honey, for example, gives a wholly different interpretation to that offered by Labov. What is of interest, however, is the tactic employed by Honey to discredit the claims of his opponent. To begin with he disputes Labov's empirical research, describing it as 'a travesty of scientific method', though it is worth noting that there is not a single shred of empirical evidence to support any of the claims made by Honey in this pamphlet. More important than that, however, is the charge laid against Labov's interpretation of his empirical data. Honey remarks that 'Labov's interpretation of what he claims is the essence of the argument of each speaker is Labov's own, and purely subjective' (*ibid.*, p.15). This is a very puzzling objection. Would Labov's results have had more validity for Honey if the interpretation of his research had been someone else's? And how is any interpretation to avoid the charge of being 'purely subjective'? Is Honey's interpretation 'purely subjective', or does it manage by some feat of ingenuity to be 'objective' and 'neutral'? In fact the charge of being 'purely subjective' in this context amounts to little more than a rhetorical smear against an academic opponent who does not share the writer's cultural and political presuppositions. If there were any discussion of what it would mean to give an objective view of the data in this case then Honey's charge might be one that needed to be addressed seriously; as it stands it is little more than a vacuous accusation.

The two principal arguments that are presented in this pamphlet against the 'new orthodoxy' then are seriously flawed in so far as they consist of a misreading of an opponent's claim and a rhetorical rejection of an opponent's interpretation. However, they are important for Honey in that they lay the basis for the central claim of his text: that 'standard English' should be taught in schools as the correct and central variety of the spoken and written language. His proposition is that:

> the ends of social justice, the promotion of the underprivileged in our educational system, and the fostering of their ability to be articulate communicators *outside* their immediate social group, require that they achieve a ready facility in standard English, even at the expense of their development in their original non-standard variety. Even at the expense, I am tempted to add, of their self-esteem.   (*Ibid.*, p.31)

It is clearly stated in this passage that one of the reasons for imposing 'standard English' is that such a process would lead to social justice. Thus the debunking of 'fantasies, fabrications, and unproven hypotheses' (*ibid.*, p.28) has to be undertaken with a view to enhancing the interests of society in a just way to a just end. However, an examination of the background to this social justice will expose a fundamental flaw in the reasoning that leads Honey to his conclusions, and demonstrate that the option he proposes is in fact one that will conserve the facts of social injustice rather than eradicating them.

Honey ranges from arguing that not all varieties of language are equal in terms of the intellectual sophistication that they allow (*ibid.*, p.11), to the contention that 'standard English' speech and writing should be taught in order to enhance the possibilities of 'social mobility' for black children (*ibid.*, p.25). It is the second argument that contains the serious flaw and reveals the political direction of Honey's proposal. It is argued that 'because our society (like all known societies) does not respect all sub-cultures equally, and because of the inescapable connexions which have grown up between the concept of "educatedness" and the ability to handle standard English, the non-standard speaker is put at an unfair disadvantage in any crucial encounter outside his own immediate speech-community' (*ibid.*, p.20). Let us accept that British society is largely intolerant of sub-cultures and that there is also a widespread belief in a certain form of the language as an 'educated' form. Let us also accept that these are 'evaluations which have long persisted across British society, show no real signs of abating, and moreover tend to be shared by the speakers of the most disparaged varieties of accent themselves' (*ibid.*, p.21). And then let us pose this question: are these 'evaluations' in the best interests of society as a whole and do they serve the ends of social justice? The answer must be no on both counts. Intolerance and hostility to difference, whether it be to a form of language, or to the colour of people's skin, or to their class background, or their gender, is both anti-social and unjust. Whether such intolerance and hostility is counted as simply 'a matter of social convention', or as a deeply rooted set of beliefs enmeshed with everyday acts of aggression and exclusion is presumably a question of political persuasion.

The contention that such 'evaluations' (prejudices as someone of a different political persuasion might call them) are of long duration is used by Honey to argue that 'insofar as adverse judgments on specific language varieties *are* merely a matter of social convention or aesthetic prejudice, the task of altering long-held and widespread opinions in any society may be a formidable one' (*ibid.*, p.22). Such an argument is essentially conservative since when faced with the complexities and difficulties of radical social change in the interests of social justice, it ducks the question and proposes instead a solution that conserves the very facts of social injustice. The intolerance and hostility are viewed as 'inescapable' and the victims of injustice are blamed for opting to resist rather than conform. A good example of blaming the victims is provided when Honey attacks Labov for promoting the 'speech patterns' of black adolescents and thereby helping them to succeed in 'opposing the norms of the wider society'. Given that the norms of the wider society do not, to give Honey's example, 'respect all sub-cultures equally', then opposing such norms might be considered by many to be in the interests of social justice.

It is, however, possible to agree with Honey on one point. That is the claim that the task of altering such 'evaluations' as those he cites is a difficult one involving much hard work, plenty of intellectual discussion of the complex points, and the arduous practice of disseminating knowledge. But of course that is what education is concerned with in its involvement with hard decisions and complex possibilities, and it should never be the role of education simply to conserve things as they are. Oddly enough this is a point made by Honey himself when he quotes Glenn Langford as arguing that 'any education worth the name sets out to change people, by, among other things introducing them to problems of which they had no previous conception. Its job is not, or not primarily, how to get what they already want' (*ibid.*, 6). Quite so. If people want to preserve structures of intolerance and prejudice then it is the role of education to change their opinions rather than pander to them. It is in the interests of social justice to do so.

Returning to Victorian values

John Honey is not the only educationalist to have proposed views on the teaching of English in the 1980s. John Rae, ex-headmaster of the exclusive, fee-paying Westminster school, has also received wide publicity for his strictures against falling standards of literacy. And an ex-pupil of Westminster, the historian of medieval philosophy and head of English studies at Trinity College, Cambridge, John Marenbon, has likewise received a sympathetic hearing in the national press for his pamphlet 'English our English: the "new orthodoxy" examined', published by the Tory think-tank, the Centre for Policy Studies (1987). Marenbon's aim is clearly to influence the Kingman Committee, set up by the Secretary of State for Education in January 1987 in order to 'make recommendations on a model of the workings of the English language to help improve teaching in schools'. Though not as intemperate as Honey's pamphlet, this text evinces many of the same premises, of which the central one is that 'when children leave English schools today, few are able to speak and write English correctly' (Marenbon, 1987, p.5).

In fact there are points when Marenbon's argument makes a good deal of sense. For example, he points to the crisis in the teaching of English studies at all levels when he argues that the concept of 'English as a distinctive subject' has been eradicated. There can be few teachers of English at any level who would disagree with that since 'English' has become the vehicle for numerous different activities and practices with no apparent consensus about aims, methods or even the subject-matter with which to work. That said, however, the view of English studies presented here is not one that seeks to understand the present variety in order to work out new aims. Rather it sees the task of English studies as that of 'teaching children to write and speak standard English correctly, and of initiating their acquaintance with the literary heritage of the language' (*ibid.*, p.18). The enormous theoretical debate that has gone on over the past twenty years or so is ignored in favour of the desire to return to the sort of shamateurism that existed before even 'practical criticism' was theorised by I.A. Richards in the 1920s and 1930s ('practical criticism' is declared to be one of the strongest 'enemies' of the literary heritage). Such shamateurism is perhaps encapsulated in Marenbon's declaration that 'beyond care, patience and precision in reading, there are no techniques which can be taught for reading literature' (*ibid.*, p.37). He also warns the teacher against 'allowing his pupils to substitute for competence in reading an ability to manipulate a critical jargon and produce seemingly impressive essays. He should be sceptical of originality in response to literature because it is most likely to betray a failure of understanding' (*ibid.*). And the net and desired effect of such scepticism towards originality is that 'the competent reader reads a work of literature much as other competent readers read it' (*ibid.*). In sum then Marenbon's view of literary training in schools is to see it as a project designed to produce 'competent readers' who will all read in much the same way, assent to the established canon of the literary heritage, and share precisely the same critical values. It is a centralising conception that has uniformity as its end.

Marenbon envisages an even more radical return to former values by arguing against the consensus that has developed over the past century in favour of English studies over and against the classics. He asserts that:

> a classical education, complemented by extensive private reading in the vernacular, would still probably be the best way of introducing an Englishman to his literary heritage, if only it were still available. Indeed, without some knowledge of classical literature, an Englishman will always be to some extent a stranger to his own culture.   (*Ibid.*, p.27)

It comes as no surprise then to discover Marenbon attacking the well-established belief (no doubt one of what might be called the 'fantasies, fabrications, and unproven hypotheses' of linguists and educationalists) that the traditional grammatical categories derived from Latin and Greek are inappropriate to modern English. Nor to find him recommending the reintroduction of traditional grammar into schoolteaching. If John Honey occasionally sounds like a Victorian linguist then it has to be said that John Marenbon goes one better by sounding like one of the high Tories of the eighteenth century.

Views such as those cited would merely be amusing and anachronistic in the light of the enormous difficulties faced in British education today if it were not for the fact that there is a likelihood that they will be influential in political circles and the Department of Education. The ideologists of the new right in education who have been briefly considered here are like their fellow travellers in seeking a return to Victorian values. No doubt there are many versions of Victorian values – child labour, mass poverty, widespread prostitution, shorter life expectancy and social turbulence for example – but the sort of Victorian values these linguists seek a return to are clear from the account of the period in the earlier chapters of this work. On occasion the contemporary right even sound like their Victorian counterparts in their incantation of the links between language, politics and morality. John Rae sees language and morality as interdependent, as a decline in one leads to a decline in the other:

The overthrow of grammar coincided with the acceptance of the equivalent of creative writing in social behaviour. As nice points of grammar were mockingly dismissed as pedantic and irrelevant, so was punctiliousness in such matters as honesty, responsibility, property, gratitude, apology and so on.   (Quoted in Milroy and Milroy, 1985, p.50)

The importance of the text books of one form of religious belief is stressed by Honey as he writes of having 'to face up to the fact that important elements of the common culture which shaped our model of the educated person's language are fast being lost – the influence of the Authorised Version of the Bible, of the Book of Common Prayer, and of *Hymns Ancient and Modern*' (Honey, 1983, p.33). No doubt Stanley Baldwin might have been surprised to learn that the influence of these texts was still being lost over half a century after he mourned the loss of the 'common culture' to which they apparently belonged. Perhaps it is simply in the nature of such reactionary nostalgic thought to think of such influences as being in a state of constant danger, always threatened with extinction from the day they were created (and in some cases even before they were created). Such reactionary nostalgia, however, has a very precise use for this imagined 'common culture' of the past: to berate whatever it is at present that they find unpalatable. Perhaps the starkest invocation of all is the ending of Marenbon's pamphlet and his appeal to 'politicians and committees' to 'keep strong in their common sense, distrustful of experts and chaste towards fashion'. He concludes with this:

> May God grant them sharpness of mind and firmness of resolve, for in the future of its language there lies the future of a nation!

The politics of discourse

Raymond Williams has commented upon the 'idealist account of language' which sees it as a 'continuous legacy . . . carrying the finest insights of the community'. He points out that this is a false conception not because of the cultural importance accorded to language, but by dint of that abstractive continuity which rests on 'what were always extraordinary historical transformations and reversals' and then proposes 'a single heritage of meanings which were held to sanction particular contemporary values' (Williams, 1979, p.177). The idealist accounts of language such as those examined in this text have obscured the real importance of language in history and history in language and have therefore also prevented the proper educational role that language could have. As with most idealist accounts, however, they do have a kernel of truth within them. Our language is a social product which is of fundamental significance since it does bear the marks of our past and present history. It demonstrates not just the finest insights of our community but also the essential bitterness and antagonism of our social history that radicals have to recall. It is the aim of conservatism to preserve the social conditions of injustice with which we live; in opposing that project by seeking to alter those conditions, it is clear that radicals too will have to pay a great deal more attention to this aspect of the politics of discourse than they have as yet.

The question of what form of education we want and need is of clear importance today because the state education system is under severe attack by the new right as they seek to introduce their buzz-words into the classrooms of our schools and make them more competitive, efficient, profitable and geared solely to fostering the ideology of the individual. We find then that we are still facing the question posed by Williams twenty-five years ago. Do we want an education system ordered 'by the free play of the market, or by a public education designed to express and create the values of an educated democracy and a common culture?' (Williams, 1961, p.176). The question is whether we want an education system geared to the complexities and difficulties of creating a tolerant and just 'common culture' in a modern society replete with potential yet fraught with difficulty. Or an education system geared to the same task of imposing a narrow code of specific values as that described by an observer of Bristol miners in 1794. The observer comments that the miners:

> were, 40 or 50 years ago, so barbarous and savage, that they were a terror to the City of Bristol, which they several times invaded: it was dangerous to go among them, and their dialect was the roughest and rudest in the Nation; but by the labours of Messrs. Whitefield and Wesley, by the erection of a parish church and some meeting-houses, and the establishment of several Sunday and daily schools, they are much civilized and improved in principles, morals and pronunciation. (Barrell, 1983, p.138)

It is clear that for some educationalists of the new right, little has changed since the late eighteenth century. For those interested in the problem of creating an alternative view of education, on the other hand, it is clear that the politics of discourse will have to be addressed again. To that end it will be worth taking note of Gramsci's claim that:

> Every time the question of the language surfaces, in one way or another, it means that a series of other problems are coming to the fore: the formation and enlargement of

the governing class, the need to establish more intimate and secure relationships between the governing groups and the national-popular mass, in other words to reorganise the cultural hegemony.   (Gramsci, 1985, pp.183–4)

Notes

Introduction

1. For an analysis of such attitudes and debates see Smith (1984).

1 A history of 'the history of the language'

1. It is in fact dubious to assert that this shift took place in any other than a general sense. Problems of representation did not disappear in the nineteenth century, as Foucault seems to suggest, but were often displaced into other fields of knowledge.
2. For a fuller treatment of the controversy see Aarsleff (1967), pp.191–210.
3. Other early works of the same order as Latham's were the Rev. M. Harrison's *The Rise, Progress and Present Structure of the English Language* (1848); G.L. Craik's *Outlines of the History of the English Language for the use of the Junior Classes in Colleges and the Higher Classes in Schools* (1851); and his *Compendious History of English Literature and of the English Language from the Norman Conquest* (1861).
4. The Society for the Diffusion of Useful Knowledge was an early-nineteenth-century educational society much derided by radicals. For an analysis of such debates see R. Johnson, ' "Really useful Knowledge": radical education and working-class culture, 1790–1848', in J. Clarke *et al.*, *Working Class Culture: Studies in History and Theory* (London, Hutchinson, 1979), pp. 75–102.

2 Archbishop Trench's theory of language: the Tractatus Theologico-Politicus

1. The motto was the title of the lectures delivered to the pupils at the Diocesan Training School at Winchester that formed the

original upon which the text was based. The motto 'Knowledge is Power' was a favourite dictum of Sir James Murray, the first editor of the *New/Oxford English Dictionary*. See K.M.E. Murray, *Caught in the Web of Words* (Oxford, OUP, 1979), p.25.

2. For an examination of these debates see Aarsleff (1967).

3. Freud's methodology is at times purely philological, as for example in the *Introductory Lectures on Psychoanalysis*. One such example is treatment of the symbolism in dreams in which he explains that to dream of wood is to dream of a woman or mother since: 'in Portuguese the word for wood is *madeira*. But you cannot fail to notice that his *madeira* is merely a modified form of the Latin *materia*, which again signifies material in general. Now *materia* is derived from *mater*-mother, and the material out of which anything is made may be conceived of as giving birth to it. So, in this symbolic use of wood to represent woman or mother, we have a survival of this idea (Freud, 1922, pp.134–5). For a discussion of related topics see John Forrester's *Language and the Origins of Psycho-Analysis* (London, Macmillan, 1980).

4. No slight is intended here on teachers of dance.

4   The standard language: the language of the literate

1. The analogy was used frequently in the eighteenth century, perhaps most notably in Clare's comment that 'grammar in learning is like tyranny in government – confound the bitch I'll never be her slave'.

2. The belief in an allegedly 'neutral' though in fact socially specific form of language is still evident today in the surprise and indignation of those students who arrive at, for example, British universities or polytechnics from their private schools and find that other students and tutors regard them as having a strong and socially identifiable accent. They usually counter by insisting that they do not have an accent; by which they usually mean that they have neither a 'provincial' nor working-class accent.

3. See the Henry Sweet Society *Newsletter*, no. 8, p.7 (Oxford, 1987).

5   Theorising the standard: Jones and Wyld

1. In case there should be any confusion for those not familiar with the deceptive terminology of British education, 'public school' actually refers to the most exclusive and fee-paying schools.
2. Originally published in 1914 but we will concentrate here on the revised third edition, published in 1927, in which there are significant differences.
3. For the classic modern linguistic reference to the 'completely homogeneous speech-community' see Noam Chomsky, *Aspects of the Theory of Language* (Massachusetts, MIT Press, 1965), p.5.
4. The tracts are 'The Nature of Human Speech' by Sir Richard Paget, SPE Tract XXII, and 'English Vowel Sounds', SPE Tract XXVI by Dr A.W. Aikin. Wyld also mentions in passing Lloyd's *Some Researches into the Nature of Vowel Sounds* (1890), and unspecified work by Sweet.

6   Language against modernity

1. Wilson described 'the barbarians' as 'really the most interesting of the three classes'.
2. Saussure's *Course* has no clearly drawn distinction between the phonetic and the phonological aspects of language. For example there are difficulties in Saussure's treatment of language with respect to natural elements (such as those discussed in the appendix entitled 'Principles of Physiological Phonetics') and the 'contrastive, regulative and negative' speech sounds at work in specific languages which he treats in his chapter on 'linguistic value'.
3. Fisher did not give such reasons for the introduction of the Bill when addressing the mercantile classes of Manchester (25 September), Liverpool (2 October), or Bradford (4 November); nor did he describe his audiences as the managers of 'hideous cities of toil'.
4. The Commissioners were Sir Henry Newbolt (Chair), John Bailey, K.M. Baines, F.S. Boas, H.M. Davies, D. Enright, C.H. Frith, J.H. Fowler, L.A. Lowe, Sir Arthur Quiller-Couch, George Sampson, C. Spurgeon, G. Perrie Williams, J. Dover Wilson. Six of the Commissioners were women, eight men. They were mostly

academics or HM Inspectors of Education. The Report was commissioned by the Rt Hon. H. Fisher, MP, President of the Board of Education in May 1919.

5. For examples of such work see Pierre Achard's 'History and the Politics of language in France', *History Workshop Journal*, 10 (Autumn 1980), pp.175–84. See also the work of Renée Balibar, *Le Français national* (Paris; Hachette, 1974); *Les Français fictifs* (Paris, Hachette, 1974); 'National Language, Education, Literature', in *The Politics of Theory*, ed. F. Barker (Essex, Essex University Press, 1982). For a discussion of these issues with respect to education see Pierre Bourdieu's *Reproduction in Education, Society and Culture* (London, Sage, 1977).

Bibliography of Works Consulted

Aarsleff, Hans, 'The Early History of the OED', *Bulletin of the New York Public Library*, 66 (Sept. 1962), 417–39.

——, *The Study of Language in England 1780–1860* (Princeton; Princeton UP, 1967).

——, *From Locke to Saussure: Essays on the Study of Language and Intellectual History* (London, Athlone, 1982).

Achard, Pierre, 'History and the Politics of Language in France', *History Workshop Journal*, 10 (Autumn 1980).

Adams, John, *Answer to Pain's [sic] Rights of Man* (London, 1793).

Aikin, A.W., 'English Vowel Sounds', Society For Pure English, Tract XXVI, (Oxford, Clarendon, 1927).

Alford, Henry, *A Plea for the Queen's English: Stray Notes on Speaking and Spelling*, 2nd edn (London, 1864).

——, *The Queen's English: A Manual of Idiom and Usage*, 3rd edn (rev. London, 1870).

Alison, Archibald, *England in 1815 and 1845* (Edinburgh, 1845).

Alston, R.C., 'An Examination of English Spelling-Reform Texts of the 16th and 17th Centuries as Sources of Evidence for the Existence of a Standard of Pronunciation' (Diss. University of London, 1964).

——, *A Bibliography of the English Language from the Invention of Printing to the Year 1800*, 11 vols (Leeds, 1965–71).

Anderson, Ben, *Imagined Communities: Reflections on the Origin and Spread of Nationalism* (London, New Left Books, 1983).

Anderson, Olive, *A Liberal State at War: English Politics and Economics During the Crimean War* (London, 1967).

Arnold, Matthew, *Culture and Anarchy: An Essay in Political and Social Criticism*, 1869, vol v, *Complete Prose Works* (Michigan, Ann Arbor, 1965).

Bakhtin, M.M., *The Dialogic Imagination* (Austin, University of Texas Press, 1981).

Balbi, Adrien, *Introduction à l'atlas ethnographique du globe* (Paris, 1826).

Baldick, Chris, *The Social Mission of English Criticism 1848–1932* (Oxford, Clarendon, 1983).

Baldwin, Stanley, *On England* (London, Phillip Allan, 1926).

——, *Our Inheritance* (London, Hodder & Stoughton, 1928).

Balibar, Renée and Dominique Laporte, *Le Français national: politique et pratiques de la langue nationale sous la révolution française* (Paris, Hachette, 1974).

——, *Les Français fictifs* (Paris, Hachette, 1974).

——, 'National Language, Education, Literature', in *The Politics of Theory: Essex Sociology of Literature Conference*, ed. F. Barker *et al.* (Essex University Press, 1982).

Barker, Ernest, *Mothers and Sons in War Time and Other Pieces* (London, Humphreys, 1915; 2nd edn rev. 1917).

——, *National Character and the Factors in its Formation* (London, Methuen, 1927).

Barnes, William, *Poems of Rural Life in the Dorset Dialect*, 3 Parts (London, 1844–62).

——, *Poems of Rural Life in National English* (London, 1846).

——, *Tiw; Or, a View of the Roots and Stems of the English as a Teutonic Tongue* (London, 1862).

——, *A Grammar and Glossary of the Dorset Dialect* (Berlin, 1863).

——, *Poems of Rural Life in Common English* (London, 1868).

——, *Poems of Rural Life in the Dorset Dialect*, 3rd collection, 2nd edn (London, 1869).

——, *A Glossary of the Dorset Dialect with a Grammar of its Word Shapening and Wording* (Dorchester, 1885).

Barrell, John, *English Literature in History 1730–1780: An Equal Wide Survey* (London, Hutchinson, 1983).

Beattie, James, *The Theory of Language* (London, 1788).

Bell, Alexander Melville, *Visible Speech: The Science of Universal Alphabetics; or Self-Interpreting Physiological Letters, for the Writing of All Languages in One Alphabet* (London, 1867).

Benzie, William, *Dr F.J. Furnivall: Victorian Scholar Adventurer* (Oklahoma, Pilgrim Books, 1983).

Blackie, J.S., *On the Studying and Teaching of Languages* (Edinburgh, 1852).

Blair, Hugh, *Lectures on Rhetoric and Belles Lettres* (Edinburgh, 1780).

Blake, N.F., *Non-Standard Language in English Literature* (London, André Deutsch, 1981).

Boorde, Andrew, *First Book of the Introduction to Knowledge* (1547); ed. F.J. Furnivall (London, 1870).

Bosworth, James, *The Elements of Anglo-Saxon Grammar with Notes Illustrating the Structure of the Saxon and the Formation of the English Language; and a Grammatical Praxis, with a Literal English Version to which are Prefixed, Remarks on the History and Use of the Anglo-Saxon, and an Introduction on the Origin and Progress of Alphabetical Writing* (London, 1823).

——, *A Compendious Grammar of the Primitive English Being a Selection of What is Most Valuable and Practical in the Elements of the Anglo-Saxon Language, with Some Additional Observations* (London, 1826).

——, *A Dictionary of the Anglo-Saxon Language* (London, 1838).

Bourdieu, P. *Reproduction in Education, Society and Culture* (London, Sage, 1977).

Boyd, William, *History of Literature, or the Progress of Language, Writing and Letters from the Earliest Ages of Antiquity to The Present Times*, 4 vols (London, 1844).

Bradley, Henry (ed.), *A Middle English Dictionary Containing Words Used by English Writers from the Twelfth Century to the Fifteenth Century* (Oxford, 1891).

Bradley, Henry and Kellner, L. (eds), *The Historical Outlines of English Accidence* (Oxford, 1895).

——, *The Making of English* (London, 1904).

——, *The Collected Papers of Henry Bradley: With a Memoir by Robert Bridges* (Oxford, Clarendon, 1928).

Browning, Robert, *The Poems*, ed. I. Pettigrew (London: Yale University Press, 1981).

Buchanan, James, *Lingua Britannicae Vera Pronunciatio* (London, 1757).

——, *The British Grammar* (London, 1762).

——, *An Essay Towards Establishing a Standard for an Elegant and Uniform Pronunciation of the English Language* (London, 1764).

Bullock, Alan, *The Life and Times of Ernest Bevin*, 2 vols (London, Heinemann, 1960).

Burke, Edmund, *Reflections on the Revolution in France* (1790); ed. Conor Cruise O'Brien (Harmondsworth, Penguin, 1969).

Burn, W.L., *The Age of Equipoise: A Study of the Mid-Victorian Generation* (London: Allen & Unwin, 1964).

Burnett, James (Lord Monboddo), *On the Origin and Progress of Language*, 6 vols (London, 1774–1792).

Burrow, John, 'The Uses of Philology in Victorian Britain', in *Ideas and Institutions of Victorian Britain: Essays in Honour of George Kitson Clarke*, ed. R. Robson (New York, Barnes & Noble, 1967).

Butcher, Lothair, 'On Political Terms', *Transactions of the Philological Society*, V (1858).

Calder, Daniel G., 'Histories and Surveys of Old English Literature: A Chronological Review', *Anglo-Saxon England*, 10 (1982).

Cameron, D., *Feminism and Linguistic Theory* (London, Macmillan, 1985).

Campbell, George, *The Philosophy of Rhetoric* (London, 1776); ed. L. Bitzer (Carbondale, Southern Illinois University Press, 1963).

Canones Lexicographici; or Rules To Be Observed in Editing the New English Dictionary (London, 1860).

Chadwick, Henry, *Studies in Old English* (Cambridge, 1899).

Chaloner, W.H., 'The Hungry Forties', Historical Association Pamphlet (London, 1957).

Chambers, R.W., 'Alexander Hamilton and the Beginnings of Comparative Philology', in *Studies in English Philology: A Miscellany in Honour of Frederick Klaeber*, ed. K. Malone *et al.* (Minneapolis, 1929).

——, 'Philologists at University College London: The Beginnings 1828–89', in his *Man's Unconquerable Mind* (London, 1934).

Chapman, R.W., 'Oxford English', *Society for Pure English*, 4, No. XXXVII (1932).

Chesterfield, Lord, *Miscellaneous Works* (Dublin, 1777).

Chomsky, Noam, *Aspects of the Theory of Syntax* (Massachussetts, MIT Press, 1965).

Clare, John, *The Letters of John Clare*, ed. J. and A. Tibble (London, Routledge & Kegan Paul, 1951).

Clark, George, *Guide to Essay Writing Specially Adapted to Meet the Requirements of Civil Service Candidates and Students for University and School Examinations* (London, 1895).

Clarke, J. *et al.*, *Working Class Culture: Studies in History and Theory* (London, Centre for Contemporary Cultural Studies; Hutchinson, 1979).

Classen, E., *The History of the English Language* (London, 1919).

Cobbett, William, *A Grammar of the English Language in a Series of Letters*, 2nd edn (London, 1819).

Cohen, Murray, *Sensible Words: Linguistic Practice in England 1640–1785* (Baltimore, Maryland, 1977).

Coleridge, Derwent, 'Observations on the Plan of the Society's

Proposed New English Dictionary', *Transactions of the Philological Society* (1860).

Cope, W.H., *A Glossary of Hampshire Words and Phrases* (London, 1883).

Cournot, M., *Essai sur les fondements de nos connaissances et sur les caractères de la critique philosophique* (Paris, 1851).

Craik, George L., *Outlines of the History of the English Language For the Use of Junior Classes in Colleges and the Higher Classes in Schools* (London, 1851).

——, *A Compendious History of English Literature and of the English Language from the Norman Conquest; with Numerous Specimens*, 2 vols (London, 1861).

Cunningham, Hugh, 'The Language of Patriotism', *History Workshop Journal*, 12 (1981).

Darwin, Charles, *On the Origin of Species by means of natural selection* (London, 1859).

Davies, John, 'On the Races of Lancashire, as Indicated by the Local Names and Dialect of the County', *Transactions of the Philological Society* (1855).

——, 'On the connexion of the Keltic with the Teutonic Languages and Especially with the Anglo-Saxon', *Transactions of the Philological Society* (1857).

Davies, Tony, 'Education, Ideology and Literature', *Red Letters*, 7 (1978).

De Carteau, M. *et al.*, *Une Politique de la langue: la révolution française et les patois* (Paris, 1975).

De Quincey, Thomas, 'The English Language', in *Collected Writings New and Enlarged*, 14 vols, ed. D. Masson (Edinburgh, 1890), vol. xiv, pp.146–61.

——, 'English Dictionaries', in *Collected Writings New and Enlarged*, 14 vols, ed. D. Masson (Edinburgh, 1890), vol. x, p.430.

De Selincourt, Ernest, *English Poets and the National Ideal* (Oxford, Clarendon, 1915).

Dickens, Charles, *Dombey and Son* (1848; Oxford, Clarendon, 1974).

Dickins, Bruce, 'J.M. Kemble and Old English Scholarship', *Proceedings of the British Academy* (1939), 51–84.

Dobson, E.J., 'Early Modern Standard English', *Transactions of the Philological Society* (1955), 25–54.

——, *English Pronunciation 1500–1700* (Oxford, Clarendon, 1957).

Donaldson, J.W., *The New Cratylus* (London, 1839).

Dover Wilson, J. (ed.), *The Schools of England: A Study in Renaissance* (Cambridge University Press, 1928).

Dowling, Linda, 'Victorian Oxford and the Science of Language', *PMLA*, 97 (1982), 160–78.

Doyle, Brian, *Some Uses of English* (Birmingham: Centre for Contemporary Cultural Studies, 1981).

Earle, John, *The Philology of the English Tongue* (Oxford, 1871).

——, *A Word for the Mother Tongue: Inaugural Lecture for the Chair of Anglo-Saxon at Oxford Nov. 17 1876* (Oxford, 1876).

——, *A Book for the Beginner in Anglo-Saxon Grammar: With Selections* (Oxford, 1877).

——, *The Peace of Wedmore and How it Touches the History of the English Language* (Oxford, 1878).

——, *English Prose: Its Elements, History and Usage* (London, 1890).

——, *A Simple Grammar of English Now in Use* (London, 1898).

——, 'The Place of English in Education', in *An English Miscellany Presented to Dr Furnivall in Honour of his 75th Birthday* (Oxford, Clarendon, 1901).

Eliot, George, Letter to Skeat in *A Bibliographical List of the Various Dialects of English* (London, 1877).

Ellis, Alexander, *On Early English Pronunciation with Especial Reference to Shakespeare and Chaucer. Containing an Investigation of the Correspondence of Writing with Speech in England from the Anglo-Saxon Period to the Present Day. Preceded by a Systematic Notation of All Spoken Sounds by Means of the Ordinary Printing Types*, 5 Parts (London, 1869–89).

——, 11th Presidential Address to the Philological Society, *Transactions of the Philological Society* (London, 1882–4).

Elphinston, J., *The Principles of the English Language Digested; Or, English Grammar Reduced to Analogy*, 2 vols (London, 1765).

Elworthy, F.T., *The Dialect of West Somerset* (London, 1875–6).

Emerson, O.F., *The History of the English Language* (New York, 1894).

Emsley, B., 'James Buchanan and the Eighteenth Century Regulation of English Usage', *PMLA*, 18 (1973), 1154–66.

English Association Pamphlets, vol. 1, nos 3–25 (Oxford, 1907–13); Vol. 2, nos 26–50 (Oxford, 1913–21);Vol. 3, nos 51–75 (Oxford, 1922–30).

English Dialect Society, 33 vols, 1873–95. (London, 1873–95).

Farrar, Frederic W., *An Essay on the Origin of Language* (London, 1860).

——, *Essays on a Liberal Education*, 2nd edn (London, 1868).

Fell, John, *An Essay Towards an English Grammar* (London, 1784).

Fenning, D., *A New Grammar of the English Language* (London, 1771).

Firth, C.H., *The School of English Language and Literature: A Contribution to the History of Oxford Studies* (Oxford, Blackwell, 1909).

Fisher, H.A.L., *Speech Upon the Introduction of the Education Bill 1917*, 10 August 1917 (London, HMSO, 1917a).

——, *The Education Act. A Speech to the Manufacturers of Manchester*, 25 September 1917 (London, HMSO, 1917b).

——, *Speech to the Liverpool Education Committee and the Liverpool Council of Education*, 2 October 1917 (London, HMSO, 1917c).

——, *Address on the Problem of National Education to the Bradford Textile Society*, 2 November 1917 (London, HMSO, 1917d).

Flügel, Eldwald, 'The History of English Philology', in *The Flügel Memorial Volume* (Standford, Cal.: Stanford University Press, 1916).

Formigari, L., 'Language and Society in the Late Eighteenth Century', *Journal of the History of Ideas*, XXXV (1974). 275-93.

Forrester, John, *Language and the Origins of Psychoanalysis* (London, Macmillan, 1980).

Foster, J., 'The Declassing of Language', *New Left Review*, 150 (March–April 1985).

Foucault, Michel, 'The Discourse on Language', in *The Archaeology of Knowledge* (London, Tavistock, 1972).

——, *The Order of Things: An Archaeology of the Human Sciences* (London, Tavistock, 1974).

Fowler, H.W. and F.G., *The King's English* (Oxford, Clarendon Press, 1906).

Free, John, *An Essay Towards a History of the English Tongue* (London, 1749).

Freeman, E.A., *Comparative Politics* (London, 1873).

Freud, Sigmund, *Introductory Lectures On Psychoanalysis* (London, George, Allen & Unwin, 1922).

Furnivall, F.J., *Proposal for the Publication of a New English Dictionary by the Philological Society* (London, 1859).

——, 3rd Annual Report of the Early English Text Society (London, 1867).

——, 7th Annual Report of the EETS (London, 1871).

——, *F. J. Furnivall. A Volume of Personal Record*, ed. J. Munro (Oxford, Clarendon, 1911).

Galsworthy, John, *On Expression*, English Association Pamphlet 59 (Oxford, 1924).

Garnett, Richard, *Philological Essays* (London, 1859).

Gilchrist, J., *Philosophic Etymology; Or a Rational Grammar* (London, 1816).

Gissing, George, *Demos, a Story of English Socialism* (1886; ed. P. Constillas, Brighton, Harvester, 1972).

Graham, G.F., *A Book About Words* (London, 1869).

Gramsci, Antonio, *Selections From the Prison Notebooks*, ed. and trans. Q. Hoare and G. Nowell Smith (London, Lawrence & Wishart, 1971).

——, *Selections From Cultural Writings*, ed. D. Forgacs and G. Nowell Smith, trans. W. Boelhower (London, Lawrence & Wishart, 1985).

Granville-Barker, Harley (ed.), *The Eighteen Seventies* (Cambridge University Press, 1929).

Greenbaum, S., *The English Language Today* (Oxford, Pergamon, 1985).

Grose, F., *Dictionary of the Vulgar Tongue* (London, 1785).

Guest, Edwin, 'On English Pronouns Personal', *Proceedings of the Philological Society*, I (1844).

——, *A History of English Rhythms*, 2 vols (1838); 2nd edn rev., ed. W.W. Skeat (London, 1882).

Halliwell, James, *A Dictionary of Archaic and Provincial Words, Obsolete Phrases, Proverbs and Ancient Customs From the 14th Century*, 2 vols (London, 1847).

Hardy, Thomas, *Tess of the D'Urbervilles* (1891; London, Macmillan, 1974).

——, *The Complete Poems of Thomas Hardy*, ed. J. Gibson (London, Macmillan, 1979).

Hare, J.C. and H.W., *Guesses at Truth by Two Brothers*, 2 vols (London, 1827).

Harris, Roy, *The Language Makers* (London, Duckworth, 1980).

——, *The Language Myth* (London, Duckworth, 1981).

——, 'The History Men: Review of the Supplement of the OED, Vol. 3, O–Scz' *Times Literary Supplement*, 3 September 1982.

Harrison, M., *The Rise, Progress and Present Structure of the English Language* (London, 1848).

Herder, Johann Gottfried, *Essay on the Origin of Language* (1770; trans.

J. Moran and A. Goode, London, University of Chicago Press, 1966).

Herford, C.H., 'The Bearing of English Studies Upon the National Life', *English Association Pamphlet*, 16 (1910) (Oxford, Clarendon, 1910).

Higginson, E., *An English Grammar Specially Intended for Classical Schools and Private Students* (London, 1864).

Hobsbawm, E.J., *The Age of Revolution* (London, Weidenfeld & Nicolson, 1962).

——, *Industry and Empire: An Economic History of Britain Since 1750* (London, Weidenfeld & Nicolson, 1969).

Honey, J., *The Language Trap: Race, Class and the 'Standard Language' Issue in British Schools* (London, National Council for Educational Standards, 1983).

Houghton, W.E., *The Victorian Frame of Mind: 1830–1870* (Yale University Press, 1957).

Humboldt, Wilhelm Von, *Linguistic Variability and Intellectual Development* (1836; Florida, University of Miami Press, 1971).

Ingram, James, *The Utility of Anglo-Saxon: An Inaugural Lecture* (Oxford, 1807).

Ivic, Milka, *Trends in Linguistics*, trans. Muriel Heppell (The Hague, Mouton, 1965).

Jespersen, Otto, *Progress in Language: With Special Reference to English* (London, 1894).

——, *The Growth and Structure of the English Language* (London, 1905).

——, *A Modern English Grammar on Historical Principles*, 6 Parts: Parts 1–4 (Heidelberg, 1909–21); Parts. 5–6 (Copenhagen, 1940).

——, *Language: Its Nature, Development and Origin* (London, 1922).

——, *Logic and Grammar* (Oxford, Clarendon, 1924).

——, *The Philosophy of Grammar* (Oxford, Clarendon, 1924).

——, *Mankind, Nation and the Individual* (Oslo, 1925).

Johnson, Samuel, *A Dictionary of the English Language in Which the Words are Deduced from their Originals, and Illustrated in their Different Significations by Examples from the Best Writers. To Which are Prefixed A History of the Language and an English Grammar*, 2 vols (London, 1755).

Jones, Daniel, *Phonetic Transcriptions of English Prose* (Oxford, Clarendon, 1907).

——, *A Chart of English Speech Sounds* (Oxford, Clarendon, 1908).

——, *The Pronunciation of English* (Cambridge University Press, 1909).

Jones, Daniel, *Phonetic Readings in English* (Heidelberg, 1912).

——, *An English Pronouncing Dictionary* (London, 1917).

——, *An Outline of English Phonetics* (Leipzig, 1919; repr. Cambridge University Press, 1922).

Jones, R.F., *The Triumph of the English Language* (Oxford, Clarendon, 1953).

Kay-Shuttleworth, James, *Four Periods of Public Education as Reviewed in 1832, 1839, 1846, 1862* (London, 1862)

Keane, A.H., *A Handbook of the History of the English Language* (London, 1860; new and enlarged edn 1875).

Kemble, J.M., 'On the North Anglian Dialect', *Proceedings of the Philological Society*, II (1845–6).

Kennedy, A.G., *A Bibliography of Writings on the English Language from the Beginning of Printing to the End of 1922* (Oxford, Clarendon, 1927).

——, 'Odium Philologicum; or, A Century of Progress to English Philology', in *Stanford Studies in English Literature and Language*, ed. H. Craig (Stanford, Stanford University Press, 1941), pp.11–27.

Ker, W.P. and Napier, A.S., *An English Miscellany Presented to Dr. Furnivall in Honour of his 75th Birthday* (Oxford, Clarendon, 1901).

Kiernan, V.G., 'Working Class and Nation in Nineteenth Century Britain', in *Rebels and Their Causes*, ed. M. Cornforth (London, 1973), pp.123–39.

——, *European Empires: From Conquest to Collapse: 1815–1960* (London, Fontana, 1982).

Kington-Oliphant, T.L., *The Sources of Standard English* (London, 1873).

Kuhlwein, Wolfgang, 'The History of Linguistics', in *Linguistics in Great Britain*, I (Tübingen, Max Niemeyer, 1971).

Labov, W., 'The Logic of Nonstandard English', in *Language in the Inner City* (London, 1972).

Land, S.K., *From Signs to Prepositions: The Concept of Form in Eighteenth Century Semantic Theory* (London, Longman, 1974).

——, 'Lord Monboddo and the Theory of Syntax in the Late Eighteenth Century', *Journal of the History of Ideas*, XXXVII (1976), 423–40.

Latham, R.G., *An Address to the Authors of England and America on the Necessity and Practicability of Permanently Remodelling their Alphabet and Orthography* (Cambridge, 1834).

——, *The English Language* (London, 1841).

Latham, R.G., *An Elementary English Grammar* (London, 1843).

——, *First Outlines of Logic Applied to Grammar and Etymology* (London, 1847).

——, *Elements of English Grammar for the Use of Ladies Schools* (London, 1849).

——, *The History and Etymology of the English Language for the Use of Classical Schools* (London, 1849).

——, *A Grammar of the English Language for the Use of Commercial Schools* (London, 1850).

——, *A Handbook of the English Language* (London, 1851).

——, *On the Importance of the Study of Language as a Branch of Education for all Classes* (London, 1855).

——, *A Smaller English Grammar for the Use of Schools* (London, 1861).

——, *Elements of Comparative Philology* (London, 1862).

——, *Essential Rules and Principles for the Study of English Grammar* (London, 1876).

Lawson, J. and Silver, H., *A Social History of Education in England* (London, Methuen, 1973).

Leavis, F.R. and Thompson, D., *Culture and Environment* (London, Chatto & Windus, 1948).

Leith, Dick, *A Social History of English* (London RKP, 1983).

Lemon, G.W., *English Etymology; Or, A Derivative Dictionary of the English Language in Two Alphabets. Tracing the Etymology of Those English Words Derived from (i) Greek and Latin. (ii) Saxon and Northern Tongues* (London, 1783).

Leonard, S.A., *The Doctrine of Correctness in English Language and Literature* (Maddison, Univ. of Wisconsin Studies in English Language and Literature, 1925).

Leroux, P., *De l'Humanité et son principes et de son avenir*, 2 vols (Paris, 1840).

Loane, M., *The Queen's Poor: Life as They Find it in Town and Country* (London, Arnold, 1905).

Locke, John, *An Essay Concerning Human Understanding* (1690; ed. P. Nidditch, Oxford, Clarendon Press, 1975).

Loewe, L., *A Dictionary of the Circassian Language in Two Parts* (London, 1853).

Lounsbury, Thomas, *A History of the English Language*, 2nd edn, rev. (New York, 1894).

Lowth, Bishop R., *A Short Introduction to English Grammar* (London, 1762).

Lysons, Samuel, *Our Vulgar Tongue* (London, 1868).

MacCarthy, E.F.M., *Address of the President of the Association of Headmasters* (London, 1915).

McKerrow, R.B., *A Note on the Teaching of English Language and Literature*, English Association Pamphlet 49 (London, 1921).

McKnight, George, *English Words and Their Background* (London, Appleton, 1923).

Marenbon, J., *English Our English: The 'New Orthodoxy' Examined* (London, Centre for Policy Studies, 1987).

Marsh, George P., *Lectures on the English Language* (New York, 1860).

——, *The Origin and History of the English Language and of the Literature it Embodies* (London, 1862).

——, *The Student's Manual of the English Language* (London, 1862).

Masterman, C.F.G., 'Realities at Home', in *The Heart of the Empire: Discussions of the Problems of Modern City Life in England with an Essay on Imperialism* (London, Fisher Unwin, 1901).

——, *From the Abyss. Of Its Inhabitants by One of Them* (London, Johnson, 1902).

——, 'The English City', in *England: A Nation. Being the Papers of the Patriots' Club*, ed. Lucien Oldershaw (London, Johnson, 1904a).

——, 'The Problem of South London', in *The Religious Life of London*, ed. R. Mundie Smith (London, Hodder & Stoughton, 1904b).

——, 'The Remedy', in *To Colonial England: a Plea for Policy*, ed. C.F.G. Masterman *et al.* (London, Fisher Unwin, 1907).

Mathews, William, *Words; Their Use and Abuse* (Toronto, 1882).

Meiklejohn, John, *An Easy Grammar for Beginners* (London, 1864).

——, *The Standard Grammar* (Edinburgh, 1882).

——, *The English Language. Its Grammar, History and Literature* (London, 1886).

——, *A Short Grammar of the English Tongue with 300 Exercises* (London, 1890).

——, *The Book of the English Language* (London, 1891).

Milroy, James and Lesley, *Authority in Language* (London, RKP, 1985).

Monboddo, Lord – *See* Burnett, James.

Morley, John, *Aspects of Modern Study* (London, 1894).

——, *Science and Literature*, English Association Pamphlet I (London, The English Association, 1913).

Morris, Richard, *Specimens of Early English: Selected from the Chief English Authors 1250–1400* (Oxford, 1867).

Morris, Richard, *Specimens of English Part II. From Robert of Gloucester to Gower 1298–1393* (Oxford, 1872).

——, *The Historical Outlines of English Accidence* (London, 1872).

——, *Elementary Lessons in Historical English Grammar* (London, 1874).

——, *English Grammar* (London, 1875).

——, 5th Presidential Address to the Philological Society, *Transactions of the Philological Society* (London, 1875–6).

Mournin, Georges, *Histoire de la linguistique des origines au XXe siècle* (Paris, 1967).

Mulhern, Francis, *The Moment of Scrutiny* (London, New Left Books, 1979).

Müller, Friedrich Max, *Three Linguistic Dissertations Read at the Meeting of the British Association in Oxford, by Chevalier Bunsen, Dr. Charles, Dr. Max Müller* (London, 1848).

——, *Suggestions for the Assistance of Officials in Learning the Language of the Seat of War in the East* (London, 1854).

——, *The Language of the Seat of War in the East. 2nd edn with an Appendix on the Missionary Alphabet and an Ethnographical Map* (London, 1855).

——, *Lectures on the Science of Language Delivered at the Royal Institute of Great Britain in 1861*, 2nd edn (London, 1862).

——, *Selected Essays on Language, Mythology, and Religion* (London, 1881).

——, *A Syllabus of Lectures on the Science of Language and its Place in General Education* (Oxford, 1889).

Müller, Georgina Grenfell, *The Life and Letters of the Rt Hon. Max Müller*, 2 vols (New York, AMS, 1976).

Munro, J. – *see* Furnivall, F.J. (1911).

Murray, James, A.H., 'The Dialect of the Southern Counties of Scotland', *Transactions of the Philological Society*, 1870–2 (London, 1870–2).

——, *The Evolution of English Lexicography: The Romanes Lecture* (Oxford, 1900).

——, *A New English Dictionary on Historical Principles*, 20 vols (10 pts) (Oxford, 1888–1928). *With Introduction, Supplement and Bibliography* (Oxford, Clarendon, 1933).

Murray, K.M.E., *Caught in the Web of Words: James A.H. Murray and 'The Oxford English Dictionary'* (Oxford, Clarendon, 1979).

Murray, Lindley, *English Grammar*, 2 vols (1795; London, 1808).

Nares, T., *Elements of Orthoepy* (London, 1784).

Newbolt, Henry, *The Teaching of English in England: Being the Report of the Departmental Committee Appointed by the President of the Board of Education to Enquire into the Position of English in the Educational System of England* (London, HMSO, 1921).

——, 'The Idea of an English Association', *English Association Pamphlet* 70 (London, The English Association, 1927, 1928).

Olden, H., *A Chronicle of Ireland* (London: 1892).

O'Neill, H.C. (ed.), *A Guide to the English Language* (London, T.C. Jack, 1915).

Palmer, D.J., *The Rise of English Studies* (Oxford, Hull University Press, 1965).

Paul, Hermann, *Principien der Sprachgeschichte, von Hermann Paul, Professor der Deutschen Sprache und Literatur an der universität Freiburg* (Halle 1880). Translated as *Principles of the History of Language* from the 2nd edn, H.A. Strong (London, 1888).

Paulin, Tom, 'Another Look at the Language Question', in *Ireland and the English Crisis* (Belfast, Bloodaxe, 1984).

Pedersen, H., *The Discovery of Language: Linguistic Science in the Nineteenth Century* (1931; trans. J.W. Spargo, Bloomington, Indiana University Press, 1959).

Peile, John, *Philology* (London, 1877).

Peyton, V.J., *The History of the English Language* (London, 1771).

Phillips, K.C., *Language and Class in Victorian England* (Oxford, Blackwell, 1984).

The Philological Society, Proceedings and *Transactions* of the Philological Society, 1842–1930, 34 vols (London, 1842–1930).

Plato, *The Dialogues of Plato*, trans. B. Jowett, Vol. 3: *Timaeus and Other Dialogues* (London, Sphere, 1970).

Potter, Simeon, *The Muse in Chains* (London, Routledge, 1937).

Priestley, Joseph, *The Rudiments of English Grammar* (London, 1761).

——, *A Course of Lectures on the Theory of Language and Universal Grammar* (London, 1762).

Proposal For the Publication of a New English Dictionary, Appendix to the *Transactions of the Philogical Society* (1857).

Quiller-Couch, Arthur, *Studies in Literature* (Cambridge University Press, 1918).

Quintilian, M. Fabius, *Institutio Oratorio*, trans. by H.E. Butler, 4 vols (London, Heinemann, 1921).

Raleigh, Walter, *On Writing and Writers* (Edinburgh, Edinburgh Press, 1926).

Renan, E., 'Qu'est que ce qu'une nation?' in *Oeuvres complètes*, 10 vols: Vol 1 (Paris, 1947–64).

Reynolds, Stephen, *A Poor Man's House*, 2nd edn (London, Bodley Head, 1909).

——, *The Holy Mountain: A Satire on Tendencies* (London, Bodley Head, 1910).

——, with B. and T. Woolley, *Seems So! A Working Class View of Politics* (London, Macmillan, 1911).

Richards, I.A., *Practical Criticism* (London, Kegan Paul, 1929).

Robins, R.H., *A Short History of Linguistics* (London, Longmans, 1967).

Russell, Bertrand, *The Philosophy of Logical Atomism* (1918 and 1924; ed. D. Pears, Illinois, La Salle, 1985).

Sampson, George, 'The Problem of Grammar', *English Association Pamphlet* 56 (London, English Association, 1924).

——, *English for the English* (1921, 2nd edn, rev. London, 1925).

Saussure, Ferdinand de, *Course in General Linguistics*, 1916, trans. R. Harris (London, Duckworth, 1983).

Sayce, A.H., *Introduction to the Science of Language*, 2 vols (London, 1890).

Schwarz, Bill, 'The Language of Constitutionalism: Baldwinite Conservatism', in *Formations: Of Nation and People*, ed. T. Bennett (London, RKP, 1984).

Sebeok, Thomas (ed.), *Portraits of Linguists: A Bibliographical Source Book for the History of Western Linguistics 1746–1963*, 2 vols (Bloomington, Indiana University Press, 1965).

Sedgwick, H., 'The Theory of Classical Education', in F. Farrar, *Essays On a Liberal Education* (London, 1868).

Sheridan, Thomas, *British Education. Or, The Source of the Disorders of Great Britain* (London, 1756).

——, *A General Dictionary of the English Language (One Main Object of which is, to Establish a Plain and Permanent standard of Pronunciation)*, 2 vols (London, 1780).

——, *A Course of Lectures on Elocution Together with Two Dissertations on Language* (London, 1781).

Simon, Brian, *Education and the Labour Movement: 1870–1920* (London, Lawrence & Wishart, 1965).

Skeat, W.W., *Questions for Examination in English Literature: With an Introduction on the Study of English* (Cambridge, 1873).

——, *Glossaries of English Dialects* (London, 1876).

Skeat, W.W., *A Concise Etymological Dictionary of the English Language* (London, 1882).

——, *An Etymological Dictionary of the English Language*, 4 parts (London, 1879–82).

——, *Principles of English Etymology* (Oxford, 1887).

——, *A Primer of English Etymology* (Oxford, 1892).

——, 'The Proverbs of Alfred' (1895), *Transactions of the Philological Society* (1895–8).

——, *Notes on English Etymology* (Oxford, Clarendon, 1901).

——, *English Dialects from the 8th Century to the Present Day* (Cambridge University Press, 1912).

——, *The Science of Etymology* (Oxford, Clarendon, 1912).

Smart, B.H., *Walker Remodelled: A New Critical Pronouncing Dictionary of the English Language. Adapted to the Present State of Literature and Science* (London, 1836).

Smart, W.K., *Reminiscences of a Soldier* (London, 1874).

Smith, Logan Pearsall, *The English Language* (London: 1912).

——, 'Robert Bridges', Society For Pure English, Tract XXXV (London: 1931).

Smith, Olivia, *The Politics Of Language 1791–1819*. Oxford: Clarendon, 1984.

Society of Pure English, *Tracts*, Vol. 1, I–X (1919–22) (Oxford, Clarendon, 1922); Vol. 2, XI–XX (Oxford, Clarendon, 1925); Vol. 3, XXI–XXX (Oxford, Clarendon, 1928); Vol. 4, XXXI–XL (Oxford, Clarendon, 1934).

Society Small Talk; Or, What to Say and When to Say it (By a Member of the Aristocracy) (London, 1879).

Spence, T., *The Grand Repository of the English Language* (Newcastle, 1775).

Stalker, James, 'Attitudes toward language in the eighteenth and nineteenth centuries', in Greenbaum (1985).

Staples, J.H., 'Notes on Ulster Dialect', *Transactions of the Philological Society* (1895–8).

Stedman-Jones, Gareth, *Languages of Class: Studies in English Working Class History 1832–1982* (Cambridge University Press, 1983).

Stevenson, John, *British Society 1914–45* (Harmondsworth, Penguin, 1984).

Swayne, G.C., 'Characteristics of Language', *Blackwoods Edinburgh Magazine* (March 1862).

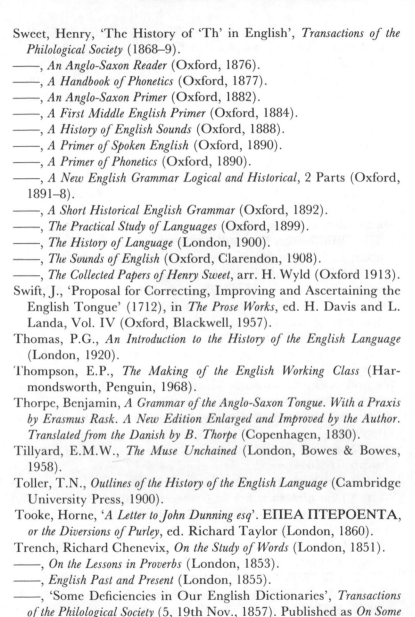

Sweet, Henry, 'The History of 'Th' in English', *Transactions of the Philological Society* (1868–9).
——, *An Anglo-Saxon Reader* (Oxford, 1876).
——, *A Handbook of Phonetics* (Oxford, 1877).
——, *An Anglo-Saxon Primer* (Oxford, 1882).
——, *A First Middle English Primer* (Oxford, 1884).
——, *A History of English Sounds* (Oxford, 1888).
——, *A Primer of Spoken English* (Oxford, 1890).
——, *A Primer of Phonetics* (Oxford, 1890).
——, *A New English Grammar Logical and Historical*, 2 Parts (Oxford, 1891–8).
——, *A Short Historical English Grammar* (Oxford, 1892).
——, *The Practical Study of Languages* (Oxford, 1899).
——, *The History of Language* (London, 1900).
——, *The Sounds of English* (Oxford, Clarendon, 1908).
——, *The Collected Papers of Henry Sweet*, arr. H. Wyld (Oxford 1913).
Swift, J., 'Proposal for Correcting, Improving and Ascertaining the English Tongue' (1712), in *The Prose Works*, ed. H. Davis and L. Landa, Vol. IV (Oxford, Blackwell, 1957).
Thomas, P.G., *An Introduction to the History of the English Language* (London, 1920).
Thompson, E.P., *The Making of the English Working Class* (Harmondsworth, Penguin, 1968).
Thorpe, Benjamin, *A Grammar of the Anglo-Saxon Tongue. With a Praxis by Erasmus Rask. A New Edition Enlarged and Improved by the Author. Translated from the Danish by B. Thorpe* (Copenhagen, 1830).
Tillyard, E.M.W., *The Muse Unchained* (London, Bowes & Bowes, 1958).
Toller, T.N., *Outlines of the History of the English Language* (Cambridge University Press, 1900).
Tooke, Horne, '*A Letter to John Dunning esq*'. ΕΠΕΑ ΠΤΕΡΟΕΝΤΑ, *or the Diversions of Purley*, ed. Richard Taylor (London, 1860).
Trench, Richard Chenevix, *On the Study of Words* (London, 1851).
——, *On the Lessons in Proverbs* (London, 1853).
——, *English Past and Present* (London, 1855).
——, 'Some Deficiencies in Our English Dictionaries', *Transactions of the Philological Society* (5, 19th Nov., 1857). Published as *On Some Deficiencies in Our English Dictionaries* (1857; 2nd edn rev. and enlarged, London, 1860).

Trench, Richard Chenevix, *A Select Glossary of English Words Used Formerly in Senses Different from their Present* (London, 1859).

——, *Poems* (London, 1865).

Tucker, Susie, *English Examined* (Cambridge University Press, 1961).

——, *Protean Shape: A Study in Eighteenth-Century Vocabulary and Usage* (London, Athlone, 1967).

Turner, Sharon, *The History of the Anglo-Saxons*, 2 vols (1799; London 1807).

Tylor, E.B., *Anthropology: An Introduction to the Study of Man and Civilisation* (London, 1881).

Vološinov, V.N., *Marxism and the Philosophy of Language* (1930; London, Seminar Press, 1973).

Waites, Bernard, 'The Language and Imagery of Class in Early Twentieth Century England', *Literature and History*, 4 (1976).

Walker, J., *A General Idea of A Pronouncing Dictionary* (London, 1774).

——, *A Dictionary of the English Language* (London, 1775).

——, *Exercises for Improvement in Elocution. Being Select Extracts from the Best Authors for the Use of Those who Study the Art of Reading and Speaking in Public* (London, 1777).

——, *A Rhetorical Grammar* (London, 1785).

——, *A Critical Pronouncing Dictionary and Expositor of the English Language* (London, 1791).

Watts, T., 'On the Probable Future Position of the English Language', *Transactions of the Philological Society* (1850).

Wedgwood, Hensleigh, *Dictionary of English Etymology*, 3 vols (London, 1859–65).

——, 'Notices of English Etymology', *Transactions of the Philological Society*, II (1844).

——, *On the Origin of Language* (London, 1866).

West, A., *The Elements of English Grammar* (Cambridge, 1893).

——, *English Grammar for Beginners* (Cambridge, 1895).

Whewell, W., *History of the Inductive Sciences* (London, 1837).

White, Richard Grant, *Words and their Uses: A Study of the English Language* (Boston, 1870).

——, *Everyday English* (London, 1880).

Whitney, W. Dwight, *Language and the Study of Language. Lectures on the Principles of Linguistic Science* (London, 1867).

——, *The Life and Growth of Language* (London, 1875).

——, *Language and its Study* (London, 1876).

——, *The Essentials of English Grammar* (London, 1877).

Whitney, W. Dwight, *Max Müller and the Science of Language: A Criticism* (New York 1893).

Williams, Raymond, 'The Growth of "Standard English"', in his *The Long Revolution* (London, Chatto & Windus, 1961).

——, *Culture and Society* (London, Chatto & Windus, 1958).

——, *Keywords: A Vocabulary of Culture and Society* (1976; 2nd edn rev. London, Fontana 1983).

——, *Politics and Letters* (London, New Left Books, 1979).

Wilson, R., *Lingua Materna: Chapters on the School Teaching of English* (London, Arnold, 1905).

Wilson, T., *The Arte of Rhetorique* (1553).

Wright, Aldis, *Notes and Queries*, 12 March 1870, 4.s.v. 271.

Wright, Elizabeth Mary and Joseph, *Specimens of an English Dialect Dictionary* (Cambridge, 1890).

——, *The English Dialect Dictionary. Being the Complete Vocabulary of all Dialect Words Still in Use or Known to have been in Use During the last 200 years*, 6 vols (London, 1898–1905).

——, *The English Dialect Grammar* (Oxford, Clarendon, 1905).

——, *Old English Grammar* (London, 1908).

——, *Rustic Speech and Folk Lore* (Oxford, 1913).

——, *An Elementary Historical New English Grammar* (Oxford, Clarendon, 1924).

Wright, Elizabeth, *The Life of Joseph Wright*, 2 vols (Oxford, Clarendon, 1932).

Wright, Thomas, *A Dictionary of Obsolete and Provincial English* (London, 1857).

Wyld, Henry C., *The Study of Living Popular Dialect and its Place in the Modern Science of Language* (Bradford, 1904).

——, *The Historical Study of the Mother Tongue: An Introduction to Philological Method* (London, 1906).

——, *The Place of the Mother Tongue in National Education* (London, Murray, 1906).

——, *The Growth of English* (London, Murray, 1907).

——, *The Teaching of Reading in Training Colleges* (London, Murray, 1908).

——, *Elementary Lessons in English Grammar* (Oxford, 1909).

——, *Evolution in English Pronunciation* (Liverpool, University Press, 1913).

——, *A Short History of English with a Bibliography of Recent Books on the Subject* (1914; 3rd edn rev. and enlarged, London, Murray, 1927).

Wyld, Henry C., *A History of Modern Colloquial English* (London, Fisher Unwin, 1920).

——, *The Universal Dictionary of the English Language* (London, Routledge, 1932).

——, 'The Best English: A Claim for the Superiority of Received Standard English', Society for Pure English, 4, *Tract* No. XXXIX, (1934), pp.603–21; published under the same title (Oxford, Clarendon, 1934).

Young, G.M., *Victorian England: Portrait of an Age* (Oxford, Clarendon, 1936).

Index